U.S.

v

Richard M. Nixon

OTHER BOOKS BY FRANK MANKIEWICZ

Perfectly Clear: Nixon from Whittier to Watergate

An Honorable Profession
A Tribute to Robert F. Kennedy
(with Pierre Salinger, Edwin Guthman, and
John Siegenthaler)

With Fidel: A Portrait of Castro and Cuba
(with Kirby Jones)

U.S.

v.

Richard M. Nixon

The Final Crisis

FRANK MANKIEWICZ

Quadrangle / The New York Times Book Co.

Library of Congress Cataloging in Publication Data

Mankiewicz, Frank, 1924-
  The U. S. v. Richard M. Nixon.

  Includes index.
  1. Watergate Affair, 1972- 2. Nixon, Richard Milhous, 1913- —Impeachment. I. Title.
E860.M4 1975   364.1'32'0973   74-81001
ISBN 0-8129-0505-9

Book design: Tere LoPrete

For Johanna

Even when the gates of heaven are shut
to prayer, they are open to tears.

—From the Talmud

I wish to acknowledge with gratitude the efforts of those who assisted in the preparation of this book. My old colleague, James Reston, Jr., was of great help in suggesting the organization of the book. In addition, at times when I was unable to cover some of the formal proceedings—trials and committee meetings—Jim provided me with excellent reporting, not only of the substance but of the mood. He is presently preparing a novel centered around the impeachment of Andrew Johnson, on which he has become an expert. His help was of great value.

Marylin Bitner performed prodigious feats of research with great skill, and was able to organize and catalog great amounts of material quickly and well. I am also greatly indebted to Betty Plaseied, who worked far beyond what duty required in typing the manuscript.

I also wish to acknowledge the patience and time of many of the participants in these events, who consented to long interviews and discussions with me. I am also thankful for the writing and comments of a many journalists—in Washington and elsewhere—whose insights have informed my own understanding and judgments.

Families often come last in these lists—which does not properly define their importance—at least not in the case of my own. Holly's contributions, both technically and substantively, were considerable, and Josh and Ben—as usual—were most supportive.

While I could not have written this book without the cooperation of others, I cannot—like Richard Nixon—assign the responsibility for any deficiency of content or style to others; it is my own.

Washington, D.C.
November, 1974

Contents

U.S.
v.
Richard M. Nixon

Introduction

How did all this happen? How did the American political system, subverted to impotence by Richard Nixon by 1972, function so strongly in 1973, and finally vindicate itself in 1974? How was it possible for a divided and demoralized people, at a time of the greatest accumulation of power in history in what has so aptly been called "the imperial presidency," to rid themselves of the very scoundrel who held that power—and to do so without violence and without recourse to any instruments save those legal and institutional ones which history and Divine Providence had placed in their hands?

This book tries to answer those questions. It will try to set forth not only how it happened, but just *what it was* that happened. I have tried to present a study of some of the institutions and how they functioned in this crisis. The office of the Special Prosecutor, the Judiciary Committee of the House of Representatives, the press, and the White House itself are examined here, not as part of some "grand design" beloved of historians, but separately—in terms of what was done, day by day, to achieve the result.

I have tried to make it clear that among all the actors in this great drama, there was little consciousness that history was being written, and that they were helping to write it. Instead, I have set forth the acts of individuals doing their jobs, because that is how the American system works. In fact, it never works worse than when its leaders and their followers in high positions become concerned about "history" and self-conscious about their roles.

In these pages, I have taken a long look at four institutions and how they functioned during this constitutional crisis. I have focused on the Special Prosecutor, the House Judiciary Committee, the press, and the Nixon White House, to see if some common threads can be found.

I think they can. Because what emerges from this study—in my view—is that those who looked at it as a *political event*—even as a *political crisis*—were proved to be wrong, and those who saw it as a *legal proceeding*, were proved to be right.

Among the press, this was particularly striking. Those "insiders," who knew politics and had good sources of information within the political establishment on Capitol Hill and at the White House, never were able to predict what would happen. On the other hand, those who were "outsiders," who didn't bother to check with "important sources," and whose analysis was based on their own perceptions and their own view of the evidence, were almost always right.

The White House "experts" who saw Watergate—indeed, who saw all of government—as a political and essentially public relations exercise, were not only wrong but defeated and shamed. What can one say, after all, about people who thought "stonewalling" would defeat a Grand Jury investigation or that something called "Operation Candor" would sway congressional votes on impeachment? Nothing really, except that their own power must have blinded them to a vision of their countrymen and how they would look at evidence of misbehavior in high places. Or one could say that these public relations men—including some of the lawyers—had forgotten the difference between a trial and a political campaign—if they ever knew it.

That difference, I hope, will come through these pages as crucial. What was going on in 1973 and 1974 was not a political or public relations event, it was a legal event, and there is a big difference. The old rules don't apply. A Grand Jury can't be filibustered; a jury verdict or a jail sentence can't be amended in a conference committee; Supreme Court justices don't honor political IOU's.

In a legal proceeding, briefs are filed, motions are made, evidence is presented—and sooner or later there are tangible results. Grand Juries indict; jurors reach verdicts on the basis of the evidence presented to them; appeals are heard and disposed of; and committees charged with considering impeachment will finally vote. These simple facts were largely ignored by the White House and the "knowledgeable" commentators, and for a while that ignorance skewed the public perception of what was happening. It is no accident that two political columnists, who are skilled at predicting how an intra-party squabble will come out in a southern state, could state within a month of the final disgraceful end of the Nixon presidency, that the Judiciary Committee was split along party lines and that a "momentum" against impeachment had developed. There was no such "momentum," the overwhelming bi-partisan vote for impeachment had been set in motion long before—by the *evidence*—but all the columnists knew was a certain aspect of politics, and they tried to force Watergate into their familiar mold.

But the *legal* institutions, the office of the Special Prosecutor and the Judiciary Committee, were successful and strong from the beginning, for no other reason than that the men and women assigned to the job did the job. Not with a "sense of history" or a mission to convict or "get" anyone, but with the knowledge that the day's work included setting in motion forces with a momentum and "time frame" of their own. If you need evidence, you ask for it; if the request is denied, you ask for a subpoena; if the witness seeks to quash the subpoena, you ask the court to affirm it by an order; if the order is appealed, you file a brief and agrue the case; it will be heard.

I have not included a systematic study of the work of the Senate Watergate Committee, of which Senator Sam Ervin was the chairman, because almost all of its work was done in public, and its impact has been felt by almost every American who either watched its work on television, or heard of it soon afterward. The Ervin Committee truly functioned as a "firebell in the night," and everyone heard it clang. There seemed to me little need to go over its hearings once again, but in any list of men and institutions which helped us survive Watergate as a free people, the members and staff of the Ervin Committee deserve an honored place.

Nixon's pardon, after the system had apparently "worked," made it clear that we cannot afford any complacency about the strength of our institutions. In E. M. Forster's phrase, our system probably deserves no more than "two cheers." For if the events described in this book gave us confidence things were working at last, the pardon given Richard Nixon less than a month after he fled the White House in disgrace dealt that confidence a heavy blow. Perhaps President Ford did not understand—perhaps he does not understand even now—that the principle of "equal justice under law" is also a part of the system, and a most important part.

In an earlier book, I argued that the uniqueness of the United States lies in the fact that, while other nations share a common language, history, and culture, we are a country only because this pluralist society shares a set of *ideals*, and that it will disintegrate once we cease to believe that we are still struggling—however slowly and hesitantly—toward the achievement of those ideals. That is why the pardon struck with such a blow at our confidence in our institutions, and at just the time we were beginning to feel that events had vindicated our faith.

In granting Nixon a pardon, his successor said he had "suffered enough." President Ford may have thought—there seems no hard evidence to support any other reason—that the pardon would somehow "close the book" on Watergate, and for that matter on Nixon himself, but it had the opposite effect. Americans would still talk, and still think, about Watergate and all the other actions that it invoked, and about Richard Nixon.

Had he really "suffered" at all? In the purely legal—almost technical—sense, he had not. He had not paid a fine; instead, the President had proposed, and Congress would vote, comparable pensions, staff allotments, and other perquisites to those paid or offered to any ex-President, including those who had finished their terms honorably.

He had not served a jail sentence, as nine of his associates had, and as more of his closest aides still feared they might. In fact, the pardon he accepted made it almost impossible that he would ever come to trial, except in the remote event that anything he did after leaving office would result in indictment.

He had not even given up anything, although there was much comment that somehow resigning the presidency was a great deprivation, and a "loss" greater than any fine or jail term might involve. But every President is sooner or later required to give up the presidency; it is not his, but ours. And this President was unique in our history. He gave up the presidency rather than face the sure judgment of his countrymen and suffer impeachment in the House of Representatives and conviction in the Senate.

His resignation, in short, was not remotely to benefit the nation whose ideals he had so clearly betrayed, but only to benefit himself. Had he stayed to be impeached and convicted, which would have happened with scarcely a handful of votes in opposition, he would have been deprived by law of his pension and other payments, and would still have had to rely on the mercy of the new President to avoid criminal prosecution and *real* penalties. For Richard Nixon, the choice was easy. In the vernacular of the time, he took the money and ran.

Nor, if one wishes to expand the definition of suffering, did Richard Nixon seem to be anguished or to feel guilt. When he accepted the pardon he hardly spoke in the accents of contrition. He spoke of the whole series of events as something that was in his mind "a complex and confusing maze of events, decisions, pressures, and personalities." This was a complex and, it would seem, deliberately confusing description from the one man who was involved in all the events, made all the decisions, exerted all the pressures, and was himself the chief personality for whose exclusive benefit and profit all the other personalities were deployed.

He described his own conduct as involving, at its worst, "mistakes and misjudgments," thus impugning the judgment and perhaps the honor of each member of the Judiciary Committee of the House of Representatives, who had by then unanimously concluded that he had committed "high crimes and misdemeanors"—including the specific crime of obstruction of justice, the specific offense of misusing departments of government for his own political purposes, and the specific constitutional violation of failure to "take care that the laws are faithfully executed." What is more, by talking of "mistakes and misjudgments," he denigrated the leadership of his own party in both Houses of Congress, who had abandoned their support for him at the end on the grounds not that he had misjudged the situation or made some mistakes—that was the language of defense they had used for months—but that the exposure at the very end of his clear deceit of them, his attorney, and his family would lead to a massive vote for impeachment and conviction.

Nixon also spoke at the time of his pardon of having been "wrong in not acting more decisively and more forthrightly in dealing with Watergate, *particularly when it reached the stage of judicial proceedings and grew from a political scandal into a national tragedy.*" (Emphasis added.)

There was the ultimate insult—this time to the overwhelming majority of his countrymen, who had seen at last that his guilt lay not in acting *indecisively*, but in acting *too decisively* to participate in a crime and then to join actively in covering it up. It was not Richard Nixon's actions when Watergate "reached the stage of judicial proceedings" that lost him, finally, whatever shreds of respect remained to him, but his actions from the very beginning. The final blow was not his defiance of the House, or even of the Special Prosecutor or of the courts, but the revelation that he had been the central conspirator in the cover-up, precisely when it *was* a "political scandal."

So this is an attempt to record the history of some American institutions which worked under stress, as written by Archibald Cox and Leon Jaworski and the staff of the Special Prosecutor; by Katherine Graham, Benjamin Bradlee, Carl Bernstein, and Bob Woodward of the Washington *Post*, and their colleagues—perceptive and dense—in the press; by Ron Ziegler, General Alexander Haig, and James St. Clair at the White House; by Peter Rodino and John Doar and their colleagues on the Judiciary Committee.

This book is, finally, a record of how the gravest crisis in one hundred years was resolved, and how it was that Richard Nixon, who liked to compare himself with Benjamin Disraeli, Charles DeGaulle, and Woodrow Wilson, would find himself linked instead by history to John Profumo, Pierre Laval, and Warren G. Harding.

Archibald Cox:
The Scholar as Prosecutor

In one of the more offensive onslaughts on the English language, H. R. Haldeman testified before the Ervin Committee of his desire to operate a "zero-defect" administration. But one of the more conspicuous defects that became apparent long before Watergate, was the inability of the Nixon people to do adequate research on who was appointed to high office.

This was particularly true at the Department of Justice, where no less than four Supreme Court vacancies were given to Richard Nixon to fill, and four nominees were turned down because John Mitchell and his colleagues had neglected to look adequately into their backgrounds.

The first was Clement Haynesworth, Jr., named to fill a vacancy created when Abe Fortas was required to resign because of serious conflict-of-interest charges. (Fortas was revealed to have arranged to receive $20,000 per year, the payment to continue to his wife if he predeceased her, for vaguely specified work for a foundation dominated by a friend in serious trouble with the law.) The Nixon people seemed surprised when it was discovered that their nominee, Haynesworth, was a major shareholder in a company which seemed to have benefited from a decision in which he took part. His nomination was turned down by the Senate, 55–45, after spirited debate.

Nixon—presumably on the advice of Mitchell—next tried to fill the vacancy with perhaps the worst Supreme Court nomination in our history, former judge G. Harrold Carswell. Carswell was a Nixon appointee to the Court of Appeals, but judges at that level get little scrutiny. When his appointment to the Supreme Court came before the Senate, it turned out that Carswell had a record ranging from subtle to blatant bigotry—including not only a crude and never-repudiated racist speech when he ran for legislative office, but also an attempt when city attorney to convert a public golf course into a private, segregated country club once higher courts had ordered the municipal course desegregated. The matter was not helped when Carswell tried to conceal the action from the Senate, and he was rejected, 51–45.

Nixon followed up this twin disaster with a greater one; he later offered the names of Little Rock attorney, Herschel Friday, and a California judge, Mildred Lillie. Both were turned down even before the Senate could consider them, in each case by the committee of the American Bar Association charged by Nixon with scrutiny of judicial nominations.

(There is an interesting footnote to history here. When Nixon was told that the ABA committee looked unfavorably on the prospective nominations, he replied "fuck the ABA." Under the circumstances, it was a surprising expletive for a man who had relied heavily upon the approval by the same committee of both Haynesworth and Carswell, but it should have served as a distant early warning to those who later seemed surprised when this and similar expletives were deleted from White House versions of transcripts of presidential conversations.)

The greatest "defect" of the Nixon administration was yet to come, however, and when it did it came in the same area as before—failure to look properly at the background of a key appointee. But this time—on October 31, 1973—the defect didn't have to do with a nominee who would be rejected, and for whom, after a public relations setback, a suitable substitute could be found. This time, the appointee was Leon Jaworski, the job was Watergate Special Prosecutor (*vice* Archibald Cox, dismissed), and the damage was not cosmetic, but fatal.

True, the "research" was not conducted by Haldeman or John Mitchell, but by General Alexander Haig, who demonstrated throughout his tour of duty as Nixon's chief of staff that in competence and sensitivity he was in every way a worthy successor to Haldeman. When he finally settled on Jaworski as the new Special Prosecutor in the wake of the "Saturday Night Massacre," as Cox's firing was to be widely called, and the "firestorm" of criticism which followed, Haig thought he was getting just the "right" man: an Establishment Texan, a former president of the ABA, a lawyer for the right Texas corporations, a man widely reported to have been an intimate friend and political supporter of both Lyndon Johnson and John Connally, and assumed at the White House to have been a Democrat for Nixon. (The assumption that Nixon thought Jaworski to have been a Democrat who jumped ship in 1972 to support him is borne out by Nixon public statements that he "had no idea" how Jaworski had voted; students of the Nixon style caught that at once as a sign that he did know, and that the knowledge was favorable.)

But what Haig (and Nixon) got was quite different. In Leon Jaworski they got a fiercely independent courtroom lawyer who had no intention, at his age (68), of selling out or of appearing to sell out. They got a man who had been profoundly influenced by two events in his life; most recently, by the life and recent death of a grandson whose doubts about the law's favoritism for the rich and the powerful had come to be shared by his grandfather, and earlier by his service on the prosecution staff at the Nazi war crimes trials in Nuremberg.

It was at Nuremberg, Jaworski was later to recall, that he saw how powerful and contented lawyers and judges had first questioned, then acquiesced in, and finally supported, the vile theories and practices of Hitler and his men. And it was that easy acceptance of evil which came to his mind in the late '60s and early '70s as Jaworski began to look at his profession and his government. He recalled, and took the trouble to memorize, what he thought were relevant lines of Alexander Pope:

> Vice is a monster of so frightful mien,
> As to be hated needs but to be seen;
> Yet seen too oft, familiar with her face,
> We first endure, then pity, then embrace.

Those lines were much in Leon Jaworski's mind as he accepted the appointment as Special Prosecutor, and he did not forget them as he did his job.

The hiring of Jaworski, of course, came against a grim background for the White House. At the time, the key figure was not the new prosecutor, not the President, and certainly not the aides charged with putting out the firestorm. The most important character in the drama was the original Special Prosecutor—the man who had been fired and against whom his successor would inevitably be measured—Archibald Cox.

The Watergate matter began simply enough. Five men were caught in the sixth-floor offices of the Democratic National Committee at the Watergate office building at 2 A.M. on June 17, 1972, and the burglary was duly reported in the press. But two Washington *Post* metropolitan reporters, Carl Bernstein and Bob Woodward, began to dig at the story, and within a few days it was clear—at least in Washington—that something more than an ordinary burglary was involved. Woodward and Bernstein, for one thing, had found the name of White House aide E. Howard Hunt in an address book belonging to one of the burglars, and had verified that he did indeed work at the White House.

The assignment of Woodward and Bernstein to the story, a routine professional journalistic judgment by the *Post*'s editors, proved to be crucial. They were good investigative reporters, with far more knowledge of how to cover a crime story than they had of national politics. In fact, it can be safely stated that if the *Post* had given the assignment to two of its political reporters, we might know very little about Watergate today—even if we knew a great deal about the social implications of burglary.

It was, of course, quite clear at the White House that something more than an ordinary burglary was involved. Within hours of the discovery of the break-in, the cover-up was set in motion. John Dean was "covering" the FBI invesigation, Maurice Stans (the Nixon finance chairman and former Secretary of Commerce) was voicing his anxiety that money found in the burglars' pockets might be traced to the Committee to Re-elect the President, John Ehrlichman and Bob Haldeman were enlisting the support of the top officials of the CIA to delay the FBI investigation, and at the Justice Department, Attorney-General Richard Kleindienst and Assistant Attorney-General Henry Petersen were beginning the close work with the White House which would keep the cover-up going until well past the November election.

Meanwhile, there were increasingly strong calls for the creation of a special prosecutor's office. Despite the statements from presidential press secretary Ron Ziegler that it was a "third-rate burglary," some elements of the press joined the calls by Democratic Party leader Lawrence O'Brien and by Senator George McGovern—who was, after all, the target of the whole conspiracy —for the removal of the investigation from the hands of the Justice Department.

For the rest of 1972 and the first months of 1973, the Nixon men were able to hold the line. Periodically, Kleindienst would dismiss the demands for a special prosecutor with the statement that a "vigorous" investigation was proceeding, and Petersen, a professional civil service lawman turned Nixon loyalist, was trotted out on September 16 to answer a charge by Senator McGovern.

The day before—September 15—the Grand Jury had returned its indictments—limiting the accused to the five men found inside Watergate (Bernard Barker, Frank Sturgis, Eugenio Martinez, Virgilio Gonzalez, and James McCord), plus E. Howard Hunt and G. Gordon Liddy. Under careful instructions from Kleindienst and Petersen, taking their cues from Dean, the U.S. Attorneys handling the case had failed to treat the case as anything but the third-rate burglary the White House had called it. No questions were asked as to why the men had committed the crime, under whose orders, or by whom they had been paid.

By September 15, any reader of the Washington *Post* knew a lot. He knew, for instance, that men in the White House and in the Nixon campaign committee were involved in the planning and the execution of the burglary. After all, James McCord had been the security chief of both the Republican National Committee and the CREP, Gordon Liddy had been general counsel of the campaign committee, and Howard Hunt had worked for Charles Colson, a White House counsel.

Inside the White House, of course, much more was known. On September 15, Richard Nixon congratulated John Dean on how well Dean had contained the Watergate matter, and at least Dean and Haldeman knew even more. John Mitchell had urged the destruction of evidence, Jeb Magruder and Herbert Porter had already perjured themselves to the Grand Jury, and the fact of that perjury was known to Dean and Haldeman and—perhaps—to Henry Petersen. What is more, Ehrlichman, Haldeman, Mitchell, and Dean, as well as Richard Helms and Vernon Walters of the CIA and Patrick Gray of the FBI, all knew that the President had ordered the CIA to delay and, if possible, prevent the FBI from determining that it was Nixon campaign money which had paid for the burglary.

On September 16, George McGovern denounced the Grand Jury indictments as a "whitewash," and called for the appointment of a special prosecutor. And Henry Petersen, within hours, became a campaign spokesman and denounced the charge of whitewash, although he must have known it to be true. The press—except for the *Post*—printed parts of both statements and, unable to believe that a criminal charge against the Nixon people could be more than campaign oratory, left the matter there.

But by spring, it was easier to believe that a criminal conspiracy had been operating inside the White House—if not yet in the Oval Office—than it had been when the charge came from George McGovern. For one thing, some of the conspirators had begun to talk. The Ervin Committee had been created and was preparing to take testimony. And on April 30, Richard Nixon dropped Dean, Haldeman, Ehrlichman, and Kleindienst over the side. Although no one could quite see it then, the dam had burst and the flood was inevitable.

The first thing that was needed, clearly, was a new Attorney-General. In the speech announcing the departure of Haldeman and Ehrlichman ("two of the finest public servants I have ever known," said Nixon, in a statement much ridiculed but almost certainly true), the President also announced the nomination of Elliot Richardson to head the Justice Department. The appointment must have seemed a good one to Nixon; in fact, Richardson, by his appointment of Archibald Cox and his own refusal to go along with firing Cox when asked, proved to be a disaster.

There was every reason for Nixon to think he had picked the right man. At the State Department as Under Secretary, as Secretary of Health, Education and Welfare, and in a brief stint as Secretary of Defense, Richardson had proved to be among the most malleable of Nixon's appointees. At HEW, he blandly reversed his own position on school desegregation when it became clear that Nixon would be exploiting the race issue for the 1972 campaign, and Richardson's acquiescence in and indeed strong support of the Christmas 1973 terror bombing of Hanoi must have convinced his boss that whatever the provocation, he would never resign.

The first task facing Richardson was the appointment of a special prosecutor, to which Nixon finally agreed—confronted by this time with a majority of the Senate demanding such an appointment as a condition of confirmation for *any* Attorney-General. But where the mere appointment of a special prosecutor —the *appearance* of fairness, an administration not investigating its own people—would once have sufficed, by May 1973 the pressures had built and *real* independence of the investigator was required. Before the Judiciary Committee of the Senate, Richardson agreed to the following language, forming a sort of compact between himself (and through him, he assured the Senators, Nixon) and the Senate:

> The Attorney-General will not countermand or interfere with the Special Prosecutor's decisions or actions. The Special Prosecutor will determine whether and to what extent he will inform or consult with the Attorney-General about the conduct of his duties and responsibilities. . . . *The Special Prosecutor will not be removed from his duties except for extraordinary improprieties on his part.* [Emphasis added.]

And with that on the record, on May 25, 1973, Archibald Cox became the first Watergate Special Prosecutor. Within five months, he was gone, taking Richardson and his deputy, William Ruckelshaus, with him. But the staff he had selected remained on the job to serve under Leon Jaworski, and that staff—and the course upon which he and they set forth—contributed as much as any other force or institution to the final shameful downfall of Richard Nixon.

Cox was a distinguished law professor from Harvard, and he had served as Solicitor-General in the administration of John F. Kennedy. He was an *appellate* lawyer (as distinguished, for example, from Leon Jaworski, who was an experienced *trial* lawyer). More to the point, he was a professor of appellate law. With very few exceptions, law school is the study of cases on appeal to higher courts, and rarely the study of the things so important to a trial practice. Thus, unless a young law student knows he wants to practice criminal law out in the real world, he is likely to learn very little about the events which precede an appeal—the whole area of investigation, presentation to a grand jury, motions to suppress evidence, pre-trial plea bargaining, etc., to say nothing of the trial itself—and he is likely to learn even less from his professors about the problems facing a prosecution than about those confronted by a defense lawyer.

In this one important respect, if there had to be two special prosecutors, Cox and Jaworski, it was fortunate that Cox came first. As a justifiably celebrated professor at the nation's leading law school, Cox had seen good students pass through his classes over the years, and had kept track of many of them through personal contact and correspondence. It was thus easier for him than it would have been for even a skilled trial lawyer like Jaworski, to assemble a staff and to be assured of the competence of the people he had hired.

The staff came together in the first few weeks of Cox's incumbency, and with very few exceptions it stayed together until the cover-up trial was over, nearly two years later. Three lawyers resigned over the arrangement struck with former Attorney-General Richard Kleindienst, and Philip Lacovara quit shortly after the pardon was given to Nixon. Except for these defections, the entire staff brought together by Cox stayed on the job under Jaworski, and after Jaworski went back to Texas they stayed to work for Henry Ruth, who had been the deputy to both his predecessors.

Lacovara was an example of the kind of lawyer Cox was able to attract to the staff. A conservative Catholic—he once chided his wife for wearing in public a dress he thought was too low-cut—Lacovara had been the chairman of Students for Goldwater when a law student at Columbia in 1964. The White House tried mightily to paint the Special Prosecutor's office as a hotbed of Kennedyite leftists, bent on "getting" Nixon, but the facts were to the contrary and the line found only a few takers.

In the early weeks, Cox felt his way, and Harvard associates Philip Heyman and James Vorenberg devoted a major part of their time to recruiting. By July, the key people were in place; Henry Ruth as deputy; Lacovara as counsel; Peter Kriendler as a sort of roving special assistant; James Neal—the man who tried the cases which sent James Hoffa to jail for jury tampering—as head of the task force on the Watergate cover-up itself; William Merrill in charge of a task force looking into the activities of the so-called plumbers; Thomas McBride, another old Justice Department hand and former Peace Corps official, leading a task force on illegal campaign contributions; Joseph Connolly heading the ITT task force; Richard Davis in charge of the "dirty tricks" task force; and James Doyle, a political reporter whose work for the Boston *Globe* and the Washington *Star* had earned him enormous respect from his colleagues, as press secretary.

There was an early challenge to Cox's credibility, and he was to discover quickly the need to avoid vulnerability from those sections of the press which were responsive to White House initiatives. Cox had begun his tour of duty with an attempt—doomed to failure—to get Senator Sam Ervin to agree to postpone his scheduled hearings. Failing in that, Cox went to court to try to delay the Ervin hearings, on the grounds (not at all unreasonable grounds to a professor of law) that the publicity would jeopardize his investigation and the right to a fair trial of anyone he might seek to indict. That failed, and it led Cox's opponents to try to use the press to bring him down.

At the Department of Justice, there was resentment in the office of the United States Attorney for the District of Columbia. Earl Silbert, the principal deputy, had tried the case of the Watergate burglars and had succeeded, whether through bungling, diffidence, or actual connivance with Attorney-General Kleindienst and Assistant Attorney-General Petersen (each theory had its adherents), in making the case seem like just a third-rate burglary with no White House connections.

Indeed, it was precisely the Justice Department's handling of the original Watergate case which had brought about the demand for an independent special prosecutor. At the trial of the Cuban-American burglars, plus Hunt, Liddy, and McCord, the United States Attorney had carefully limited the matter to the burglary itself and, over the mounting irritation of Judge John Sirica, failed to get into such potentially explosive questions as who had paid for the burglary, who had ordered it or approved it, and to whom the criminals had reported.

So at the threshold of his tenure as Special Prosecutor, Cox had the problem of what to do with Earl Silbert, Seymour Glanzer, and Donald Campbell, the assistant U.S. attorneys who had tried the case. The obvious course was to take the matter away from them, and put the new prosecutorial force in full charge of all Watergate matters. But Cox felt his way slowly, and spoke to the prosecutors about the problem.

That gave an opening to the White House. Leaks about the struggle over Silbert's role began to appear in the press, fed by White House staff people to friendly members of the press. Once the leaks appeared, other White House staff men would denounce the leaks, and demand that Cox stop them. It was a good technique, one Nixon and his people were to use later, and it all contributed to an image of Cox as ineffectual and a man who didn't know his way around Washington.

The real Cox, it finally appeared, was a man who knew his way around very well, and by the time he left—after a masterful press conference the day he was fired—and for a long time before that, the press treatment of the Special Prosecutor and his office was a model of respect and accuracy.

The Cox operation—as the Jaworski and Ruth operations which followed—relied heavily on the principle of collegiality. Unlike most prosecutorial forces at the county, state, or federal level, there was no one man calling the shots. By all accounts from those associated with the Watergate Special Prosecution Force (the official name), all the major decisions were taken after consultation had created at least a rough consensus.

The system of regular meetings—usually among Cox, Kriendler, Ruth, Lacovara, Neal, Merrill, McBride, Connolly, and Davis—began early, and was the major method of conflict resolution. Probably because none of the lawyers were in any way "career" government employees, and because each of them had volunteered for the assignment, there was very little of the Washington gloss on the operation.

Thus, according to those who were there, "office politics" were at a minimum, no one was concerned about the sort of thing on which any bureaucracy inevitably spends a lot of time (size of office, rank of secretary, color of carpet, amount of sick leave accumulated) and what is more, absolutely no reports of any differences within the office ever emerged.

Positions were argued, even lobbied intensely, but once a decision was made it was operative, and the press, which found a mother lode of inside information at both the Ervin Committee and the House Judiciary Committee, never had much to report from the Special Prosecutor's office except—once the legal wheels began to turn—a steady stream of indictments, guilty pleas, and convictions.

The treatment of John Dean was a good example. Ever since he first began to talk to the federal prosecutors—before Cox's appointment—Dean and his attorneys had tried to get some kind of immunity. The negotiations were at two levels, with the Senate Watergate Committee and with the U.S. attorney, and later with Cox.

Dean and his counsel were on strong ground. He had a great deal to tell, he was the first really "inside" witness, and the early conversations with him made it clear that he came closer than anyone else to an ability to identify the precise ways in which not only Haldeman, Ehrlichman, Colson, and Mitchell were involved in Watergate and the cover-up but also the degree of Nixon's own complicity.

The immunity temptation was too great for the Ervin Committee, finally, to resist. The Committee, after all, was not a law enforcement agency, but a legislative investigation charged with putting as full a story as possible before Congress and the public. So the Senators finally agreed, in return for his testimony, to grant Dean what is legally known as "use immunity."

Use immunity differs from total or "transactional" immunity from prosecution in that it forbids only prosecution based on the testimony which is forthcoming. With the grant, Dean could testify before the Committee about any incriminating matter and know that he could not be prosecuted for that testimony.

But use immunity does not cover any evidence obtained by any other method than the testimony covered by the grant. Thus, Dean could still be prosecuted for the crimes in which he was admittedly involved, if the evidence could be demonstrated to have come from anywhere but his own testimony before Senator Ervin's committee.

Against this background, a continuing discussion was proceeding within the Cox office. James Neal, as the head of the main Watergate task force, was the man with the most at stake on the question of John Dean's immunity. Neal felt, and expressed himself strongly, that Dean *was* his case against the other conspirators, and if it took immunity from all prosecution to get his testimony, then Dean should have immunity.

But Cox and Neal's colleagues weren't so sure. During the summer of 1973, the main line of Nixon's defense was that the whole Watergate matter came down to a conflict between the President

of the United States and the "turncoat" Dean. The press was full
of leaks that Dean was unreliable, and at one point the White
House press people reached a temporary new low with the planted
rumor that Dean would "say anything" to avoid going to jail, so
great was his fear of homosexual rape.

The "Nixon v. Dean" line was a strong one through July, August, and September, until the prosecutor's office began to collect
more evidence. Columnist Joseph Alsop, whose early admiration
of Nixon and his men as sensible and "long-headed" (dolico-
cephalics rate high in Alsop's anthropology; no one seems to know
why) was equaled only by his dislike for Nixon's critics, began to
refer to Dean as a "bottom-dwelling slug."

And if Dean was indeed an unreliable fellow with grudges
against his former colleagues, if his testimony—as was darkly
hinted by the Nixon men—would be destroyed by the famous
tapes, as yet unrevealed, then why, ran the reasoning in the Cox
meetings, grant immunity to this bottom-dwelling slug?

Before the question was resolved by Cox, the Special Prosecutor
took an important step. On the eve of Dean's testimony before the
Ervin Committee, where he had immunity for everything he might
say or confess to, Cox went into the court of Judge John Sirica and,
under seal, deposited all the evidence against Dean which his
office had already collected. Cox was saying, in effect, "Okay,
Dean is immune from prosecution for all that he says before the
Committee, but he is *not* immune from any prosecution based on
what is in this file." It was an important battle in the war of nerves
being conducted between Dean and his lawyers, anxious to trade
the former counsel's bombshells for his freedom, and Cox, still
wary of Dean's revelations and sternly anxious not to let any mid-
dle- or large-sized fish swim entirely away.

Neal finally yielded, Dean didn't get the immunity he sought,
and the deal finally worked out probably better served the ends
of justice. Dean pleaded guilty to one felony count of conspiracy to
obstruct justice, for which he was sentenced to one to four years
in prison, and agreed to testify fully at all future trials in return
for Cox's agreement to drop all other charges (except, of course,
any perjury which might later be proved).

The controversy over Dean's immunity—as it turned out—was
resolved on the day before Nixon fired Cox, and may even have
helped to trigger the decision. With Dean having pleaded guilty

and facing a stiff sentence, his full testimony was guaranteed, and could no longer be attacked on the ground that he had traded it for lenient treatment.

The Dean decision was an excellent example of the high degree of professionalism involved in the work of the Special Prosecutor's office. If Cox and his colleagues had been, as Ziegler and other Nixon publicity men like Kenneth Clawson and Patrick Buchanan repeatedly tried to picture them, Kennedy men out to get Nixon and reverse the result of the 1972 election, then Dean would have been granted immunity at the beginning. His testimony was obviously so crucial to the job of implicating Nixon in the conspiracy, that Dean would have been paid any price by men out solely to convince the public of that involvement.

But these were *legal* problems being discussed and overcome, and it was in that framework that the discussions proceeded and the decision was finally taken. It is no accident or vast conspiracy that no member of the Special Prosecutor's staff ever spoke of a "historic mission" or of "convicting" Nixon, or indeed of anything except the day-to-day legal problems of filing briefs, examining actual or potential witnesses, or researching the cases whose precedents would affect the trials and appeals and motions always on the agenda.

One other key decision of the Special Prosecutor's office deserves discussion, to demonstrate in another way that these were lawyers, making legal decisions, and not political figures deciding how best to remove a sitting President whose "mandate" they resented.

On July 16, 1973, a former White House staff assistant to H. R. Haldeman, droning on in his testimony before the Ervin Committee, was asked whether to his knowledge any conversations of President Nixon in his offices in the White House had ever been taped or otherwise recorded. "I was afraid you'd ask that question," Alexander Butterfield began, and the remainder of his detailed testimony led, of course, to the shattering of the Nixon presidency.

Although the staff of the Senate Watergate Committee, and Senators Ervin and Baker, had been aware for three days of what Butterfield's testimony would be, it was heard by Cox and his associates with as much surprise as it was throughout the country. If the President's conversations in the Oval Office, the Executive Office Building, Camp David, and the Cabinet Room, plus all of his telephone calls, had been taped and the tapes stored in the White House, then all evidentiary conflicts could be resolved. Or at least that was what went through the mind of every lawyer who saw and heard the testimony—including those at the office of the Special Prosecutor.

In those cluttered offices, the effect of Butterfield's testimony was immediate. Key staff members—Ruth, Lacovara, Neal, Vorenberg, Heyman, Kriendler, Doyle—gathered in Cox's office to hear the rest of the testimony and make plans for immediate action. The action, of course, related to the testimony of John Dean. Neal, with principal responsibility for the cover-up case, in which Dean's testimony would have to be tested, took the lead.

When Butterfield revealed the extent of the Nixon taping system, the reaction of the Cox lawyers was much the same as that of other lawyers around the country. Here was "the best evidence," proof which would resolve the Nixon–Dean conflict and determine which man was telling the truth. For the Cox lawyers—particularly Neal—it was crucial to listen to the tapes as soon as possible, not only to test Nixon's involvement in the cover-up, but to test Dean's credibility on other matters.

If, for example, Dean's testimony held up as to his conversations with Nixon—it would be given a higher credibility as to his version of his conversations with Haldeman, Ehrlichman, or Mitchell, which were unrecorded.

Dean, for example, had told the Ervin Committee publicly, and Cox investigators privately, of conversations with Nixon on at least two occasions which—in Dean's view—implicated Nixon directly. On September 15, Dean recalled, he had interrupted a Haldeman–Nixon conversation already in progress in the Oval Office to be told by the President what a good job he was doing "containing" Watergate. Since it was the day that only the small-fry burglars had been indicted, with no grand jury action touching the White House, and only six weeks before the election, the conversation was significant.

In addition, Dean had spoken of conversations in March 1973, when he first told Nixon of a "cancer growing on the presidency" and where he had talked of the involvement of key White House staff men in the obstruction of justice. It was in the conversation of March 21, according to Dean, that Nixon agreed to the payment of "hush money" to Howard Hunt and the other defendants.

So, sitting in Cox's office watching the amazing testimony of Butterfield unfold, the prosecution lawyers began to act, almost instinctively, like lawyers. Neal and a few others began quickly to look through Dean's testimony, in order to pull out the key dates of conversations. Once this was done, a letter was prepared to the White House asking Nixon for nine specific tapes and some additional memoranda.

The letter was carefully drafted, because it had occurred to Cox and his people that one defense available to Nixon was that of executive privilege, which he had often threatened to invoke on a much broader scale than any President had ever outlined. Earlier in the year, Richard Kleindienst had deliberately baited a Senate committee with the astounding claim that the President, if he wished, could prevent *any* of the millions of federal employees from testifying before a congressional committee simply by invoking executive privilege.

Senator Muskie could hardly believe his ears, and challenged Kleindienst on the matter. Kleindienst, who would later plead guilty to lying to a Senate committee when he *did* testify, stuck to his guns. "If you don't like it," he said, "you can always impeach him." Muskie, still incredulous, asked, "on what charge?" "You don't need any grounds," Kleindienst replied, "you just need the votes." As it turned out, the House and the Senate had both the votes and the charges when the time came—and one charge was precisely that withholding of information which Kleindienst had defended.

In order to avoid a successful executive privilege challenge, James Neal and his colleagues asked not just for the tapes, but for other documents as well. They asked for a notice transferring Howard Hunt from the White House staff to the Nixon campaign committee, and copies of "political matters memoranda" passing to H. R. Haldeman from Gordon Strachan, his assistant, for the year preceding the 1972 election.

The purpose of including these items with the request for the tapes was, among other things, to blunt the executive privilege and national security defenses. These were clearly political memos, and by no stretch of presidential power could they be included within a protected ambit of privilege.

The tapes themselves, first described in a letter which went to the White House two days after Butterfield testified, were also carefully selected. Six were conversations to which John Dean had testified. Two were meetings in June 1972, within days of the Watergate burglary, among Nixon, Haldeman, Ehrlichman, and Mitchell. One was a telephone conversation between Nixon and Mitchell three days after the burglary.

But even as the letter went to the White House, Cox and his co-workers sensed that a major confrontation was developing. It was all too pat, somehow. How could one expect Nixon, who until then had been pursuing a steady course of deceit, evasion, and concealment, suddenly to yield up the records of the very conversations which would determine his guilt or innocence? If the tapes were exculpatory of Nixon, Cox's people believed, Nixon would have made their existence known long before.

So there was little hope that the tapes would be forthcoming when the letter went out on July 18, and still less when a reply was received on July 20, turning Cox down. At that point, a subpoena was prepared, listing the documents in a more formal way, but for the first time Cox understood the dimensions of the historical confrontation in which he was involved, and also had some intimation of the result—at least the personal result.

By the time the subpoena was served on Nixon, just one week to the day after Butterfield's testimony, James Vorenberg told Cox he thought the inevitable end of this controversy would be Cox's firing, and Cox said he thought the same thing. Both knew the matter would have to be fought out in the courts—not only Judge Sirica's but the Court of Appeals and the Supreme Court. Cox thought strongly that he had the right side of the argument and would win, but both knew Nixon would not yield the tapes without using every weapon he had. And anyone who had followed the career of Richard Nixon knew that he would never confine himself to clearly defined legal weapons.

The decision to fight—and be fired as a likely result—was taken on legal grounds. Curiously enough, if Cox had really been thinking in political—or "get Nixon"—terms, he would have picked other tapes. As it was, the nine tapes under subpoena, and over which the Saturday Night Massacre would be conducted, did the job, from a lawyer's point of view. They would—if delivered—prove or disprove Dean's account of his conversations with Nixon on September 15, 1972, and on March 13, March 21, March 22, and April 15, 1973. (Indeed, when transcripts of these conversations were finally released by the White House, considerably edited and sanitized, they showed that Dean had in fact been telling the truth and that Nixon had not.)

In addition, in an attempt to pin down Haldeman, Ehrlichman, and Mitchell, and confirm or negate Dean's account of early cover-up activity, Cox subpoenaed a June 20, 1972, Nixon meeting with Haldeman and Ehrlichman, a June 20 Nixon phone conversation with Mitchell, and a June 30 meeting, again with Haldeman and Ehrlichman. Two of these three turned out to be the result of good analysis by the Cox team; when Cox was fired and the resulting wave of national disgust forced Nixon to yield and present the subpoenaed tapes, the June 20 conversation with Mitchell was mysteriously missing, and the June 20 conversation with Haldeman—which concerned Watergate, according to Haldeman's memorandum of the conversation—was obliterated by a manually created hum of 18½ minutes, precisely the length of time in which the two men discussed the burglary.

But there was another tape which more politically minded prosecutors would have asked for, which turned out to be the one that finally gave the country all the evidence it needed to know Nixon had been lying all along.

That was, of course, the tape of June 23, 1972, in which Haldeman and Nixon cooked up a fake story about CIA activity in Mexico, and agreed to force CIA director Richard Helms and his deputy, General Vernon Walters, to halt an FBI investigation then in progress.

By June 23, 1972, the FBI was tracing the money found in the pockets and in the hotel rooms of the burglars. It was about to trace it to a bank in Mexico City, where a Mexican lawyer had helped to "launder" the money on its way from a wealthy Texas contributor to the Nixon campaign in Washington. Haldeman and Ehrlichman testified that on Nixon's instructions they had ordered Helms and Walters to stop the FBI investigation on the pretext that it interfered with CIA work in Mexico, although both Helms and Walters knew there was none.

(Oddly enough, it proved to be Walters, the "political" appointee who owed his job to a previous friendship with Nixon, who first called a halt to this part of the cover-up and told the FBI, after a delay of a few weeks, that there *was no* CIA activity with which the Watergate investigation was interfering. Helms, the "professional" at the CIA, was perfectly willing to continue the deception Nixon wanted, and once even put in writing the need to limit the inquiry to those arrested in the burglary. At this writing, Helms is serving—if that is the word—as U.S. Ambassador in Iran.)

The June 23 tape, when it was finally released on August 5, 1974, was devastating and caused whatever limited support Nixon still had to vanish. If Cox had asked for it initially, it would have been revealed as early as October 1973 that Nixon was indeed a conspirator in the effort to obstruct justice, the whole impeachment proceeding would have been cut short, and Cox would have stood alone as the man "who cracked the case."

But the legal judgment was otherwise, the subpoena for the tapes was a legal document based on lawyers' reasons, and not a fishing expedition with the purpose of finding enough "dirt" on Richard Nixon to bring him down.

The subpoena, of course, was met with a motion to quash—to void the subpoena on the grounds that the material sought would somehow breach both national security and executive privilege—and Judge Sirica's decision was pivotal. In a long and carefully researched opinion, Sirica held that the limited privilege the law gives to the President to protect confidential conversations on matters of state would have to yield in the case. He ordered Nixon to deliver the tapes to him.

Sirica would then, according to his decision, listen to the tapes and excise those portions which he felt properly to be protected by national security considerations. Then, if either side objected to his decisions, they could listen to the questioned portions and argue the matter anew, in private. It was, on the whole, an excellent decision, properly narrowing the scope of the privilege but not destroying it.

Nixon appealed to the Court of Appeals for the District of Columbia, and in due course that court affirmed Sirica's decision and ordered Nixon either to comply by October 19 or file an appeal with the Supreme Court.

For weeks, as the date approached, there was speculation, some of it raw and political and some of it learned and legal, over what the Supreme Court would do. Meanwhile, the Nixon forces kept up a steady drumfire of criticism of Cox, the major theme of which was that plenty of evidence was available without the tapes, and why didn't the Special Prosecutor go ahead and press for indictments before the Grand Jury?

The answer, of course, was that so long as the tapes remained at least theoretically available, the indictments would have to be delayed. If any of the possible defendants were to be indicted, they could then claim with justification that the government had not considered all the available evidence, some of which might have been exculpatory. So the work of the Grand Jury stalled temporarily, and awaited the Nixon appeal to the Supreme Court and the subsequent decision.

One reason the White House's hypocrisy on this argument was so apparent to the lawyers in Cox's office was that the White House had, by this time, engaged the services of an expert in constitutional law, Charles Alan Wright of the University of Texas Law School. Wright had been brought in by Nixon to argue the case in the Supreme Court, and it may be that it was his advice that Nixon would surely lose in the Supreme Court which finally convinced Nixon that defiance was better—or at least less damaging—than compliance.

In any event, whatever Wright's advice, he must have known that indictments would have to await the final court determination with respect to the subpoena. Thus, the White House's needling of Cox about the delay in indictments implied strongly that Wright himself had become part of the Nixon public relations apparatus.

Wright lent himself to another curious ploy during those weeks leading up to what was thought to be the deadline for filing a Supreme Court appeal. Assistant press secretary Gerald Warren—who had taken over the daily briefings once it became clear that Ron Ziegler had lost whatever credibility he had ever had—said one day in an official presidential statement that Nixon would comply with any "definitive" decision by the high court. This gave rise to considerable speculation, centering chiefly on what kind of vote on the Supreme Court would count as "definitive." Wright's silence in the face of this selective "rule of law" stance by the chief executive further diminished his legal stature, much as James St. Clair, his successor was by his unabashed appearances as a Nixon publicist and by his refusal to concede that Nixon would obey *any* court decision.

In fact, throughout this whole proceeding, one effect was to tarnish any lawyer who sought to represent Nixon. The legal profession has suffered through Watergate, mostly through the actions of Nixon's lawyers. Wright, St. Clair, White House staff counsels Leonard Garment and J. Fred Buzhardt—all found out sooner or later that to serve Richard Nixon diminished them professionally.

But the heaviest blows fell on other lawyers who had served Nixon before and during Watergate. Of the two men who acted as Attorney-General, John Mitchell is on trial for conspiracy, obstruction of justice, and perjury and Richard Kleindienst pleaded guilty to lying to a Senate committee. All three of those who held the title of counsel (Ehrlichman, Charles Colson, and Dean) have been convicted of crimes done in his service, and two (Dean and Colson) are now serving prison terms. And Nixon's personal attorney, Herbert Kalmbach, is also in a federal prison for his actions while a Nixon man.

It raises a question. We are ready to criticize a lawyer if, for example, his last six clients have been indicted, convicted, or jailed for offenses precisely in his specialty. We say he is a bad lawyer, or worse. But what are we to make of Richard Nixon, a *client* whose last six *lawyers* have either been indicted, convicted, or jailed, and for offenses not only in his area of specialty but committed directly in his service?

As the deadline of October 19 approached, other matters were occupying Nixon and his legal advisors. For one thing, there was the matter of somehow disposing of the enormous embarrassment created by Vice-President Spiro Agnew. The Department of Justice had discovered what it regarded as incontrovertible proof that Agnew had been on the take for years, continuing to extort and collect money from Maryland state contractors after he became governor and—worse—even after he had become Vice-President.

Agnew was strongly resisting an offer to plead guilty and resign, in exchange for the dropping of more serious charges and a plea for leniency by the government. He was even urging the House of Representatives to start impeachment proceedings, a course which Nixon thought fraught with peril. Once the House finds out the impeachment machinery works, it was thought, there is no telling what they might do with it. In addition, it had occurred to Elliot Richardson, then serving with some difficulty as

Attorney-General, that an impeachment proceeding against the President for obstruction of justice would be intolerable while the Vice-President was being tried in the federal courts for bribery and extortion.

So, in October, the deal was finally struck with Agnew. Full of defiance, he pleaded "no contest" (the judge was quick to point out this was equivalent to a plea of guilty) to one substantive count of income tax evasion, the government dropped the bribery and extortion charges (but not without filing a devastating 40-page summary of the evidence it would have introduced had Agnew been so unwise as to go to trial). The judge sentenced him to three years unsupervised probation and a $10,000 fine, and Agnew disappeared forever from the Nixon administration and—it would seem—from the consciousness of the American people. If ever a major American political figure became an un-person overnight, it was Spiro Agnew on October 10, 1973.

But while the Agnew matter was being resolved to Nixon's satisfaction, the Cox investigation was proceeding in a decidedly unsatisfactory manner. With the Special Prosecutor's office fully staffed, Cox was beginning to look into some of the areas of possible criminal conduct which had not been readily apparent in May when he received his mandate, but which were clearly within its ambit.

For some time reporters had been looking into allegations that campaign funds left over from the 1968 Nixon campaign had been used to purchase the Nixon property at San Clemente, and there had been other reports that the funds for the purchase came chiefly from the Teamsters' Union. There was little on the record (beyond the pardon for Jimmy Hoffa, a *quo* for which the *quid* had not been fully determined), but since the Nixon spokesmen had come up with three different stories as to how the property had been purchased, and had refused to make the relevant deeds, mortgages, and other documents available, the area was certainly one that Cox was required to probe.

One other area too close to the White House bone was also coming under Cox's scrutiny—the financial dealings of Charles "Bebe" Rebozo. Rebozo was Nixon's closest friend, and by the fall of 1973 his involvement with Howard Hughes and other Nixon money-men was under investigation by both Cox and the staff of the Ervin Committee.

Rebozo, who had no official connection with the Nixon campaign and thus had no authority to receive contributions, had reluctantly (after it was about to be made public) revealed that he had received—in 1969 and 1970—the sum of $100,000 from Hughes, and others had testified that there were substantial Hughes contributions in 1972.

Rebozo, according to his own story, had put the money—in cash—in a safety deposit box and had not removed it until 1973, when he returned it to the Hughes organization. The story was hard to believe. Rebozo, whatever else he might be, was at least a shrewd banker, and even un-shrewd bankers do not store cash in safety deposit boxes for three years unless they think the money is "hot."

There were questions to be asked. Why had Rebozo taken the money personally, at San Clemente, instead of having it contributed to some official Nixon or GOP committee? Why was the money given in cash? For what campaign was it intended, and why was it not used for that campaign? Why, if as Rebozo claimed, he had kept the money because he feared the split within the Hughes organization would make the money somehow tainted, had he not returned the money until the authorities began to close in?

Some answers began to emerge in early 1974 as the staff of the Ervin Committee revealed that Herbert Kalmbach had testified to a quite different use of the Hughes funds. According to Kalmbach, Rebozo told him that some of the money had gone to Nixon's secretary, Rose Mary Woods, and some of it had been paid to Nixon's brothers, Donald and Edward. Kalmbach's version had a credible ring, made more credible later by the discovery by the Ervin Committee staff that Rebozo had laundered $5,000 of campaign money from 1968 in order that Richard Nixon himself might use the funds to buy his wife some earrings for her birthday.

Early in December 1974, a hitherto unrevealed conversation among Nixon, Haldeman, and Ehrlichman was read to the cover-up trial jury. In it, Nixon offered the two men money up to $250,000 from a fund Rebozo was keeping for him—suggesting a further reason why Nixon wanted Cox to stay away from a thorough investigation of Rebozo and his bank accounts.

Whatever the facts about San Clemente and Rebozo's role in

the financial affairs of Richard Nixon, they were two areas of Cox's probe which made the White House furious. Elliot Richardson recalled that during the height of the Agnew bargaining, he was told by the President that after Agnew, the next target was Cox, and that Alexander Haig had complained about a news report that Cox was getting into the whole San Clemente financing question.

During the week preceding October 19—the deadline for filing a Nixon appeal on the tapes with the Supreme Court—Nixon and Haig (with the active connivance of the constitutional scholar Charles Alan Wright) were indeed plotting how to get rid of Cox. Richardson had simply refused to do the deed, on the reasonable grounds (although it seemed a surprising attitude to Nixon and Haig) that he had given his word, publicly, that he would not.

So Haig, Nixon, and Wright, through the course of that eventful week, began to develop a scenario which they thought might ease Richardson's conscience, or at least seem palatable enough to the public. What they had in mind—put bluntly—was to defy the law, refuse to yield the tapes, and declare the suit over the tapes moot since Cox would have been fired and the Special Prosecutor's office dissolved.

Since Richardson would not agree simply to fire Cox—he had not been guilty of "extreme improprieties," the only legal ground available—he was appealed to on grounds of pride. Somehow, the Middle East crisis following the Yom Kippur war was invoked. Haig, particularly, kept hinting darkly to Richardson that Cox's looking into money Bebe Rebozo might have washed for his friend in the White House would weaken the United States in its global struggle for peace. Richardson, who had bought a lot of shabby political merchandise from the White House before, wasn't buying this time.

Next, Wright tried out a "compromise" on Cox, but one which he knew the prosecutor could not accept. If Nixon would deliver to the Special Prosecutor an edited summary of the tapes sought by the subpoena, Cox would accept that in lieu of the actual tapes and, what is more, would thereafter refrain from seeking any additional evidence from the White House.

Wright even began the offer to Cox with the sentence, "I have a proposal I don't think you'll agree with," and he was dead right.

Meanwhile, Haig was refining the Nixon proposal for "compromise," and doing it less than honestly. Senator Ervin and Senator Howard Baker, the ranking Republican member of the Watergate Committee, were summoned to the White House. There, they were told that Senator John Stennis would be given the *verbatim* transcripts of the tapes, and would verify, by listening to the tapes, their authenticity. Then, the Senators were told, Cox would be given the transcripts, less any sensitive "national security" portions Stennis and the White House *and* Cox had agreed might be deleted.

Nothing was said to Ervin and Baker about the plan to restrict Cox from further information; they were directly deceived by Haig as to the nature of the transcripts to be delivered—whether *verbatim* or *edited*—and indirectly deceived as to Cox's acquiescence, Haig speaking constantly of a "compromise."

The use by Haig, as well as the other Nixon men throughout the controversy which followed, of the word *compromise,* was typical of the way these men operated (and, inferentially, of their contempt for the English language). There was, of course, at no time a compromise, merely a proposal by Nixon and Haig to avoid the law, a proposal which Cox—as Wright had anticipated—totally rejected.

But Ervin and Baker, misled by Haig, went along with what they thought was a compromise which would see verbatim transcripts released by the White House. One reason they agreed was that Judge Sirica, who had ruled *for* Cox on the subpoena for the tapes, had ruled *against* the Ervin Committee on the grounds their mandate from Congress was not broad enough in scope to include this kind of subpoena power. The compromise, the Senators felt, would at least yield *some* tapes.

Once Cox had turned down the proposal to allow Nixon to defy the law and substitute laundered transcripts for evidence, and to require him to cease his investigation of the White House, Nixon and Haig went public with what they (and, dutifully, the news media) were now calling the "Stennis compromise." The use of Stennis was a nice public relations touch. The Senator, although nominally a Democrat, was Nixon's strongest supporter in the Senate, and a short time before had publicly urged him to "tough it out" (the phrase stuck, and contributed in a small way to the further debasement of the language). In addition, Stennis was still recovering from gunshot wounds suffered a few months before in the course of a street hold-up by two teen-age blacks; to suggest that his performance as authenticator of the tapes might involve a pro-Nixon bias was at that time as un-American as to oppose the serving of apple pie at a White House dinner.

And as a final touch, Nixon took to referring to Stennis as "Judge" Stennis. Although he had served more than a quarter-century in the Senate, Stennis had a few years of service before that as a circuit judge in Mississippi; it was enough for the PR men in the White House.

As the deadline for appeal to the Supreme Court passed, and the evening TV news programs began to be beamed across the country, the "Stennis compromise" was set forth by Nixon. It had all the best of appearances. Distinguished Judge Stennis would listen to the tapes and authenticate the version of the transcripts to be delivered, after concurring in any national security deletions. Justice would be served, since Cox would then have all the "relevant" Watergate evidence he needed. Once this was accomplished, Cox would have no need to go into more time-consuming legal proceedings to get more evidence, since he would have all he needed. Senators Ervin and Baker approved this generous compromise. One would hope Cox would not object, because it would show his lack of good faith.

It was, all in all, vintage Nixon. Half-truth mixed with flat lies, all designed to avoid and evade the plain rule of law. Had he put it truthfully (never once in the whole long history of Watergate an option even considered by Nixon), the statement of October 19 would have gone something like this:

"As you know, today is the last day to appeal to the Supreme Court from Judge Sirica's decision that I must give Mr. Cox the nine tapes he has subpoenaed. I will not appeal that decision because I am sure to lose in the Supreme Court, and I have said I would abide by their 'definitive' decision. Since the information on the tapes is too incriminating to me, I refuse to give them to the prosecutor. Instead, I have worked out an alternative method which I hope, but hardly expect, he will approve. I will edit the transcripts, taking out anything I would rather not have Mr. Cox hear. Then I will ask my friend and loyal supporter, Senator John Stennis, to agree publicly that everything I removed was in the interests of national security.

"In return for getting my version of what I said, Mr. Cox will never ask for anything more. If he refuses, I will fire him, and hope no one notices that it would be illegal to do so. In my behalf, General Haig has deceived Senators Baker and Ervin, telling them that I plan to give Mr. Cox *verbatim* transcripts of the tapes, and that Senator Stennis's job is only to verify their accuracy. Since Senators Ervin and Baker believe that false story, they have approved the plan. Thank you and good night."

Not bloody likely.

Later the same night, Ervin and Baker denounced the use of their "support" for something they had never approved, and Cox scheduled a press conference for the following day. It seemed clear that Cox would reject the proposal, and it also seemed clear that he would be fired. But how? and when? and by whom? were still very much open questions.

By Saturday, October 20, the Nixon public relations campaign was starting to come unstuck. For one thing, the timing of the *démarche* was suspicious. Not only was October 19 the last day to file an appeal to the Supreme Court (a time which could easily have been extended), it was a key day for other reasons. On that day, his deal to testify having finally been struck with Cox and James Neal, John Dean pleaded guilty to one felony count of obstruction of justice. On the same day, H. R. Haldeman went before the Grand Jury again, and the questions he was asked must have filled the Nixon men with foreboding. In addition, that day's Miami newspapers headlined the news that Cox's people were looking into Rebozo's financial transactions, and Rebozo himself came to Washington. It didn't seem like a time for a generous compromise from the White House, and indeed it was not.

All of this speculation, and more, was in the air as Cox got ready to face the press on Saturday. There were premonitions of disaster on his own staff as the press conference approached. As one insider remembered it, "Archie has projection problems when he's relaxed. His voice is often squeaky and he can come across to the public as a—well—as a Harvard professor."

Another worry to the prosecution force was the attitude of Richardson. He had turned down the compromise the night before, which in retrospect made it clear he would stand tough when ordered to fire Cox, but there was still some doubt. In fact, as the scenarios spun out before Cox threw down the gauntlet, it was hard to see where it would all lead. Much depended on Richardson, and only slightly less on William Ruckelshaus, a respected Indiana Republican who was Richardson's Deputy Attorney-General.

Cox would turn down the Nixon proposal, so the theorizing went. Then Nixon would ask Richardson to fire Cox. If Richardson refused, Nixon would have to fire Richardson. Then he could ask Ruckelshaus to do the job, and if *he* refused, then Nixon would have to fire him. After Ruckelshaus, there was only Solicitor-General Robert Bork, and it had not occurred to Cox's people that Bork would do the job. It also had not occurred to them that Richardson and Ruckelshaus would *resign*. In fact, until Cox's press conference, it wasn't clear to either Cox *or* his advisors that Richardson would stand by Cox. They *thought* he would, and his actions until then had certainly indicated the strong likelihood that he would, but they were not sure.

Cox's press conference was, in many ways, a turning point in the controversy, and made a foregone conclusion of the nation-wide reaction of fury at Nixon over the Saturday Night Massacre. The fears of his staff were resolved; Cox was superb. He looked and talked strong, and he put the matter so simply that the issue never became Nixon v. Cox. By the time he finished explaining why he would not go along with Nixon's defiance of the law, and by the time he had explained his dislike for confrontations and the strong possibility that "maybe I'm getting too big for my britches," Cox had already won the day.

Only ABC didn't carry Cox's challenge live (there was, after all, a college football game scheduled whose advertising spots had already been sold). All the networks were set to carry large portions of the press conference on the evening news. The message was plain: Cox was going to abide by his charter and by the law. There was no compromise, and he could not agree not to seek more evidence. And by his clear discussion of the week's events, and the messages he had received from the White House and from Wright, and by his references to the terms of his appointment, Cox—without intending it that way—made it obvious, if it had not been obvious before, that Elliot Richardson would also not go along with the White House.

And so it was that Americans, at home Saturday night in front of their television sets (most of them, as usual, watching CBS's four comedy half-hours between 8 P.M. and 10 P.M.), were treated to the extraordinary spectacle of program interruptions by network White House correspondents, out of breath from having raced from the briefing room to the White House lawn, conveying a series of astonishing bulletins.

The President, we learned, had asked Elliot Richardson to fire Cox, and Richardson had resigned rather than do it or see it done. Then the President had asked Ruckelshaus to do the job, and *he* had resigned rather than be a party to the firing. Finally, the President had asked Bork, by now the acting Attorney-General, and he had agreed. Cox was fired, said the White House announcement, the Special Prosecutor's office had been abolished, and the Department of Justice would conduct the investigation. Finally, it was announced that agents of the FBI were surrounding and had occupied the offices of Richardson, Ruckelshaus, and Cox. Henry Ruth, who was later to become Special Prosecutor himself, summed it up that night for most Americans, referring to the title of a a ten-year-old melodramatic novel describing a *coup d'état* by the U.S. Army. "It may not have been *Seven Days in May*," he said, "but it was one night in October."

In retrospect, it could have been different. If Richardson, for example, had simply refused to fire Cox, but had not resigned, would Nixon have fired him, and then Ruckelshaus? In any event, if Bork had not caved in and performed the deed, which he must have known was illegal, there would have been no way to remove Cox. The law did not provide for any further succession in the Department of Justice, and it is clear the Senate would never have confirmed another Attorney-General without the assurance that Cox would remain.

But Bork did the White House's dirty work (and in the process started a small movement to enrich the language with a new verb, "to bork," meaning to do another man's dirty work, no matter what the moral price) and as of Saturday at 8:45 P.M., Cox was out as Special Prosecutor. Bork, however, did more, and it went unnoticed in the confusion of the weekend. His order removing Cox did nothing about the other half of the job—eliminating the office of Special Prosecutor entirely and transferring its functions to the Justice Department.

Whatever the reason for Bork's action, it was crucial to the continuance of the existence of the Special Prosecutor. The original announcement by Ron Ziegler was explicit—Cox had been fired by Bork and the office was abolished. But, in what must be an unprecedented event, that was the last anyone heard of the abolition of the office. Whether Bork took note of the flood of criticism which broke and which was to increase as the days went by, or whether he was suddenly afflicted with pangs of conscience, or whether he simply acted like the politician who "would go in the kitchen but wouldn't go upstairs" is unknown. But the office of Special Prosecutor survived the massacre, and its survival was crucial.

Cox, looking down the road to confrontation, was uneasy and did nothing to forestall his own removal. For that matter, a few weeks later, when his removal was found illegal by federal judge Gerhard Gesell, Cox refused to do anything about it. His reasoning, although alien to Nixon's, was sound and patriotic. The contest as perceived by the nation, Cox felt, should never be one of Cox against Nixon, or even of the Special Prosecutor against Nixon, but rather one of Nixon against the rule of law. That had been the theory with which he began, and it was the one with which he left.

Within days, that concern of Cox's had been thoroughly understood and acted upon by the rest of the lawyers on the staff he had put together. It turned the controversy from one of personality into one of principle, and from a furious turmoil over procedure into a steady and calm concern over substance. But for a few days, once the Saturday Night Massacre had in fact occurred, it was a near thing.

After the press conference, the Coxes (Mrs. Cox had accompanied her husband at the press conference) walked back to the office on K Street with James Doyle and his assistant, John Barker. Cox remarked on the way that while he was aware of the regulation against the consumption of spiritous beverages on federal property, perhaps the rule could be bent slightly that day to accommodate a few six-packs of beer. Barker complied.

Back at the office, almost the whole staff sat, drank the beer, and talked. Most people there thought the next step would come on Tuesday, October 23, since Monday was a government holiday. (In the course of the steady homogenizing of America over the past several years, Armistice Day had become Veterans' Day, and the date had moved from November 11 to the last Monday of October, no one wishing to honor veterans on a day too close to Thanksgiving and the beginning of the Christmas retail season.)

It did not occur to the staff assembled in Cox's office that the firing was only a few hours off, on Saturday night, because no one in the office, Cox included, knew that the decision to fire Cox, for any reason—or as it turned out, no reason—had been taken at least one week before. And when it was all over, Elliot Richardson recalled what he thought was a light remark during the discussions about Agnew that when that matter was concluded "we'd have to get rid of Cox." At the time, he didn't take it seriously, at least not seriously enough to tell Cox.

As the prosecutors started to drift apart toward their homes late Saturday afternoon, Doyle stayed behind to give the news-magazines what he called their "ticktockers," hour-by-hour, sometimes minute-by-minute, accounts of the events of the day, and then he went home. There, he was joined by Barker, whose family was out of town. The two men watched the news and news analysis programs, and Doyle interrupted his relaxation long enough to call a local Washington station, where commentator George Will had just speculated that if Cox were fired, it would increase his already large fee for private cases before the Supreme Court. Doyle told the producer that there were no fees, large or small, and that the last time Cox had appeared before the Supreme Court it was on behalf of an accused murderer, for no fee at all. Will corrected his remarks, and Doyle and Barker went back to watching and taking occasional calls from newsmen, most of them seeking interviews with Cox.

Sometime after 8 o'clock, a reporter from the Washington *Post*, Peter Milius, showed up at Doyle's front door with the story. The *Post* had sent him in person because no one could reach Doyle by phone. According to Milius, Cox had been fired, the office of Special Prosecutor had been abolished, and the FBI was moving in.

In all of this, the detail of sending the FBI to take over the offices of Cox, his assistants, Richardson, and Ruckelshaus was the detail that registered. It gave the whole event an un-American, almost Gestapo-like theatricality, and for most Americans, changed strong opposition to fury and disgust. It was unthinkable that the mild-mannered, impeccably correct, law-abiding man they had seen on television that day required the presence of the FBI in his office, to prevent—what? It was the working of the Nixonian mind again—the assumption that the whole world shared the Nixon mentality and moral level. After all, the reasoning must have gone, if *Cox* had fired *Nixon*, it would have taken more than FBI men to keep the files from being removed and perhaps doctored at the White House. The takeover of the offices by the FBI was ordered by General Haig (one more reminder of *Seven Days in May*) and demonstrated once more his total lack of understanding of American public opinion.

On the night of the Massacre, after Richardson had refused to fire Cox, and had resigned instead, Haig called upon Ruckelshaus to carry out the President's illegal order. When Ruckelshaus seemed to waiver, Haig told him it was "an order from the Commander-in-Chief." Ruckelshaus's reply has not been recorded; he says only that he told Haig he would resign rather than carry out the order. Ruckelshaus wasn't even allowed that dignified act; he was dismissed promptly, even as his resignation was on its way to Nixon.

(Haig was confused about more than the nature of the role of military and civilian in the United States. Later, when it was pointed out to him that a portion of one of the tapes had been manually obliterated, and that only Nixon, Nixon's secretary, and Nixon's appointments secretary had held custody of the tape, Haig replied that the erasure must have been done by some "sinister force." And when, a few weeks later, in a television interview, he said that history would look kindly on Nixon's "vicarship," it seemed fair to conclude that Haig was also confused about the separation of church and state.)

When the Washington *Post* reporter told James Doyle what had happened, Doyle called Cox. The Special Prosecutor told him that the White House had called to ask directions to Cox's home, and that a special messenger had just arrived from the Justice Department with the letter from Bork telling Cox he was fired.

Cox said he had hoped that, since neither Richardson nor Ruckelshaus would do Nixon's bidding, Bork wouldn't either, but that evidently he had. But Bork, perhaps in some final instinct of propriety, had merely notified Cox of his own firing and,

despite Ziegler's statement that the Office of the Special Prosecutor had been abolished, no official notification of that had as
yet been made, nor would it ever be made. But Doyle, and Cox,
and all the other members of the prosecution force believed the
office had been abolished, since that was the official announcement Ziegler had put out, and it was the one being carried on
all the news programs.

Over the phone, Cox gave Doyle a statement to release to the
press, composed on the spur of the moment. It was brief, and
said that the issues involved were now for Congress and the
country. Although Cox did not intend it as such, it was a clear
adumbration of impeachment, since it had long since become
obvious that impeachment was the only remedy available to
reach the offenses of a President who had decided to defy the law.

Another curious footnote to the Cox statement was that the
press—unanimously—amended it. Cox had concluded his conversation with Doyle by settling on ". . . now it is for Congress and
the country." The wire services who received the statement added,
almost by reflex, the words "to decide," giving the sentence
somewhat better meter but ever-so-slightly hardening the meaning.

By 10 o'clock on the night of the Massacre, nearly the entire
Cox staff, lawyers and secretaries, had gathered at the K Street
offices. No one had called the meeting, but the instinct to huddle
together was strong. The offices were crawling with FBI men. In
addition to the FBI, the Department of Justice had sent over some
marshals, and the regular Executive Protection Service guards were
on duty. According to Doyle, " the rage level was extremely high."

The press was also present in large numbers, and permission
was finally worked out for the reporters to gather in the library,
their customary retreat. It was at that gathering of press people
that Henry Ruth made his remark about *Seven Days in May*.
When Doyle was asked what *he* was going to do, the press secretary replied that he would go home "and read about the Reichstag
fire." It was that kind of night; even Ralph Nader had somehow
gained admittance and held an impromptu press conference.

After the meeting with the reporters, the staff gathered with
Ruth in the eighth-floor conference room. It was, by all accounts,
a quiet but intensely emotional meeting. Ruth began the meeting
by asking anyone who would not be at work Tuesday morning

to raise his hand; no one did. Monday would be Veterans' Day and a court holiday, but Tuesday, October 23, there would be motions to file—specifically a motion to hold the President in contempt for not responding to Judge Sirica's subpoena, which had become final through the failure to appeal.

It was still assumed by all present—from Ruth and Doyle down to the most recently hired secretary—that the office had been abolished. Just how they would continue with their work had not been thought through; some thought the office might be "folded" into the Justice Department, and there was considerable apprehension about being placed under the authority of Henry Petersen, who had attacked the need for a Special Prosecutor even as recently as in his testimony before the Ervin Committee in late summer.

But it was the *legal* situation which was uppermost in everyone's mind; there were, after all, cases pending, motions to be made, testimony to be presented to the Grand Jury, appeals to be forwarded, subpoenas to prepare.

The integrity of the records was the immediate problem. If the members of the Special Prosecutor's office couldn't take papers out of the office—and those were Haig's orders—at least there should be assurances that the FBI would prevent anyone else from taking them out. That arrangement was finally worked out Saturday night, and the staff—prepared to go to work *somewhere* on Tuesday unless each was individually fired—went home.

On his way home, Doyle thought to stop in his office and take a few family pictures from his desk and a framed copy of the Declaration of Independence from his wall. Angelo Lano, the FBI agent in charge of the occupation detail, had also been the Bureau liaison with Cox's office and was a friend of the men and women who worked there, including Doyle. Tonight, however, he had his orders and told Doyle he could take nothing out of his office. "It's the Declaration of Independence, Angie," said Doyle. "Just stamp it 'VOID' and let me take it home."

By Sunday, the firestorm was beginning to rage. The flood of more than a million calls and telegrams was beginning to engulf the White House, and angry Congressmen and Senators were beginning to feel the heat and to generate some. Senator Edward Kennedy had issued a statement containing the dread word, "impeachment," members of the Senate Judiciary Committee were calling for an early meeting to discuss how to preserve the office of the Special Prosecutor. In the House, Speaker Carl Albert was clearly signaling a new attitude toward the early impeachment resolutions from Representative Robert Drinan of Massachusetts and Representative Jerome Waldie of California, both of which had been routinely pigeonholed earlier.

Against that background, Doyle observed that no official document had yet been issued or delivered which abolished the office of Special Prosecutor, or even affected its operation in any way, save for the dismissal of Cox. "To bork" might mean "to perform dutifully the dirty work of a powerful master," but it might not—it began to appear—extend to the performance of *any* act, however distasteful. Doyle, concerned about the scope and enforceability of the agreement with the FBI not to allow the documents in the office to be removed by anyone, decided to test the White House's resolve.

Accordingly, he went down to the office on Sunday. He found network news camera crews outside the door and an FBI man guarding it. Operating, he says, largely on instinct, Doyle motioned to the newsmen to follow him and started in the door. The FBI man said he couldn't come in; the cameras started rolling. "What do you mean, I can't come in?" inquired Doyle. "I work here, here's my pass."

To which the FBI man replied that the office was closed. "Not to me," said Doyle, "I work here. What's your name?" When he was refused entry once more, but sensed that perhaps he could be admitted but not the press, Doyle showed his badge. It was, he remembered later, a bigger one than the FBI man's. "Of course they can come in; I'm the public affairs officer—it says so right here—and they are the press. There is a press room on the tenth floor and that's where we're going." The FBI man, who had probably read the newspapers that morning, let them in. The whole episode, after all, was on film.

The press went up to the makeshift press room in the tenth-floor library to wait, and Doyle went to his office. As he turned on the television set, there was the face of Melvin Laird, formerly Secretary of Defense and now a Nixon counselor at the White House, blandly assuring the audience that there were no FBI men at the Special Prosecutor's office.

Doyle picked up the phone, and called the producer of "Meet

the Press" to point out that the office was crawling with FBI agents. The producer replied that the agents had been withdrawn. Doyle responded that he was *in* the office, and that he would, if requested, read the names of the agents he could see. Lawrence Spivak didn't put Doyle's denial on the air, but he must have told someone, because within a short time the FBI agents were withdrawn, to be replaced by federal marshals.

Once the marshals were in place—Doyle had shooed them out of Cox's office on the grounds they were violating security regulations—Doyle called a press briefing for 4 P.M. Sunday. No sooner did the announcement of the briefing move on the wires than the Justice Department was on the phone. Jack Hushen, the department's press officer—he is now serving as deputy White House press secretary—wanted to know what the briefing was about. "Housekeeping matters," said Doyle. Hushen repeated that he wanted to know the real subject and added, "You know, you work for me now." Doyle replied, "I haven't seen any piece of paper on that. If you have such a piece of paper, please send it over here so we'll know who works for whom." At that, Hushen backed away and said only that Henry Petersen wanted to know what the briefing would be about. "Housekeeping matters," said Doyle, "so the press will know that there's still a government."

The briefing, in Doyle's recollection, was alternately civil and surreal. Mainly it consisted of the reporters' (true to form, most of them knew only what they had read in the others' newspapers) telling Doyle the office had been abolished, and his telling them he was still there. Finally, the briefing ended with a reporter once more saying, "Come on, Jim, you've been abolished," and Doyle, somewhat exasperated, saying, "Look, if the White House puts out a press statement describing someone as green, and you look up and he's blue . . ." The following morning, papers around the country carried the story—"Watergate Prosecutor Spokesman Says Office Not Abolished, Will Carry On."

It was a direct challenge to Nixon, as it turned out, and as always through the whole sordid history of Watergate, when Nixon was challenged head-on by strength, he backed down. Nothing more was ever heard about abolishing the office of the Special Prosecutor.

By Monday morning, there was strategy to be considered. On the last business day before the Massacre, Henry Ruth had ob-

tained assurances from all the lawyers that no one would resign
even if Cox were fired—that each would have to be fired in turn
before they would leave. Now that pledge would have to be
reconsidered if there was still a threat to move the office to the
Justice Department. It was, after all, one thing to stay on the job
Cox had begun, even without Cox but with the rest of the
force intact; it was quite another to work for Henry Petersen.

On Monday, the senior staff began to meet in Ruth's office
to discuss strategy, but the thought was that it might be improper
to use the offices and, in any event, the press and the force of
U.S. marshals was milling about. So the meeting adjourned to a
suite of private law offices down on Connecticut Avenue, in a
law firm with which Joseph Connolly, then the head of the ITT
task force, had previously been connected. (A client of one of
the other lawyers in the firm, there to discuss the precise form a
business enterprise might take and its tax consequences, was surprised that holiday morning to open the door to the conference
room and discover Henry Ruth presiding over a meeting of some
30 lawyers from the Special Prosecutor's office.)

At the start, there were reassurances needed. Some of the
lawyers felt that Doyle's statement that the office would continue
somehow constituted a betrayal of Cox. Doyle, who had spoken
to Cox on Sunday, and Ruth were able to calm those fears.
Indeed, Ruth felt strongly that resignation of the Cox staff was
probably the aim of the White House action, since it would be
extremely difficult to fire them all.

(Doyle's conversation with Cox on Sunday was a good indicator
of the mood. On that day, one of the security men came to Doyle
and said the Attorney-General was on the phone. Doyle, thinking
of Richardson, said he'd be pleased to talk to him. No, he was
told, this is Mr. Bork and he wants Mr. Cox's phone number.
Doyle refused, saying he didn't know if Cox wanted to talk to
"this fellow" or not. Some angry words were exchanged, after
which Doyle called Cox to tell him someone named Bork wanted
to talk to him.)

At the Monday meeting it was finally agreed that no one would
resign, and that the following day everyone would go about his
professional responsibilities as though Cox were only absent, not
fired, and as though no one had even heard of Ziegler's statement
of Saturday that the office had been abolished. That meant that

Richard Ben-Veniste and Jill Wine Volner (Ben-Veniste had taken charge of the main Watergate cover-up task force on Friday; James Neal had gone back to Nashville after taking John Dean's guilty plea) would be in Judge Sirica's court to seek a contempt order on the grounds of non-compliance—the Stennis compromise having been rejected by the government.

On Tuesday, there was still no word whether the White House would carry through on abolition of the office; none ever came. The protest had reached the proportions of the firestorm (the term was Haig's, and the measure of Nixon's lack of touch with reality was that he continued to rely on Haig for advice). On Capitol Hill, the Senate Judiciary Committee was getting hearings under weigh with the aim of coming up with legislation to make the Special Prosecutor a permanent office, so that Cox's successor could not be fired by the very forces he was charged with investigating.

Also on Tuesday, Elliot Richardson had a press conference, and, despite fears by some that he might bork, strongly backed Cox and defended his own and Ruckelshaus's refusal to fire him. Richardson also destroyed whatever credibility Haig had left by denying convincingly that he had ever approved the plan by which Senator Stennis would approve the edited transcripts. (Haig would later tell the Judiciary Committee that Richardson had indeed had reservations about the compromise, and then suggested, not too subtly, that Richardson thought better of the whole plan after he had had a few drinks.)

On Tuesday, Archibald Cox came into his office for the last time, to pick up a few personal belongings and to say good-bye to his staff. The press wanted the staff to come to the library where cameras were ready to film Cox's farewell but both the lawyers and Cox, true to their own standards, thought it looked too artificial and turned it down. Cox left to go to the Supreme Court library to do some research, and heard on his car radio that Nixon had caved in and agreed to obey the subpoena and deliver the tapes.

In Judge Sirica's court that day, there was a lot going on. In a most important act, the significance of which none of the White House lawyers comprehended, Judge Sirica signed a protective order requested by the Special Prosecutor. The order made it illegal for anyone to handle or otherwise remove the files of the

Special Prosecutor, "except for members of the Watergate Special Prosecution Force employed before October 19, 1973." Once the order was signed, another firing became most unlikely, since no one else sent into the Prosecutor's office—not even the FBI or the marshalls now there—could remove any of the files. The willingness of Judge Sirica to sign the order gave some indication of *his* state of mind and added to the strong possibility that he would find Nixon in contempt if he persisted in the Stennis compromise when it clearly constituted non-compliance with Sirica's order.

There was much speculation over that long weekend as to just what Judge Sirica would do when court reconvened. He could, of course, accept the "Stennis compromise" as substantial compliance with his order. He could, if he wished, grant an additional extension of time in which to comply. Or he could note Nixon's refusal to comply, and perhaps go so far as to hold the President in contempt of court.

Sirica had already made up his mind, and only the 180-degree turn in White House tactics in offering at the last minute to comply with the subpoena, kept the judge from acting. Unknown to the White House, Sirica had kept a long-standing family commitment on the holiday Monday, and took his college-bound daughter to Connecticut to visit the campus of Fairfield University.

While his daughter was being escorted around the school by some of the undergraduates, Judge Sirica visited the university's president, an old friend of his from Georgetown University in Washington. Naturally enough, they discussed the momentous decision the judge would have to make the next day and Sirica, somewhat somberly, told his friend he would probably be the first federal judge in our history to hold a President in contempt.

Charles Alan Wright faced a difficult job on that Tuesday. For months he had argued that the President need not comply with the subpoena, and had used his considerable legal skills in an attempt to support that argument. He had lost before Judge Sirica and he had lost in the Court of Appeals. He was prepared to re-argue the matter, and even to attempt to show that the Stennis compromise somehow constituted compliance, although even Wright's skills would have hardly been equal to the task of making an edited copy seem equal to the unedited original—in short, of making defiance seem to be compliance. But Wright received surprising orders Tuesday morning. He was told to abandon the defenses—national security, executive privilege, all of them—and yield. Nobody was talking, and nobody has talked since, and we shall probably never know why Nixon once more abandoned his position of stated high principles and yielded, but it came as an enormous surprise in the courtroom. Perhaps it was the firestorm, perhaps the beginnings of a rumble of impeachment from the leadership of the House of Representatives, but whatever it was, Archibald Cox had his victory—the delivery of the "best evidence" in response to a legal subpoena. And he heard the news as he was driving away from his office, fired because he had insisted on the rule of law.

In the courtroom, even the prosecution attorneys were stunned as Wright announced that President Nixon would indeed yield and comply with the subpoena. (As it turned out a few days later, compliance was far from complete; two tapes were "missing" and one had an 18½-minute buzz just as Nixon and Haldeman's voices began to discuss Watergate.)

It remained for Wright to add the final absurd touch. After having participated in every step of the firing of Cox, an act every one of his lawyer's instincts must have told him was illegal, and after having urged defiance upon his client in developing the Stennis compromise and in having his view adopted, Wright told the press, after leaving the courtroom in defeat, "This President does not defy the law." As Wright well knew, "this President" did very little else.

For the remainder of the week after the decision to deliver the tapes, the prosecution force was under the general direction of Henry Petersen, yet remained independent. Petersen's general direction was for the prosecution lawyers to remain in place and continue with all their cases. But even that passivity raised problems.

For example, during the week of uncertainty in which Petersen —as Assistant Attorney-General in charge of the criminal division —was in charge of the special prosecution force, he was told that former Attorney-General Richard Kleindienst had informed the prosecutors in charge of the ITT matter that he had lied to the Senate Judiciary Committee. Under cross-examination at his confirmation hearing, Kleindienst had told the Senators that he had

had no communication with President Nixon about the ITT case.

Now, according to Kleindienst, it appeared there had indeed been communication. ITT (originally a company which owned foreign telephone companies and was now one of the largest conglomerates) had been in anti-trust trouble in 1970 and 1971. The government had brought suit, seeking a divestiture of some of the companies owned by ITT. ITT had won in the lower court, and in the course of the negotiations over a settlement the company had offered $400,000 to the Republican Party to help defray the cost of the 1972 convention.

The immediate question, and this was what the Senators had wanted to know, was whether the White House—perhaps influenced by the $400,000 offer—had intervened with pressure to drop the case against the conglomerate. Kleindienst had assured the Senators that there had been no such pressure, and that the decisions had been taken entirely within the Justice Department.

The facts, as Kleindienst finally truthfully told the prosecutors, were sharply different. He had received a call from John Ehrlichman, in which Ehrlichman asked him not to appeal, and to let the pro-ITT decision stand. Kleindienst then told Ehrlichman he could not do that, and that the appeal—in order at least to preserve the government's bargaining position—would have to go ahead. Ehrlichman was not pleased, and told Kleindienst the matter was not closed.

Within a few moments, according to Kleindienst, he received another call from the White House, this time from Nixon himself. (With the tapes and transcripts to guide us as to the elegance of language customarily used by the President and his close advisors, one wonders what the tape of the intervening Ehrlichman–Nixon conversation would yield in the way of expletives.) Nixon was explicit. "You dumb son-of-a-bitch," he began, "don't you understand the English language?" It was a natural enough question, coming as it did from a man who demonstrated regularly his own difficulty in understanding the language, and Nixon went on to order Kleindienst to drop the appeal.

To Kleindienst's credit, he did not follow orders, and even threatened to resign if the appeal did not go forward. It did, and there was subsequently a settlement highly favorable to ITT, in which Kleindienst did not participate.

But the Kleindienst revelation put considerable pressure on Petersen. When he heard of Kleindienst's testimony, he said that of course he would have to withdraw from that matter (the high-class reflexive verb for this act has lately come to be "recuse"; one hopes it will soon disappear along with other Nixon-era verbiage such as "incursion" and "time-frame"), but that otherwise the office should continue as before.

The week was full of surprises. Only days after announcing that Nixon would, for a change, not defy the law, Charles Alan Wright had to come into court and tell Justice Sirica that of the nine tapes ordered by the subpoena, only seven would be delivered, since the other two were missing. One was a June 20, 1972 phone conversation with John Mitchell, the explanation for the absence of which was that Nixon had used a telephone in the private family quarters at the White House, from which conversations were not automatically recorded. The other was a conversation on April 15 with John Dean; the explanation was that since it was at the end of a day of long conversations in the White House, the tape had simply run out and the Secret Service people in charge of the tapes had not prepared for this contingency by providing another reel. Secret Service sources doubt the accuracy of this story, but the actual tape has never been found.

In other words, of nine tapes ordered to be delivered, the White House had produced seven. This was bad enough, but there was to be worse. The day following a clear statement by Nixon to some assembled Republican governors that there were to be "no more bombshells" it was announced that one more tape, if not missing, was at least defective. It was a June 20 conversation between Haldeman and Nixon, just three days after the burglary. Haldeman's notes showed that much of the conversation was in fact about Watergate, but Nixon's attorneys were forced to admit in court that more than 18 minutes of the taped conversation had been obliterated by a loud hum, and that none of the conversation about Watergate remained. It was too much, particularly since no explanation fit the facts except that one of the Nixon people—perhaps the President himself—had manually erased incriminating evidence.

Testimony was later taken, in Judge Sirica's court and before a Grand Jury, as to how the evidence came to be destroyed, and a panel of experts jointly named by the White House and the

Special Prosecutor analyzed the tape at exhaustive length. Their unanimous opinion was that the 18½ minutes had been manually erased, by a series of at least five erasures. Since only Nixon, his new appointments secretary Steven Bull, and his secretary Rose Mary Woods had access to the tape, the circle of suspicion was not very wide.

In the course of accounting for the "18-minute gap," as it came to be called, Rose Mary Woods became less a suspect of having done the deed than a figure of fun. She originally testified that perhaps she had accidentally erased the conversation by placing her foot on the wrong pedal while listening to the tape and transcribing it, in the course of taking a phone call. (Curiously, it was one of the few phone calls she did not painstakingly log.) But the absurdity of this attempt to take the rap appeared at once when she re-enacted the scene at her office. The location of her desk, the phone, and the pedals of the transcribing machine were so placed that it would have required one of the great contortionists of history even to have obliterated a few seconds, let alone 18 minutes. Ms. Woods herself saw the hopelessness of it all, thought for a few days that the White House lawyers were setting her up to take the blame, and changed her story. The phone call, she now remembered, was only for five minutes, and she couldn't have erased the missing portion of the tape.

Little more was heard from Nixon's secretary; at this writing the Grand Jury has yet to indict anyone for the destruction of evidence conceded to have been done by erasing part of the tape. But the image of Rose Mary Woods at her desk, leaning back with her head cocked to take a phone call, her left hand around the phone, her right straining to reach the keyboard of the tape recorder, and her foot under the desk vainly pulling her body off balance as she reaches for the wrong pedal, is one which will accompany her forever.

Once the story was out about the destruction of evidence covered by the subpoena (and few could be found who believed that the other two tapes were indeed missing, and not destroyed), the firestorm resumed its intensity. The furor over Cox's firing had yet to die down, the Senate was pursuing ways to re-appoint Cox or in any event to make permanent the office of Special Prosecutor and insulate it from presidential interference, and

Congressmen and other Nixon supporters were reconsidering their support in light of the new information.

In the middle of all this came the Great Worldwide Alert, in which the administration—including the usually non-political Henry Kissinger—tried to distract national attention by placing U.S. forces around the world on a war alert, allegedly in response to Russian moves in the Middle East. Hardly anyone believed the crisis was real—and no evidence has ever been adduced to show that it was—but it bought Nixon a few days of time in which to make a new move, and he used it, as we have seen, not wisely but too well. He decided to appoint Leon Jaworski as Special Prosecutor.

Now Jaworski must have seemed nearly ideal to Nixon and Haig, as usual the "point" man on the mission. Jaworski was a prototype of the Establishment lawyer. In addition, he had become rich and powerful by representing precisely the new *arriviste* moneyed clients Nixon so much admired, rather than the older wealth he distrusted.

He had been a close friend of Lyndon Johnson's and had continued to be after LBJ left office, doubtless indicating to Nixon and Haig that he would be free of any taint of association with "peace" radicals. In addition, he was believed to be close to John Connally, a Democrat-turned-Republican whom Nixon had made Secretary of the Treasury and whom he was thought to be grooming as his successor. (Jaworski, in fact, had not been very close to Connally, and what acquaintance he had did not prevent him later from seeking, and getting, an indictment of Connally for accepting a bribe and for perjury.)

In short, Nixon and Haig thought Jaworski would appear to be continuing the work of the Special Prosecutor while in fact selling it out. They were resigned to indictments of some of the highest White House figures (Haldeman, Ehrlichman, Mitchell) in the cover-up; what they desperately wanted at this point was someone who would stop there, who would rein in the Special Prosecution staff, and above all who would not pursue evidence as far as the Oval Office. So they turned to Jaworski, the pillar of the bar and the symbol of nouveau-rich aristocracy whom they saw as their savior. He turned out to be the tough prosecutor who pursued the evidence and, in the end, was their nemesis.

The view of Jaworski as a wise Nixon choice was shared by others. Over at the Special Prosecutor's office itself and elsewhere in Washington there was great apprehension. Texas, ABA, corporation lawyer, Connally, oil, LBJ—we live increasingly by symbols and these all read wrong. One man on the prosecutor's staff who had been in the thick of the Cox firing said it was like the wartime joke where the new submarine commander comes aboard and he has a German accent.

The Middle East crisis bought Nixon only a few days' time, and by the second week after the Massacre events were closing in. Cox's firing had been held illegal by federal judge Gerhard Gesell (in a suit begun by Ralph Nader), who found that the Justice Department's own regulations had not been complied with, but the matter was moot since Cox himself had said he would not use the decision to try to return. This event, although little noticed in the continuing drama being fought out in the Senate Judiciary Committee and in Judge Sirica's court, offered a nice contrast in both style and substance.

Could anyone imagine, for example, that Nixon or any of his partisans would not have taken advantage of the Gesell decision to return to the job? If Cox were really, as Nixon hatchet men Buchanan, Clawson, and Haig were regularly telling anyone who would listen, a Kennedyite (or worse, a McGovernite) out to get Nixon and reverse the 1972 mandate, would he not have leaped at the chance to be reinstated? The answer is that Cox was primarily a man of the law. He saw clearly that, however it might please his partisans (and himself) to return, the issue would thereafter clearly be cast in terms of Nixon v. Cox, and not of a search for the evidence and the truth. So, true to his principles, Cox passed up victory in the battle and left the field to others—who went on to win the war.

History, one can be sure, will be more than kind to Archibald Cox. In less than five months, he formed what is unquestionably the finest prosecution staff ever assembled, and by his dedication to duty and the law, he drew a deadly contrast with the criminal forces arrayed against him and the American people. In the final resolution of what became the gravest constitutional crisis since the Civil War (and perhaps including it) he played a major, decisive, and honorable role.

Leon Jaworski:
The Prosecutor as Scholar

Within ten days of Cox's firing (October 29), the Nixon people had some news. Simultaneously, the appointments were announced of Senator William Saxbe of Ohio to be Attorney-General and of Jaworski to be Special Prosecutor. Saxbe was a first-term Republican with a conservative voting record but a reputation for straight talk, who often attacked Nixon. At the time of the Christmas terror bombing of Hanoi in 1972, Saxbe wondered publicly if Nixon "had gone out of his mind," something many others in Washington were wondering privately.

But Saxbe was a Senator, and a friendly and convivial one, and thus sure to be confirmed. It was a measure of White House desperation in those days that Nixon would take into the Cabinet a Republican Senator from a state with a Democratic governor who would certainly appoint someone from his own party to fill the vacancy. But *somebody* had to be nominated who could be confirmed, and Saxbe was the man.

The Jaworski appointment was handled differently. Haig telephoned Jaworski at his Houston office on Ocotber 30 to offer him the job. By now, Cox had been out of office for ten days, one week had gone by since Nixon had agreed to deliver the tapes, and the White House now knew, although the prosecutors and the country did not, that two of the tapes would be announced as missing.

Jaworski's first reaction to Haig's offer was negative. He had been approached about the job back in June, before Cox was named. An emissary of Richardson's had talked to Jaworski then, and had said the ultimate control of the Special Prosecutor's functions would be in the Department of Justice. Jaworski said then that no good man would take the job unless the degree of independence was far greater, that the quality of the Prosecutor would be a direct function of his ability to operate his office independently of the Attorney-General. When Cox was appointed, Jaworski knew that additional independence must have been worked out. But the firing of Cox seemed to negate any independence at all, so his first reaction to Haig was that he would not take the job.

Haig talked the language of patriotism. He told Jaworski, "I'm going to put the patriotic monkey on your back." He even talked darkly of revolution, although the country was probably further from revolution than at any other crisis time in history. What Haig saw as revolution was in fact the constitutional process at work, creakingly at first but every day more surely. Lawyers of the prosecution force were in court, pressing for the delivery of the tapes they had subpoenaed and which they had been told would be delivered. On the very day on which Haig saw revolution, Chairman Peter Rodino of the House of Representatives Judiciary Committee, having been given a reluctant approval by the House leadership to move ahead with impeachment proceedings, was talking to senior committee members about procedures. The Ervin Committee, having concluded the taking of testimony, was considering further staff investigation and discussing the shape of its final report.

Perhaps, in retrospect, Jaworski should have attached more significance to Haig's talk about revolution. It might have prepared him more for "stonewalling," the refusal of the White House, led by Nixon and Haig, to participate in the constitutional process. Because if Alexander Haig saw the American political process only as either doing the President's will ("it's an order from the Commander-in-Chief") or as revolutionary, then Richard Nixon must have seen it that way, too.

During the telephone conversation, which lasted an hour, Jaworski told Haig that he had turned the job down once, and was disposed to turn it down again, unless the Special Prosecutor could have the degree of independence Jaworski demanded and which the American people expected. To Jaworski, Haig seemed desperate, and said he was ready to agree to almost any degree of independence. Jaworski thought the firing of Cox demonstrated how unlikely that seemed, and continued to say no. Finally, Haig asked if Jaworski would at least come to Washington for a day (Haig had a plane waiting at nearby Ellington Air Force Base) and let the President's men convince him that the situation had changed. Jaworski agreed to that, feeling that it was his patriotic obligation to go that far.

In Washington the next day, Haig talked again of how desperate the situation was. There *was* desperation at the White House of a different kind than the insurrection and revolution spoken of by Haig, but it was concealed from Jaworski; later that same day it would be announced that two of the nine tapes were missing.

Haig told Jaworski he had been investigated at length and that everyone agreed he was the man for the job. Jaworski talked of the need for independence, and Haig said "write your own ticket." Jaworski then spoke of two of his concerns: how to insulate the Special Prosecutor from the kind of impetuous and illegal firing which had happened to Cox, and how to guarantee that he would have the right to "sue"—to seek evidence through service of civil process—the President.

As to the first, Haig and Jaworski worked out a "buffer" between the Special Prosecutor and the President. The President could not fire the Prosecutor without a "substantial concurrence" from a group of eight men—the Majority and Minority leaders of the Senate, the Speaker and Minority leader of the House, and the chairman and ranking Republican of both the House and Senate Judiciary Committees. Translated into human beings, that turned out to be not such a good bargain, and it is probable in retrospect that Nixon and Haig had worked out this new compromise in advance. The eight men involved would be Senators Mike Mansfield, Hugh Scott, James Eastland, and Roman Hruska, and Representatives Carl Albert, John Rhodes, Peter Rodino, and Edward Hutchinson. Of this group, five (Eastland, Scott, Hutchinson, Hruska, and Rhodes) had demonstrated throughout the whole Watergate controversy a total unwillingness to consider seriously any facts unfavorable to Nixon, and Scott had even repeatedly allowed himself to be used as a channel for the most improbable of the White House evasions. Mansfield and Albert could probably be counted on to stand fast in a showdown, although neither had demonstrated a particular awareness of the magnitude of the controversy, and both had reached their present positions by avoiding fights rather than by winning them. Only Rodino might be counted a sure vote for the Prosecutor if the President once again were to contrive a showdown.

As to the second question, it was by far the more important. It was the issue over which Cox had been fired, and Nixon had even gone so far as to "order" Cox not to seek any further evidence. Haig asked Jaworski if he would like to put the question to Nixon, or talk to him about any other aspect of the Prosecutor's assignment. Jaworski refused, on the grounds that to talk to the President would seem improper if he later decided to take the job. He did not speak to Nixon on that occasion, and has yet to do so.

But Haig took the question into the Oval Office, and came out with the news that the President had agreed to both the "buffer" (not surprising, it had all the earmarks of a Nixon scheme from the beginning) and to the right of the Prosecutor to sue the President.

Then Bork (the acting Attorney-General) and Saxbe (whose nomination as Attorney-General would be announced the next day) joined Haig and Jaworski, and both agreed to the two principles. They also urged Jaworski to take the job. Bork and Saxbe were followed by White House counsels Leonard Garment and J. Fred Buzhardt, who gave their approval. After that, White House counselors Melvin Laird and Bryce Harlow ("Counselor" was a new title in the Nixon administration—one of the devices by which he was able to make it appear that the largest White House staff in history was somehow engaged in serious business) came in and gave their approval as well. Once more, Haig urged Jaworski to take the Prosecutor's post, and this time Jaworski accepted. His appointment was announced—along with Saxbe's—the next day.

It is doubtful if Alexander Haig had ever heard of Michael Moncrief—known to his family as "Mike"—and it is doubtful if he has yet heard of him. But Mike Moncrief was a significant influence on Leon Jaworski, at the time he became Special Prosecutor and during the time he held the job. Mike was Jaworski's grandson, and from the time the boy's parents divorced when Mike was very young, Jaworski helped his daughter (now Mrs. W. H. Worrell) raise her son.

Jaworski and his grandson became very close, hunting and fishing during school vacations at the Jaworski ranch at Wimberley, Texas, and during long sessions of talk as the boy grew to maturity. Mike was a brilliant student at Kinkaid High School in Houston, winning debate championships in his last two years. He was a star performer on the inter-school quiz program contests, and had virtually his choice of colleges to attend. He selected Duke University, and had completed his freshman year and was working on the Wimberley ranch when he was killed in a freak automobile accident on July 4, 1972.

Michael's ideas had impressed Jaworski, particularly his ideas about the law. When a friend suggested to the young man that he take up law as a career, because the law was "a source of power in our society," Michael had replied that that was precisely why he did not want it as a career. And in the course of many philosophical discussions with Mike, Jaworski says now that he began to question seriously some of the standards of his profession and, for that matter, of American society. A thoughtful boy, Mike had begun to articulate some of the early ideals which had brought Jaworski to law as a young man, but some of which had begun to seem remote as he rose to a position of prominence at the bar.

Jaworski had served as president of the American Bar Association in 1971 and 1972. That accolade from corporate Establishment America must have caught Haig's eye, but in Jaworski's view the most influential contact with the ABA came in the year before he assumed the often ceremonial presidency. In that year, as president-elect, he was charged with supervising the activities of a law students' association which the ABA supports.

In 1970, Jaworski recalls, he was as dubious of the young law students as any other Establishment corporate lawyer would be. Their predominantly anti-war stance troubled him; like his friend Lyndon Johnson, from whom he had turned down appointments as Attorney-General and to the Supreme Court, he shared more or less uncritically the Pentagon's assessment of the Vietnam war.

In addition he felt, almost subliminally, that the aggressive, activist law students with whom he was to deal were too radical and, indeed, that they were far from committed to the American legal system. In their expressed concern for justice and equality before the law, he saw instead a desire to tear down the system which he felt, with all its imperfections, had stood the nation and society in good stead for nearly two hundred years.

But as he spent his year with these young activists, Jaworski came to see that their concerns were quite genuine, and that their analysis of the state of the legal profession and the administration of justice was more keen and precise than his. He came, in short, to feel that their commitment to the system was strong—in fact, a great deal stronger than that of his contemporaries, many of whom were willing to ignore the obvious injustices around them.

He began, he says, to share their concern and anger over the frequent hypocricy of the law. He began to see that one becomes a participant in injustice by ignoring it. The law students were concerned about what Jaworski once thought of as "causes"—disparity in sentencing procedures between rich and poor, the frequent harassment and denial of civil rights to minority racial groups, the inability of poor defendants to obtain competent lawyers (or, for that matter, the inability to gain even access to the law in non-criminal matters), conditions in prisons and jails. He came to see them as ills to be cured, as the proper concern of the leaders of the bar, and their continued unchallenged existence as equal a danger to the American system of justice as the early Nazi excesses were to the German system.

Now, after his service as Special Prosecutor, Jaworski speaks publicly only to groups of law students or young lawyers, and his message is much the same as that of the "radical" students he met in 1970. He is firmly convinced that what separates the United States from other countries is not particularly our language or institutions but the system of individual rights and freedoms. If this system is not protected by men of the law, then all else will fail.

Near the end, when Jaworski was seeking a Supreme Court ruling that Nixon must yield more tapes, he observed that when he entered the Supreme Court building for the final oral argument, a crowd had gathered on the steps, and that he was cheered as he entered. Two things about the crowd impressed Jaworski, he says. In the first place, it was largely composed of young people, and in the second, what they were shouting were not crude anti-Nixon slogans, but "Go, U.S."

"Those young people weren't vindictive, or out to 'get' anyone," he recalled. "They wanted desperately to think that a rule of law was working here, that somehow we could return to a time when no one was above the law, and when the system really worked."

But there was no applause when Leon Jaworski was first appointed. Not only Haig and Nixon, but those fearing a sell-out, were of the opinion that Nixon had picked the "right" man. Nothing in Jaworski's public background reassured them. And that attitude extended into the special prosecution force itself.

"We didn't know what to expect," said one high-ranking member of Cox's staff, "but we didn't think it would be good. Here comes a guy in who's pure Establishment, and we knew Haig had been filling him with the standard bull about all the Kennedy men up there out to get the President, and we were worried."

In addition, the Cox men were worried about possible staff changes. It would seem reasonable, after all, for Jaworski to bring with him a new deputy, or at least a young man from his law office to perform the job Peter Kriendler did for Cox, that of special assistant tying together the work of the different task forces, or perhaps a legal counsel, or at the very least a secretary.

Instead, as James Doyle put it, "he came with a garment bag. Period." Before coming to Washington to start his duties, Jaworski made only one telephone call to the staff; he called Henry Ruth, whom he had known on one of the LBJ-era commissions on criminal justice. He assured Ruth he wanted him to continue as deputy prosecutor. He brought no legal talent with him, he planned no staff changes, and he made none. In all the time Jaworski served as Special Prosecutor, no one was added to the staff, and only four men left. (Joseph Connolly and two of his associates from the ITT Task Force resigned over disagreement with the "deal" struck with Richard Kleindienst, and Philip Lacovara resigned in protest over the pardon given by President Ford to Nixon. But none of the protestors "went public" with their grievances.)

Jaworski was determined at the start to see what kind of a staff he had, and refused to let Nixon and Haig characterize them for him. He came to Washington and spent his first several days meeting the staff, and quickly discovered that the anti-Nixon bias he had heard about at the White House was simply not present.

That discovery, and Jaworski's mounting irritation at the continuing effort by Ron Ziegler and others (chiefly Patrick Buchanan and Kenneth Clawson) to keep the calumny alive, led to a letter from Jaworski to Ziegler. Taking note of Ziegler's ill-concealed floating of charges that the prosecutor's staff was biased and out to get Nixon, Jaworski wrote Ziegler denying the charge, asking Ziegler to be specific and produce evidence in support of the charge or, in effect, to shut up. Jaworski also offered to talk to Ziegler about the matter, at either man's office, if Ziegler ever came up with any evidence. Ziegler, who like the rest of the Nixon men knew superior power when he saw it, backed down and began to attack the Judiciary Committee instead.

Jaworski's early moves may not have been designed to calm the fears of the staff, but they had that effect. He spent the first few days in intensive briefing with the different task forces, hearing the evidence and absorbing the legal issues. In the middle of the briefing, a news correspondent he had known in Texas dropped by to say hello, and Jaworski—after only two days on the job—told him he was very impressed with two things: the calibre of the staff members and the evidence.

Jaworski also made a few symbolic acts. He announced that the staff would remain intact, and within the first two weeks he personally went into court to file and argue a motion prepared by William Merrill in the case of Egil (Bud) Krogh. Krogh was one of the "plumbers," and had helped plan the burglary of the offices of Dr. Lewis Fielding, Daniel Ellsberg's psychiatrist. His defense in court was that the action was really legal, because it was done for reasons of "national security." As the later release of the Nixon transcripts would demonstrate, this was a false argument cooked up by Nixon and his aides to cover their guilt in planning and executing a burglary whose only aim was political —to discredit Ellsberg by getting some "dirt" on him, at the time logic was the only weapon available to attack the defense argument.

The Jaworski staff had prepared a legal argument to the effect that the act of the burglary was illegal in any event, and that the whole assault on Ellsberg was politically motivated. Jaworski took the argument as drafted, went to court to argue it, and prevailed. It was impressive evidence, as far as the staff was concerned, that he was ready to back them up and continue the legal processes which Cox and they had set in motion.

But the Cox staff was not the only place where suspicion of Jaworski (in this case, enhanced by suspicion of Nixon) was rampant. The Senate Judiciary Committee, despite the Jaworski appointment, was still busily pursuing a statutory remedy for the firing of Archibald Cox. Senators Birch Bayh, Edward Kennedy, John Tunney, and Philip Hart were taking the lead in working out a satisfactory piece of legislation which would guarantee the existence of a Special Prosecutor wholly independent of Nixon, the White House staff, and the entire executive branch.

A number of avenues were pursued. Assuming legislation could be drafted adequately insulating the prosecutor from executive interference, setting a fixed term, and describing his duties and extending his writ as broadly as possible without running afoul of the constitutional separation of powers, one big question remained. Who would appoint the prosecutor? If the President, it put Nixon back in control, and, it was thought, the Jaworski appointment was another demonstration of how this could be used to frustrate the intent of those who framed the legislation.

Appointment by Congress was unwieldy—who would in fact name the appointee?—and possibly unconstitutional. In any event, it would be hard to deny a temporary majority the right to change prosecutors, and would make the incumbent's tenure too dependent on the election returns. So the Judiciary Committee activists, led by Bayh, turned to a third alternative. They would draft a statute properly insulating the prosecutor, giving him an ample writ, and provide for his appointment by the federal district judges in the District of Columbia. They didn't know if they had a majority for the bill in the Senate or House, and there was opposition from backers of other plans even in the committee, but they were ready to make a push in committee and on the floor.

While all this was going on, Jaworski was moving into the job, and to the general approval—after the initial suspicion had worn off—of the old Cox staff. Unknown to Bayh and his colleagues, a solid majority of the staff had reached a consensus— let the matter drop and support Jaworski. Thus, while angry rhetoric was coming each day from the Senate, from men who had every right to believe they were fighting for the independence and integrity of the prosecutor, the former Cox staff people were becoming more and more convinced each day that Jaworski himself was a sufficient guarantee of that independence and integrity.

The controversy was resolved against the Senate liberals by decisive action by the Washington *Post*. This was a curious result, since the *Post* had generally been counted on the liberal or, at any rate, anti-White House side on Watergate. In this case, the *Post*'s editorial page managers, Philip Geyelin and Meg Greenfield, were beginning to get the feeling, from their contacts in government and particularly from their sensitivity to the problems of the Watergate prosecutors, that any initial suspicion of and opposition to Jaworski was rapidly dwindling among the former Cox loyalists.

Meg Greenfield, accordingly, called James Doyle at the prosecutors' press office and told him the *Post* was disposed to write an editorial which would call on the Judiciary Committee to abandon its effort to write into law new guidelines for the Special Prosecutor and, instead, to be content with Jaworski and support him. She asked Doyle if it were not generally true that the staff was having second thoughts about Jaworski, and that they were all positive.

Doyle, after a moment's reflection, said that was a fair analysis of the views of the top staff people with whom he had talked, and that if there was still resentment and suspicion of Jaworski at lower levels it was without any evidence to support it. So the *Post* wrote a strong editorial for Washingtonians to read with breakfast, commenting favorably on the way Jaworski was proceeding and the confidence he seemed to have from the top people on his staff, and calling on the Senate Judiciary Committee members to recognize that ultimately this was a matter of trust, and that, anyway, no statute could do what they wanted it to.

That very day, influenced by the editorial, the Senate Democratic leadership dropped the bill from active consideration and Senator Bayh, after surveying the bleak scene with his colleagues, decided not to make what would have surely been a losing fight of it. Jaworski was on his own.

He *was* impressed with the evidence. And as it came to be

enhanced with the six tapes Nixon had yielded, it became more impressive. As the early weeks of his incumbency passed, Jaworski became more and more convinced that the White House cover-up of Watergate included even the occupant of the Oval Office.

Once Jaworski was in place, with the acceptance—and, later, the enthusiasm—of his staff and the pressure therefore cooled for legislation to make his place, or that of another prosecutor, more secure, the pace of activity quickened. Partly this was due to the natural accumulation of cases and evidence developed under Cox, but in large measure it was due to Jaworski's natural bent for litigation in court, rather than the more abstract questions involved on appeal.

If the Nixon forces meant what they said and truly wanted Jaworski to "get on with it" and seek indictments so that Watergate could be "put behind us," they picked the right man. What they really wanted—even as 1973 ended—was another Henry Petersen, who could help contain the case. If it couldn't stop at Liddy, the White House strategy ran now, at least let it stop at Haldeman and Ehrlichman.

But in Leon Jaworski they had a prosecutor who was not interested in containment, and who was later to tell the press that it was not long after he assumed office that he began to realize that the trail of crime led straight and true to the Oval Office. Methodically, the prosecution staff took the legal steps necessary to gather evidence, indict, and, if possible, convict. At this writing they have yet to lose a case or an appeal.

"One year of Watergate is enough," proclaimed Nixon at his State of the Union speech in January 1974, and he was only wrong by six months. Once again, Nixon misjudged both the mood of his people, and their intelligence as the pace of litigation quickened. On November 1, 1973, Donald Segretti was sentenced to six months in prison; he had masterminded the "dirty tricks" operation in the 1972 campaign, during which time he was supervised by appointments secretary Dwight Chapin and paid by Herbert Kalmbach. It was only the beginning.

Later that month, Chapin himself was indicted on four counts of lying to the Grand Jury about his connection with Segretti. He pleaded not guilty, and there were complaints from some of the Nixon publicists in the press about persecution of this "fine young man." He was convicted on two counts on April 5, 1974, and sentenced to 30 months in prison. The conviction of Chapin was psychologically important to the prosecution staff—it was their first—since it demonstrated to any waverers the advantages of pleading guilty and testifying to the truth.

The day after Chapin had been indicted, Egil Krogh abandoned his "national security" defense, which Jaworski had already shredded, and pleaded guilty to his part in the conspiracy to burglarize the offices of Dr. Fielding. Krogh was no mere hired gun, like Segretti, nor was he, like Chapin, a total creature of Bob Haldeman's. He had served in the White House under Ehrlichman, he had been chief of the "plumbers," he had been appointed by Nixon as Under Secretary of Transportation at a time when the President knew of Krogh's part in the Ellsberg burglary, and he had been active at the White House in District of Columbia matters.

Jaworski was pleased with Krogh's recantation; he had lectured the young man long and hard, mainly on the parallels between the easy acceptance of criminal activity in the White House and what he had seen in post-Nazi Germany. Although Krogh, by all accounts a devout Christian Scientist, was believable in his statements, there is also reason to believe he did not tell quite all he knew about Nixon's knowledge of the Fielding break-in. In any event, his guilty plea and sentence, six years, was a bitter blow to the White House, because with his admission went most of the strength of the national security defense. Krogh was probably not surprised later to read transcripts of Nixon conversations in which it was made clear that the national security defense was made up by Nixon and his aides as a cover in case the story ever became public.

Late in January 1974, Herbert Porter pleaded guilty to lying to the FBI, and was sentenced to 15 months in prison, of which all but thirty days was suspended. Those who had watched Porter before the Ervin Committee in the summer of 1973 recalled an argument between him and Senator Baker in which Porter estimated that he had been a supporter of Richard Nixon "longer than any one in this room," his fealty having begun in a campaign when Porter was 8 years old. Baker quickly established that his own record of support for Nixon went back further than Porter's; both men would probably now concede the honor.

On February 21, by indicting Jake Jacobsen in what appeared

to be a collateral proceeding, the Jaworski forces struck a seemingly unimportant blow which must have seemed, however, ominous indeed to Nixon. It must have seemed particularly so to John Connally, once Nixon's Secretary of the Treasury and the active well-publicized head during the 1972 campaign of a paper organization known as "Democrats for Nixon." (The times had not been easy for the "Democrats for Nixon." Connally's vice-chairman was Dale Anderson, the man who succeeded Spiro Agnew as County Executive in Baltimore County. In between denunciations of the "leftists" who had taken over the Democratic Party, Anderson had apparently been busy in other ways; he was convicted of 32 counts of tax evasion, extortion, and bribery, mostly involving the same men who had regularly paid off Agnew.)

The indictment of Jacobsen, on one charge of lying to a Grand Jury, was significant because of rumors that Jacobsen had told the prosecutors of a $10,000 cash payoff from the milk producers, which he had delivered to Connally in return for Connally's services in persuading Nixon to raise the price of milk in 1972. Jacobsen was not a Nixon man—he had served in the Johnson White House—but he *was* a Connally man. His indictment was dismissed on May 3, on a technicality, but it was thought only a matter of time before a new indictment would be returned to which Jacobsen would plead guilty. On July 29, 1974, while the House Judiciary Committee was debating the second impeachment resolution, both Jacobsen and Connally were indicted, Jacobsen for making an illegal payment to a public official and Connally for accepting the payment, conspiracy to commit perjury, and lying to a Grand Jury.

The record of indictments, guilty pleas, and sentences continued, against a background of quickening activity in the House Judiciary Committee. Two weeks before the Jacobsen indictment, the House voted, 410–4, to proceed with the impeachment investigation and to grant plenary subpoena powers to the Judiciary Committee, which promptly asked for a number of the Nixon tapes.

Four days after Jacobsen's first indictment, Herbert Kalmbach pleaded guilty to two charges. One was a felony count arising out of the Federal Corrupt Practices Act; he had presided over the contribution and disbursement of enormous sums in 1970 to pro-Nixon Senate candidates, an activity directed from a down-town townhouse in Washington and largely unreported, in viola-tion of the law. The other count charged Kalmbach with offering an ambassadorship in exchange for a contribution. The guilty plea made it possible for the prosecutors to name Kalmbach as a conspirator in the main cover-up case, but to leave him unindicted in return for his testimony in that and other pending cases. Kalm-bach, who had built a substantial law practice in California largely on his reputation as Nixon's personal attorney, was sen-tenced to 18 months in prison and fined $10,000.

One week later, on March 1, 1974, came the long-awaited in-dictments for the Watergate cover-up itself. In all, the Grand Jury indicted seven men, and named eighteen others as a part of the conspiracy. But only the names of those indicted were made public, and it was an impressive list. We had come a long way from the third-rate burglary.

• Charles Colson, special counsel to the President and a stout, tough, and resourceful Nixon operative and defender, indicted on one count of conspiracy and one of obstruction of justice.

• H. R. Haldeman, the "zero defect" advocate as White House chief of staff and a Nixon confidante and political companion since the California campaigns, indicted on one count of con-spiracy, one count of obstruction of justice, and three counts of perjury. (One of the perjury counts charged that he had lied when he told the Ervin Committee that he had listened to a tape in which Nixon told John Dean that money could be raised to buy the burglars' silence, "but it would be wrong.")

• John Ehrlichman, another veteran of the California days and Nixon's chief domestic advisor, indicted on one count of con-spiracy, one count of obstruction of justice, one count of lying to the FBI, and two counts of lying to a Grand Jury.

• John Mitchell, Nixon's law partner, campaign manager, and Attorney-General, indicted on one count of conspiracy, one count of obstruction of justice, two counts of lying to a Grand Jury, one count of perjury, and one count of lying to the FBI.

• Gordon Strachan, former aide to Haldeman and later gen-eral counsel of the United States Information Agency, indicted on one count of conspiracy, one count of obstruction of justice, and one count of lying to a Grand Jury.

• Kenneth W. Parkinson, attorney for the Committee to Re-

Elect the President, indicted on one conspiracy count and one count of obstruction of justice.

• Robert C. Mardian, formerly Assistant Attorney-General in charge of (of all things) internal security and a hard-line law-and-order man, indicted on one count of conspiracy.

In addition, the Grand Jury named eighteen others as unindicted co-conspirators, but did not make their names public. There was good reason not to do so; one of those named by the Grand Jury as a co-conspirator in the scheme to obstruct justice was the President of the United States. The list of the other unindicted co-conspirators, once it became known several months later, contained no surprises. The four Cuban exiles who had been in on the burglary and who had been paid to remain silent were named—Bernard Barker, Eugenio Martinez, Virgilio Gonzalez, and Frank Sturgis. So were Howard Hunt and G. Gordon Liddy, as well as Hunt's wife, who had been killed in an airplane crash in Chicago a few months before, at a time when she was carrying some of the hush money. Also included was Hunt's attorney, William Bittman.

From the Nixon campaign, Frederick LaRue and Jeb Magruder, deputy chairmen of the campaign, made the list, as well as Paul O'Brien, a lawyer who had represented the CREP. Herbert Kalmbach was named, as was Anthony Ulasewicz, an assistant of Ehrlichman's who had been used to collect and pass on the hush money given Kalmbach by largely unsuspecting donors. John Dean was on the list, by his own admission a co-conspirator but unindicted because of his earlier guilty plea and his forthcoming testimony, and so was James McCord, who was in on the original burglary in his capacity as security chief of the Nixon campaign. John Caulfield, another Ehrlichman sleuth at the White House, was among the unindicted co-conspirators, and the list also included the only woman so far to surface as involved in the cover-up (except for Mrs. Hunt). She was Liddy's secretary, Sally Harmony, who had typed the original wiretap transcripts. (Watergate prosecutors indicated during the cover-up trial that they might add one more name, White House aide Richard Moore.) That was the whole list, except for one name.

That name, of course, was Richard Nixon, and Jaworski was determined to keep the fact of Nixon's having been named as a co-conspirator a secret. He thought its release would be regarded, and quite properly, as prejudicial not only to the defendants but to the President himself in any impeachment proceeding. At the very least, he was anxious that any release of this information not come from the Special Prosecutor.

The origins of the naming of Nixon as an unindicted co-conspirator are interesting. The category is almost always reserved for a conspirator whose prosecution, for whatever reason, the prosecutors wish to avoid. Customarily, the unindicted co-conspirator is a former member of the conspiracy who has become a government witness, almost always in exchange for immunity from prosecution or for an agreement to accept a plea to a lesser charge. Sometimes the unindicted co-conspirator is someone against whom the prosecutors have something less than a case they can bring to trial, but who they are convinced played a part in the conspiracy. Occasionally, the unindicted co-conspirator—as in the case of some of the radicals and peace groups prosecuted by John Mitchell—is simply someone the Justice Department wants to harass.

But Richard Nixon presented a special case. The evidence given to the Grand Jury convinced its members, unanimously, that the President was a member of the conspiracy to cover up the Watergate burglary, and that he had been a leader in it from almost the day of the crime. All other things being equal, he would have been indicted along with the other defendants.

But all other things were not equal. The prosecution staff was confronted with a delicate constitutional problem. The Constitution, in a somewhat ambiguous provision, states (Art. I, Sec. 3) that "Judgment in cases of impeachment shall not extend further than to removal from office and disqualification to hold and enjoy any office of honor, trust or profit under the United States; but the party convicted shall nevertheless be liable and subject to indictment, trial, judgment and punishment, according to law."

Obviously, that section had never been tested as to a President. But Jaworski and most (but not all) constitutional scholars read it as forbidding the indictment of a sitting President unless he had *first* been impeached and convicted. Otherwise, he reasoned, what is the meaning of the permission to indict and try "the party convicted"? In any event, he so instructed the Grand Jury, which would otherwise certainly have indicted Nixon.

Later, when the fact of the Grand Jury's having indeed named Nixon as a co-conspirator, albeit not an indicted one, began to leak out, Jaworski flatly denied to the Washington *Post* that the Grand Jury had voted unanimously to indict Nixon, and had changed its mind only because of Jaworski's persuasion. The denial, although cited by *Post* editor Benjamin Bradlee as "the one time Jaworski wasn't honest with us," was correct. The Grand Jury never voted, unanimously or otherwise, to indict Nixon, but it surely would have had Jaworski not persuaded the members to proceed otherwise.

After the major cover-up indictments, Jaworski's prosecutors began to mop up the Fielding burglary cases. One week after he had been indicted with his co-defendants for the cover-up, John Ehrlichman was indicted again for his role in the earlier burglary in Beverly Hills. Along with Ehrlichman (who was indicted on one conspiracy count, one count of lying to the FBI and three counts of lying to the Grand Jury), Liddy, and three of the Cubans (Barker, Martinez, and Felipe De Diego), were also named in the indictment.

On July 12, Ehrlichman, Liddy, and two of the Cubans (the indictment of De Diego was dismissed on technical grounds; the prosecutor has appealed) were convicted after trial of all the charges, except that in Ehrlichman's case he was acquitted on one of three counts of lying to the Grand Jury, and the charge of lying to the FBI was later dismissed by the trial judge. Ehrlichman was sentenced to five years in prison.

Former Special Counsel Charles Colson was also indicted for conspiracy in the Fielding burglary, on evidence that he was aware of the operation and had raised the money to pay for the transportation of the burglary team to California and back. Along with the other defendants, he pleaded not guilty, and continued to play the role of Nixon loyalist and deny his guilt for any part of Watergate or anything related to it.

But Colson had joined a religious group headed by Senator Harold Hughes of Iowa, and had begun to undergo what he called a "conversion to Christ." After weeks of discussing the problem with his colleagues in the evangelical group, he decided the Christian path was to confess his guilt.

Colson's brand of Christianity however, does not forbid a

certain amount of plea bargaining, and his attorneys and the prosecutors began to search for the right formula. Finally, on June 3, he pleaded guilty to one count of obstruction of justice, admitting that he set upon a course of conduct designed to defame Dr. Ellsberg, who was then on trial. At his sentencing, Colson said he had been instructed in this course by President Nixon; he was sentenced to three years in prison and fined $5,000. The other charges were dismissed.

Later, in May, came the case Jaworski was to say was the toughest decision he had to make. Richard Kleindienst had told the prosecutors, before Cox was fired, that he had lied to the Senate Judiciary Committee when he said he had not been contacted by the White House with respect to the ITT case. He had been contacted by the President himself, a conversation he concealed at the time from the Senators.

The question before the prosecution force was what to do about it. Some of the lawyers, led by Joe Connolly, the head of the ITT task force, saw a clear case of perjury by the highest ranking law enforcement officer in the nation, an act clearly warranting indictment and trial. If the Attorney-General is not prosecuted—and hard—for perjury, then how can the prosecution of lesser men in the government for the same offense be condoned? It was a strong argument, and most lawyers agree with it even now. The whole system of law depends, after all, on its observance by the strong and powerful, and who is more strong and powerful than the Attorney-General?

But Jaworski did not entirely agree, at least as to the particular facts of Kleindienst's case, however much he might agree to the general principle. Three things about the Kleindienst case troubled him. First of all, in talking with the former Attorney-General, Jaworski became convinced (others were not) that Kleindienst was genuinely contrite, and that he had suffered for his actions more than anyone else caught in the toils of Watergate. While Kleindienst certainly went along with the efforts in 1972 to limit the prosecution so that it would not expose the White House or CREP involvement, he did not initiate or participate in any of the overt events of the cover-up.

In fact, when Gordon Liddy came to him the day of the burglary, probably sent by John Mitchell, and asked that McCord be released from jail before his cover was blown and it was discovered that he had given a false name and was really employed by CREP, Kleindienst turned Liddy down cold.

Jaworski was also impressed by the nature of Kleindienst's perjurious testimony. It was the opposite of self-serving, he felt. Most perjurers, after all, including those involved in Watergate, lie to save themselves or to make themselves look good. Kleindienst, Jaworski noted, had lied only to help save Nixon, and in the process had turned down an opportunity to make himself look good. Although Nixon had cursed him and ordered him to abandon an appeal against a decision favorable to ITT, Kleindienst had refused to do so, and had even threatened to resign if he were not permitted to go forward. He could have told *that* to the Senators, and in the climate then existing it might have saved his job. As it was, he was let go with Haldeman and Ehrlichman on April 30, 1973, when Nixon first spoke publicly about the scandal.

Finally, although neither man will talk much about it, there appears to have been at least a tentative understanding worked out between Kleindienst and Cox that, in return for Kleindienst's coming in with the evidence against himself and the help that may have been to the ITT task force, he would be permitted to plead guilty to something less than the felony of perjury. The distinction was important to Kleindienst; a plea of guilty to a felony—particularly perjury—would almost certainly have resulted in his disbarment, and probably a jail term as well.

Whatever the compelling reason (no one will ever know; it seems to have been a combination of all three, with perhaps the Cox connection uppermost), Jaworski overruled his staff and permitted Kleindienst to plead guilty to an obscure misdemeanor, failure to tell the truth to a committee of Congress. The public was unable to figure out the difference among not telling the truth, lying, and perjury—and there was no reason why it should. Kleindienst had lied, there were—in the opinion of the Special Prosecutor—mitigating circumstances, and so he came into court and pleaded guilty to a misdemeanor with which no one had ever before been charged.

But what neither Jaworski nor Joseph Connolly (nor probably Kleindienst) was prepared for was the sentence the former Attorney-General received. Even the misdemeanor carried a possible prison term and a substantial fine, if the judge cared to impose it. But Judge George Hart of the District Court treated Kleindienst as if he had done the Republic a favor by appearing for his sentencing. He spoke of Kleindienst's government service as though it were wholly admirable—he had, after all, been head of the Department of Justice during its most shameful period, the time from the Watergate burglary until Kleindienst's inactivity forced the appointment of a Special Prosecutor—and he described the "universal respect" in which Kleindienst was held at the bar. When it was all over, Judge Hart sentenced Kleindienst to a prison term of thirty days and fined him $100—and then suspended the prison term. Some observers were surprised Judge Hart did not volunteer to raise a gold purse for the defendant.

But if the Kleindienst case was the low point for the Special Prosecutor's office, there were at least *three* high points, and they demonstrated at its best the operation of the rule of law. They were, respectively, the maintenance of secrecy over the Grand Jury's naming of Nixon as an unindicted co-conspirator, the ultimate unanimous decision of the Supreme Court that Nixon yield some 64 tapes subpoenaed by Jaworski, and the legal proceeding by which the evidence gathered by the Grand Jury was made available, after the indictments had been handed up, to the House Judiciary Committee for use in its impeachment investigation.

1. By March 1, when the Grand Jury had returned its indictments, and named the co-conspirators, the Special Prosecutor's office saw two objectives. One was to keep the information about Nixon from becoming public as long as possible, in order to avoid any appearance of prejudicing any case—either against the President or any of his men. The other was to transfer, in a legal way, the evidence which supported the indictments *and* the co-conspirator status of Nixon, to the House Judiciary Committee.

For whatever the strength of the constitutional argument against indicting Nixon, it rested on the simple proposition that as to a President, the only appropriate legal and constitutional remedy was *impeachment*. And by March 1, it seemed quite clear that the House Judiciary Committee was seriously investigating that possibility. It seemed equally clear that to require the Committee to subpoena, fight through the motions against the subpoena, and otherwise take by testimony the same evidence which the Grand Jury had found so compelling, would be a useless legal exercise and one which the orderly processes of law could not require.

The first objective, to keep the naming of Nixon secret, required that the report and evidence of the Grand Jury be sealed. It further required absolute secrecy from the entire staff of the Special Prosecutor's office, all of whom, of course, were privy to the information. It is an enormous tribute to that staff—attorneys, secretaries, administrative people—that the secret of Nixon's conspirator status was kept from the world from March 1 until the middle of May, and even from Nixon himself and his attorneys.

It might even have remained a secret until the jury had been sequestered in the trial of the indicted conspirators, except for some overreaching by Nixon's attorney, James St. Clair. St. Clair brought on the calamity by challenging Jaworski's right to seek additional tapes for use in the cover-up trial.

On the most solid ground, legally, that either he or Cox had been since the office was created, Jaworski on April 16, 1974 asked for a subpoena for 64 White House tapes to use in the trial, then set for September. Jaworski, in his motion requesting the order from Judge Sirica, pointed out that these were tapes which any of the defendants could request, under applicable law, on the grounds that they might contain exculpatory material as to them, and that in addition they might furnish evidence which chief trial prosecutor James Neal might use as part of the government's case. On a showing of that kind, Neal and Jaworski were convinced, the legal authority was so overwhelming that no defense of executive privilege could prevail. On April 18, Judge Sirica signed the order, and set May 1 as the date for delivery of the documents.

On May 1, true to form, Nixon's attorneys said they would not deliver the tapes and other documents. At the same time, they filed a motion to quash the subpoena, not only on the specious grounds of executive privilege but also the astounding grounds that Jaworski, as an executive branch appointee, had no right to sue the President for the materials, or anything else. The next day, Judge Sirica set May 6 as the date to file legal briefs and May 8 as the time for the hearing.

Jaworski, who had taken the post as Special Prosecutor only after General Haig's assurance that he *could* sue the President, now moved to cover his flank. He dispatched a letter to the Senate Judiciary Committee, pointing out that St. Clair's argument in court flew squarely in the teeth not only of the assurances he had received, but also the guidelines laid down for the Special Prosecutor by acting Attorney-General Bork—and subsequently ratified by William Saxbe. The Senators took notice of the complaint, and let Jaworski know he could count on their assistance if trouble persisted.

The prosecutors now played what they thought was a trump card. Until May 6, not even St. Clair knew that Nixon had been named an unindicted co-conspirator, and clearly the House Judiciary Committee did not know either. But that fact was a key argument in the prosecutors' brief in support of the subpoena for Nixon's tapes.

The law is clear that testimony of one conspirator—even, in some cases, hearsay testimony if it concerns the statements of another conspirator—may be used against the others; it is the main reason the unindicted co-conspirator device is used in conspiracy prosecutions. So on May 6, the brief of the Special Prosecutor contained—for the first time—the fact of Nixon's status, and it came as a surprise to St. Clair.

When St. Clair was advised that the prosecutors would have to use the Nixon status in their arguments, St. Clair asked for more time to file his brief. It was simply a device to permit him to talk to his client, to determine if perhaps the public relations damage in the information's becoming public—"Grand Jury Named Nixon as Co-Conspirator, Court Papers Reveal"—might not outweigh whatever delay in delivery of the tapes would be obtained by continuing to argue against the subpoena.

Accordingly, both St. Clair and Jaworski asked for a week's delay, and Judge Sirica granted it, citing "discussions leading to possible compliance with the subpoena." The discussions, of course, consisted of St. Clair and Nixon trying to figure out what hurt least, giving Jaworski the tapes, or delaying delivery until the Supreme Court finally ordered it but suffering meanwhile the public knowledge that the Grand Jury thought Nixon was in on the conspiracy to obstruct justice.

We will never know what advice St. Clair gave Nixon, or

whether it was taken. As a lawyer—and a good one, by all accounts—St. Clair must have known the fight against the subpoena
was a losing one, as the unanimous opinion of the Supreme Court
was later to confirm. Whether he had become so trapped by the
political and public relations aspect of representing Nixon that
he did not give that advice must remain an unknown. But whatever the advice, the decision was to stand fast on the tapes, even
if it meant public knowledge of the conspirator status of the
President. Considering what was on the tapes, it was a wise decision, but one which only postponed the inevitable public and
congressional awareness of Nixon's role.

So St. Clair advised Jaworski and the court that the White
House would not yield the tapes, and the legal issue was joined.
Judge Sirica, after a hearing, denied the motion to quash and
ordered that the tapes be turned over. The order, of course, was
appealed.

But the prosecutors did reveal in their brief that the Grand
Jury had included Nixon among the conspirators. The brief was
filed on May 10, under seal, Jaworski still determined that if
the matter became public it would not be through the office of
the Special Prosecutor. Judge Sirica set a hearing for oral arguments for May 13. Naturally, all of the attorneys for the cover-up
defendants were also served with copies of the prosecutors' brief,
and thus they too became aware for the first time, of the Grand
Jury's action.

One of the defense attorneys—which one has never been revealed—"went public" with the list of unindicted co-conspirators,
in the belief that the hearing on May 13 would be public, and
that the information would be known at that time anyway. As
it turned out, Judge Sirica held that hearing *in camera*, without
the public or the press, so that the secret information about Nixon
could have been held for a while longer, but by that time the
press already had the story.

But Jaworski had accomplished his purpose; he had been in
possession—and so had every member of his allegedly "anti-
Nixon" staff—of the most damaging information about Nixon yet
to emerge from Watergate, and had not revealed it for two and a
half months. It was certainly a record for a Washington secret of
any kind; for an important secret, the record will undoubtedly
stand for some time.

2. The second objective to be pursued was, of course, the transfer to the House Judiciary Committee of the evidence which had been presented to the Grand Jury. When Jaworski had explained to the Grand Jury that he was convinced by the constitutional argument that Nixon could not be indicted prior to impeachment and conviction, the members of the Grand Jury were anxious that the evidence presented to them be made available to the impeachment investigation. So Neal, Jaworski, and the grand jurors set about to find a legal method of accomplishing the Grand Jury's desires.

At the threshold, they were confronted with the fact that they could not simply transfer the material once the indictments were handed up, nor could they make them public. A Grand Jury is a curious institution in American law, and its records are ordinarily sealed. Since the proceeding before Grand Juries is not to determine guilt or innocence, but only whether probable cause exists to believe that a crime has been committed and that certain named individuals committed the crimes, it follows that considerable evidence presented to a Grand Jury, if made public, might be extremely damaging to innocent persons (including those indicted, who remain innocent until convicted by a *petit*, or trial jury).

In this case, however, the House Judiciary Committee was proceeding along precisely the same track—to determine whether probable cause existed to believe that Richard Nixon had committed impeachable offenses, so that the full House of Representatives could vote on impeachment (likened to an indictment), so that the Senate could determine guilt or innocence in a trial. In the Senate, as before a trial jury, the standard of proof is that the evidence must prove guilt "beyond a reasonable doubt." Before the House of Representatives, as before a Grand Jury, the standard is only that the members must assess the possibility of guilt only on the basis of "probable cause."

So the grand jurors, anxious that the constitutional processes proceed without the unnecessary delay which would be caused by requiring the Judiciary Committee to travel precisely the same evidentiary ground as they had, requested James Neal to turn the material over, under seal, to the Judiciary Committee. Neal so informed Judge Sirica, after the indictments were handed up on March 1.

On March 6, Judge Sirica held a hearing on the proposal by the Grand Jury, and the efficacy of the strategy developed by Jaworski and Neal became apparent. St. Clair could not publicly oppose the transfer of the documents, by now sealed in a briefcase. To do so would have have been too obvious a continuation of the cover-up. The Nixon men had been maintaining for weeks that the Judiciary Committee was the appropriate forum to determine the President's fate, and ritualistic assurances had been given of "full cooperation." To oppose at this point the transfer of the Grand Jury's evidence would be too much stonewalling, and so St. Clair interposed no objections at the hearing.

But the White House had a few more pieces of ammunition left. Haldeman's lawyer, John Wilson, carried the ball for Nixon at the hearing, as he seemed to have been doing for some time. Back in the summer of 1973, he had not only represented both Haldeman and Ehrlichman before the Ervin Committee (an action seen by many lawyers as a clear conflict of interest), but he had also on at least two occasions been to the White House for secret meetings with Nixon to discuss the case and his clients—after they had "resigned."

So Wilson, ostensibly for Haldeman (and the attorney for Gordon Strachan), argued that the materials should not go over to Peter Rodino's committee. It didn't work. On March 18, Judge Sirica ordered that the Grand Jury's wishes be respected and the material transferred to the Committee. Two days later, Wilson and his colleague—Strachan's attorney—appealed to the Court of Appeals; the hearing was held in the appellate court the next day, and the appeal was rejected. On March 25, the now-famous "briefcase" was delivered in court to Judiciary Committee counsel John Doar, and the Grand Jury was satisfied that justice would be done in the new forum.

3. The final problem, of course, was the tapes themselves. Neal, Richard Ben-Veniste, and their task force had carefully culled the list, and had come up with 64 tapes they deemed essential to the conduct of the cover-up trial. Following the previous procedures, they asked for the evidence and, inevitably, the White House refused.

On April 16 the prosecutors asked Judge Sirica for, and got a subpoena. On the return date, St. Clair refused to deliver the tapes, and sought an order quashing the subpoena. After hearing the arguments, Judge Sirica confirmed the order on May 20. On May 24, St. Clair noticed an appeal in the Court of Appeals, and it began to appear that, at the very least, Nixon had succeeded in postponing the cover-up trial.

The reason lay in the court calendars. Under normal circumstances the Court of Appeals, even if it expedited the oral arguments and the decision, would not decide the matter for a few months. Then, St. Clair was sure to take an appeal to the Supreme Court, which does not sit to hear cases from the end of May until the beginning of October. The trial, scheduled for early September, would surely have to be put off, which meant that it would have to wait until the entire impeachment proceeding—committee hearings, House floor debate, and a Senate trial—had been concluded.

The prosecutors moved swiftly to prevent the delay. On the same days as the Nixon appeal was filed, May 24, using a seldom-invoked procedure, Jaworski went to the Supreme Court and sought a writ of *certiorari*, which would take the case directly to the high court and bypass the Court of Appeals. Jaworski cited the trial date and the necessity of a quick decision, and asked the Supreme Court not only to issue the writ, but to stay in session into the summer so it could hear the case and decide in time for the evidence—if the decision was favorable—to be used at the trial.

The Supreme Court agreed, and heard arguments on July 8. The decision on July 24 was almost an anti-climax. It was unanimous, and held that Judge Sirica's order was proper, and that whatever executive privilege meant, it could not protect evidence of presidential conversations which might reveal the existence of a criminal conspiracy. In order to achieve unanimity, Chief Justice Burger virtually tailored the decision to fit the facts of this particular case, and avoided any firm outlines of what constituted executive privilege. The case, of course, was entitled "U.S. *v.* Nixon," a most apt title, and there seems little doubt that the Chief Justice was correct in narrowing its scope to the precise facts which that title suggests. It *was* the United States versus Richard Nixon, and the exceptional language and reasoning of the opinion—which said little more than that Richard Nixon, at *that* time, must yield *those* tapes for the purpose of the forthcoming trial of his assistants—was entirely appropriate.

Even in "victory," Jaworski and his assistants were looking squarely at the legal problems. Once the Supreme Court ruled, St. Clair said publicly that the White House would *begin* preparation of the evidence it had been ordered to turn over. That preparation and delivery, St. Clair said, would take a long time.

Jaworski and Neal would have none of it. Two days later, on July 26, they were in Judge Sirica's court again, on a motion requesting expedited delivery. Judge Sirica, properly annoyed at St. Clair's projected dalliance and apparently furious at the discovery that Nixon's lawyer had not even listened to the tapes himself (although he had been prepared to argue the damage their release would do to the national security and the power of future presidents), immediately instructed St. Clair to begin delivery. The first tapes were turned over on July 29, and additional ones on August 2.

It was the delivery on August 2 of the "smoking gun," the tape of June 23, which finally sealed Richard Nixon's doom; the legal system, used by dedicated lawyers, had worked—and worked well.

As for Leon Jaworski, he felt his job was done and he resigned as Special Prosecutor once the jury in the cover-up trial had been selected and sequestered. In the year he was on the job, almost all of what the office of Special Prosecutor had been created to do, had been done. The trial remained, and appeals would unquestionably follow, but James Neal and Richard Ben-Veniste would handle the matter in court. Some indictments and trials (or guilty pleas) would still be forthcoming from Thomas McBride's task force on campaign contributions; Jaworski had participated in some of the early plea bargaining with Maurice Stans.

Jaworski had strongly urged that Henry Ruth be appointed to replace him, and Ruth's appointment was announced on October 26, 1974; the same high standard of professionalism would prevail. Ruth's first acomplishment was to complete the renegotiation of the deal struck between President Ford and Richard Nixon at the time of Ford's pardon, which gave Nixon control over the remainder of the tapes, and would have required a new subpoena to get any of them for further use. Ruth signed a new agreement with the Ford White House; the Special Prosecutor could have access to any tapes he wished for the investigation.

When Jaworski resigned, there was some criticism, most of it centered around his "acceptance" of the Ford pardon. He should have challenged its legality and its constitutionality, it was said, by moving to indict Nixon anyway, and forcing the former President's lawyers to plead the pardon as a bar to prosecution. But Jaworski was convinced that a President's power to pardon under the Constitution is absolute, and extends even to crimes with which the pardonee has yet to be charged. He felt the procedure would have been idle, and he did not practice law, he said, to vindicate abstract principles—particularly when he did not believe there was a chance of success.

Back on the ranch in Wimberley, Jaworski could reflect that while we may never know all the truth of Watergate, we learned a great deal through his efforts as Special Prosecutor. Powerful men were brought to justice, the constitutional process of impeachment proceeded the way the Founders had thought it would, and Leon Jaworski could remember Michael Moncrief, and know that he had used the law for more than power.

The Press:
First Rumblings

Richard Nixon never came to terms with the fact of a free press.
When it was on his side—which was most of the time—he took it
for granted as just another campaign tool. When it wasn't, he
and his people treated it like an enemy. Thus, one of the endur-
ing myths of the Nixon years is that the press was somehow out
to "get" Nixon, and finally succeeded. It was a natural conclusion
for the Nixon men, since large portions of the American press
did chronicle, however imperfectly, the facts which ultimately
drove Nixon from office in disgrace. But myth must eventually
yield to reality, and the reality in this case is that the press had
very little to do with the ultimate result, and certainly did not
will it.

I have refrained here from the use of the plural word, "media,"
because its meaning changes depending upon who is using the
word. Generally, it has came to mean television, as opposed to
newspapers, and while there should be some distinction * "media"
doesn't quite do the job. In addition, it has acquired almost a
pejorative gloss—hardly anyone uses the word in the course of
praising the performance of whatever it is that makes up the
media. "The press" conjures up visions of courageous editors in
the tradition of John Peter Zenger and Elijah Lovejoy, fearlessly

---

* Newspapers, for example, operate under the constitutional shield of the First
Amendment, and television stations do not; newspapers generally try to contain
as much news as possible in order to draw advertisers; television stations generally
offer *as little* news as possible, in order to draw advertisers. Newspapers' main job
is to purvey *news;* television's main job is to entertain.

risking community disapproval, whereas "media" calls to mind
slick eastern elitists busily slanting the news.

Both images are, of course, wide of the mark, and nowhere was
this better demonstrated than in the events leading up to the
resignation of Richard Nixon. Editors and publishers rarely defy
their communities (when they are not absentees); for the most
part they are a part of the local power structure precisely because
they mirror the local business community prejudices and interests. And network television executives, when they are not the
same people as the newspaper executives, have no interest in
"slanting" the news, but only in providing as little of it as possible,
and then as blandly as possible, because experience has shown
them that local car dealers and savings and loan associations are
more anxious to buy time on game shows and re-runs of earlier
popular entertainment programs.

Nevertheless, the press had an information job to perform as
the Watergate scandal unfolded, and once the news was out in
the open, it performed it adequately, although all through 1973
and 1974 there was an enormous amount of self-congratulation
in the press, most of it undeserved.

The scandal itself went largely uninvestigated and unreported
(except, of course, for the Washington *Post*). While the *Post* was
reporting the clear links between the original burglars and the
Nixon campaign and, later, the White House itself, the rest of the
press was doing little or nothing. Ben Bagdikian estimated, in
the spring of 1973, that of the thousands of correspondents in
Washington, only 14 could be said to be "covering" the Watergate story.

During the 1972 campaign, when the cover-up was functioning
precisely because the election campaign was in progress (John
Mitchell told the Ervin Committee he would have done "anything" to prevent Nixon's defeat, and he was evidently telling
the truth), the *Post* was almost alone in digging away at the truth.
CBS did a comprehensive two-part summary of the evidence so
far uncovered, in October 1972, but otherwise there was very
little. Most newspapers, after all, do not like to run front-page
stories which begin "the Washington *Post* said today," and television news (which regards a "piece" which lasts one minute and
forty-five seconds as an "in-depth treatment") preferred to keep
a "balanced" view of the campaign. This usually consisted of a

minute of George McGovern campaigning and, since Nixon was not campaigning, one minute of somebody, anybody, campaigning against McGovern.

But once the facts came from *within* the conspiracy, the job of the press became simpler. It was far easier, and far more defensible in the community, to report what James McCord or Jeb Magruder or John Dean had *said* in public under oath, or what a Grand Jury or the Special Prosecutor had *charged* in an indictment, than it had been to find out and report what Haldeman or Mitchell (or even Nixon) had *done* under cover and had denied.

So there is some basis for the belief that the press played a major role in the downfall of Nixon, but only because the news *happened* day after day and the papers and television reported it. It wasn't *The New York Times* or CBS, after all, which exposed the fact that Haldeman and Ehrlichman had, on instructions of President Nixon, ordered the CIA to stop the FBI investigation of Watergate because if the FBI were not stopped, it would discover that Nixon campaign funds paid for the burglary. That information was given, under oath, before the Ervin Committee. It wasn't NBC or *Newsweek* that dug out every swindle in Nixon's tax returns; it was the Joint Committee on Internal Revenue Taxation. Once the official institutions began doing their job in the spring of 1973, it was a downhill race for the press and, to be sure, the "media."

But special mention needs to be made of the Washington *Post*. The *Post* did take the story seriously—from the day of the original burglary. Reporters Carl Bernstein and Bob Woodward have already received great credit; they deserve it all, and more. As David Broder, himself a Pulitzer Prize winner, wrote early on, they made one proud to be in the same profession.

But the *Post*'s success at breaking the Watergate story was not just the story of two gifted and brave reporters. It involved editors like Barry Sussman and Howard Simon, and above all it involved Executive Editor Benjamin Bradlee and Publisher Katherine Graham. There were plenty of opportunities to flinch, particularly once it became known, in Washington and on Wall Street, that the Nixon administration was out to destroy the *Post*, by attacking the stock (the company is publicly held) and by malicious challenges to television licenses the company owned in Miami and Jacksonville. Bradlee and Graham, after all, were being asked to go along with a continuing news story alleging a criminal conspiracy being conducted from the White House, at a time when a vindictive President, who had gathered more power into his hands than any other in our history, had just been triumphantly re-elected.

Bradlee was—and is—an unlikely character to play the role of bitter-end ideological Nixon-hater to which he was assigned by the White House. He is an essentially conservative, anti-political man with a natural horror of being involved in "causes." In appearance, he would have been a perfect actor to play Jay Gatsby, coming across as a faintly disreputable ex-aviator.

Bradlee has a strong distaste for passionate politicians ("Bobby Kennedy scared the hell out of me," he says), and confesses to a liking for the kind of politician who is precisely the enemy of the liberals he is accused of supporting. Bradlee says he admires political rogues—not crooks, but rogues—and has a built-in distrust of reformers.

He covered Nixon in the 1960 presidential campaign, during and after which he confessed to an admiration for the detached and cool irony of John Kennedy (Bradlee freely admits his taste in politicians runs more to style than to substance), and in 1962 as a *Newsweek* reporter he wrote a cover story on Nixon after his unsuccessful run for Governor of California. After that, in John Ehrlichman's phrase, Nixon went off his screen.

In fact, until Watergate the *Post*'s coverage of the 1972 campaign was remarkably restrained, for the hometown newspaper in the most political city in the world. If the *Post* had a favorite in those days, it was probably Senator Edmund Muskie; its White House coverage was properly respectful. The paper has traditionally had at least a part of its self-image as a court circular, and until the departure of Russell Wiggins as editor in 1968, the *Post* almost always supported the President, any President.

Even during Bradlee's incumbency, the tradition of reverence for the Chief Executive softened only slightly. As to the major issue of the time—the war in Vietnam—it was not until well into the Nixon years that the *Post* began to oppose the war. Even then, it never assumed as strong a voice as, for example, *The New York Times*, and in editorial positions it reflected a generally Establishment tone.

But the *Post*'s editors and reporters were, above all, professional, and once they began to dig under the surface of the official Watergate story the open clash with the Nixon White House became inevitable.

One example of that professionalism is worth noting. On June 25, 1973, John Dean began his testimony before the Ervin Committee. He spent that whole first day reading his prepared statement, which ran 465 pages, and he did not finish until nearly 6 P.M. Even at the time, and certainly in retrospect, that was probably the beginning of the end. In remembering that day a year later, Bradlee recalled the problem Dean's statement posed for him and the *Post*. It was, he said, a *technical* problem—how to compress the highlights of 465 pages into the available news hole of only a few pages, and do it completely, accurately, and fairly, with only a few hours to go. As it turned out, the job was done—lots of Dean's testimony appeared, with appropriate comments and responses from those accused. But the *Post*'s problem—with Dean and later—was seen from the inside almost always as a *news* problem and not as an ideological one.

By October 1972, the break was open and the battle was joined. On October 25, there was a Page One story identifying H. R. Haldeman as one of those in charge of a secret fund used to pay for campaign sabotage.

It seems a narrow focus now—Haldeman seems to have been not only a paymaster for campaign sabotage but also for the cover-up of which he was a prime architect—but from that day on the *Post* was considered not an opponent of the Nixon administration but an enemy, to be treated as such. The charge against Haldeman turned out, by the way, to be the final exposé of the campaign and the last time Watergate made the front page before Election Day. The next day the administration brought Henry Kissinger out to say that "peace is at hand" in Vietnam, and Watergate moved to the inside pages.

From then on, Bradlee now says, the *Post* had "some rough moments." "What kept us tough," he adds "was that they were lying." There was a lot at stake beyond the reputation of a newspaper. Woodward and Bernstein, after all, had already accomplished a great deal and if a story turned out not to be entirely true they could probably find work elsewhere; Bradlee felt his whole career was on the line, and he was right. Someone was not just going to lose, but be humiliated, and it was not at all clear in the months after the 1972 election that those humiliated would all turn out to be the President's men.

The importance of the Washington *Post* in the unraveling of the conspiracy cannot be overstated. It was not simply a case of a good newspaper getting a great story and getting it right. It was crucial that the newspaper, to break the Watergate story and to hammer away at it, *be in Washington.*

Much is made, for instance, of the role of Judge John Sirica at the first trial of the Watergate burglars. Sirica was scornful of the work of the Justice Department, and kept complaining that the truth was not emerging, and flatly refused to believe the idea that Hunt, Liddy, and the hired Cubans were the beginning and the end of the story. Who paid them? Why did they do the job? What were they told? By whom? Who authorized Liddy to go ahead? Who funished all the $100 bills? He got no answer to these questions it was quite proper for him to ask, and he gave the defendants very stiff provisional sentences in the hope they would cooperate in telling somebody—the Ervin Committee, the Grand Jury—the truth.

His tactic paid off when first McCord, then Magruder, then Dean finally came forward with some answers.

But it is doubtful if Judge Sirica would have known what questions were *not* being answered had it not been for the Washington *Post.* There had to be a confluence of crime, judge, and newspaper in the same city, and there was. If Woodward and Bernstein had been working, not for the *Post* but for the Washington bureau of a newspaper in the West, for example, or if Howard Hunt's advice had been followed and the burglary had taken place, not at the Watergate but at the Hotel Fontainebleau in Miami Beach—it is most likely that the Justice Department could have carried off the "containment" of the crime to the level of Gordon Liddy and we might never have learned more.

For that matter, the presence of the *Post* (and the burglary) in Washington paid off in other ways. Is it not possible that the Senate would not have been so quick to set up a Select Committee to investigate what its members had read about—if they had not read about it in their hometown newspaper? Would Sam Ervin's questions have been half so devastating had he not been aware—through the *Post's* daring stories—of what had been covered up?

(On August 9, 1974, as Richard Nixon flew to San Clemente as an ex-President, a printer in the *Post's* composing room ran off a proposed ad for the "Help Wanted" pages. Against a background of classified ads, he pasted up a smiling picture of Gerald Ford, and underneath it the legend, "I got my job through the Washington *Post*.")

Once the Ervin hearings were begun, the whole country began to get the news, during the day and at night on television—and in the newspapers the next day. The question—as Ervin's committee produced witness after witness and as Archibald Cox began the legal proceedings which would bring the guilty to trial —was the one of remedy. In that spring of 1973, people were still asking "what did the President know, and when did he know it?"—even after Nixon's own statements had made it "perfectly clear" that as to some crimes, including obstruction of justice, the answers were, respectively, "all" and "from the beginning."

But one year later, impeachment had become a probability, and a few months after that, Nixon was gone. Even by the end of the Ervin hearings, less than 25 percent of Americans and probably fewer Congressmen were thinking about impeachment. That change, occurring over less than a year, had to do as much with what people were saying about the news as the news itself.

For during that whole year and a half of Watergate, it seemed at times as though the circuits of information were being overloaded. Stories—major, damning ones—came and went before they could be evaluated. Taxes, wiretaps, secret funds, the tapes, Vesco, Segretti, John Dean's honeymoon money—news which would have been a sensation in 1972 would make one day's newspaper and be supplanted the next day by something else. The 18-minute gap, the May 22 statement, "but it would be wrong," ITT, impeachable offense—on it went, and the men and women who would decide, the Congress, were as unable as all the rest of us to keep up and to sort it all into an orderly whole.

Thus it becomes important, in tracing the change in public opinion which was ultimately reflected in Congress, to look at the news analysis—the syndicated columnists and editorialists, and particularly the ones the Congressmen and Senators were reading. What emerges from the following month-by-month survey of that analysis, as it appeared in the *Post, The New York Times,* the

Chicago *Tribune* and *Sun-Times,* and the *Los Angeles Times,*
shows that if there was a press conspiracy to get Nixon, it was
remarkably well concealed. The pundits were almost all behind
public opinion, and some of the most respected of them, as late
as June and July of 1974, were discounting the possibility of impeachment. It was events which made the news, and not—as Nixon
would like to remember it—the other way 'round. In Emerson's
phrase, "things are in the saddle, and ride mankind."

By May of 1973, Senator Ervin was beginning his hearings, and
the first major Nixon statement was on the record. On April 30,
Nixon had announced to the nation the "resignations" of Haldeman and Ehrlichman, the departure from the cabinet of Attorney-
General Kleindienst, and the firing of John Dean. He had also
pledged to "get to the bottom" of Watergate, and said there would
be no "whitewash at the White House."

John Dean was talking to the prosecutors, and so was Jeb
Magruder. But the revelations continued. John Mitchell and
Maurice Stans had been indicted in connection with a concealed
$250,000 campaign contribution from Robert Vesco, who had fled
the United States in the face of a fraud prosecution. They were
later acquitted, in a proceeding brought by the Justice Department, not by the Special Prosecutor.

In May came the first mention of impeachment by any national
columnist. It came, not surprisingly, from Joseph Kraft, who had
seen Watergate as a *legal* proceeding, and had concentrated on the
evidence, from the beginning. On May 6, 1973, Kraft wrote that
"Watergate raises the suspicion (to use a term even the Marquis
of Queensberry would probably find excessively gentle) that the
President of the United States has been deeply involved in criminal
activities. So inevitably there is talk of impeachment."

Kraft went on to say, to be sure, that the "logic of national
politics" went overwhelmingly against the possibility of impeachment, but he made the point strongly that it was an alternative—
and perhaps an inevitable alternative—to a failure on the part of
the White House to yield up the story of what actually happened.

Kraft discussed a recent warning by Melvin Laird—at that time
between jobs, having resigned as Secretary of Defense and having
not yet been brought back aboard for a salvage operation at the

White House—to the effect that if President Nixon were involved in Watergate, which he doubted, he (Laird) would not want the country to know about it.

To Kraft, this was a warning from a shrewd Republican strategist that anyone who wanted to push hard on Watergate, would be subject to a strong counterattack which would include the charge that national unity was being destroyed for a partisan advantage.

This charge, that the "enemies" of Mr. Nixon and, ultimately, all proponents of impeachment, were truly out to destroy national unity and to leave America defenseless in the presence of its enemies, was to find an echo not only in further statements by Laird but by all of the White House strategists, and those in the press who were responsive to their suggestions. Thus, as we shall see, General Haig was able regularly to sell Joseph Alsop, and Haig and Laird were able to convince columnists Rowland Evans and Robert Novak, that strong attacks on Nixon were attacks on the national defense.

Kraft also took note on May 6 that the Watergate investigation was being managed by Henry Petersen. Kraft pointed out—and it was not being widely pointed out at the time—that Petersen had called the original Justice Department noninvestigation of Watergate "among the most exhaustive I have seen in 25 years as a prosecutor." Kraft correctly observed that Petersen was suspect, and could not "possibly have a straightforward arms' length relationship with the White House and the President," particularly in such matters as the proposed grant of immunity to John Dean in exchange for his testimony. Kraft could not know in May that the subsequent playing of the White House tapes would reveal precisely the truth of what he was saying about Petersen and Nixon, but he was able to put together what was known at the time, in order to show that the relationship was, at the very least, suspect.

Concluding this distant early warning of impeachment, Kraft felt confident "that the truth can be forced out," and that "we can make our system of checks and balances work without going to the political equivalent of nuclear war—impeachment." But he concluded that to make the system work everyone would have to concentrate on getting out the facts. It appeared he was not optimistic that the White House would join in that effort.

On the same day, James Reston in *The New York Times* was suggesting that Watergate, grave as the crisis was, might perhaps demonstrate "the uses of adversity," in that it would be difficult for President Nixon now to continue to oppose such overdue reforms as those connected with campaign financing.

Reston pointed out that new laws on campaign financing would not "really resolve the present crisis in our political life. They would help, but the crisis is much deeper. It is not mainly political but philosophical, and the corruption is not only here in Washington with Maurice Stans and his black bags full of laundered money out of Mexico, but with the people and institutions that produce the cash."

Reston in his May 6 column did touch on one aspect of the Nixon men's behavior that was later to reach greater proportions:

> Nothing has hurt the President and his closest aides in the White House more than their assumption of moral superiority, their lectures on patriotism and defending the flag, which they carry in their buttonholes—all this followed by disclosures that the root assumptions of fair play and decency in the American system is being corrupted by self-righteous manipulators, managers, hucksters and burglars working out of the White House.

By May 15, 1973, David Broder of the Washington *Post,* who had been, off and on, a strong defender of Nixon's, particularly on the question of Vietnam, pointed out that Watergate described a "double drama." The public drama, according to Broder, was the "gradual revelation of the dimensions of the conspiracy, in which increasing numbers of high officials are accused of subverting, for their own aims, the electoral, judicial, and governmental processes."

But the other part of the drama, Broder felt, was more interesting. It involved, he thought, "the shrouded scenario unfolding in the mind of Richard Nixon."

Broder drew some historical parallels—Herbert Hoover, Harry Truman, Lyndon Johnson—of Presidents beleaguered and rendered politically impotent inside their last two years in office. But he pointed out that none of the prior cases was a parallel to

Nixon because "calamity has overtaken him earlier in his term than it did his predecessors, and the option of seeking or declining re-election was already removed for him by the two-term limitation in the Twenty-second Amendment."

Broder concluded, at least from the evidence of some psychological studies of Nixon, that he would try to ride out the storm, using "mammoth denial as a defense against unacceptable impulses and feelings." Broder's point here was that Nixon was denying not only the events of Watergate in which he might or might not have been involved, but "any realistic appraisal of its consequences for him and his administration." No mention of impeachment, to be sure, but an indication that grave and probably irreparable damage had already been done to Nixon's reputation. This unusually harsh assessment of Nixon's position by Broder must have come as a bitter blow at the White House. In 1969, when the peace movement was preparing its major marches against the Vietnam war, Broder had written of "the breaking of the President," a process, he said, which had proved successful against Lyndon Johnson and which was—in 1969—about to be used against Richard Nixon. The Nixon people took great heart from this article of Broder's, and used it repeatedly as justification for the acts—many of them illegal—which they took against war protesters and which they were to expand and enlarge upon against their enemies in the larger political society.

Through all of June 1973, there was no talk of impeachment; indeed, it was widely believed (and to a great extent, correctly) that most Democrats in the Congress didn't even want to think about impeachment, since it would elevate Spiro Agnew to the presidency and leave him eligible for re-election.

But from Regina, Canada, in the middle of the month came a Canadian press report that Nixon "was on the road either to resignation or impeachment over the Watergate issue." The prediction came from Clark Mollenhoff, the bureau chief in Washington of the Des Moines *Register,* who had served a tempestuous year in the Nixon White House as a sort of corruption finder. As Mollenhoff looked back on his term of loyal service to Nixon (he had stoutly defended the nominations of both Judge Carswell and Judge Haynesworth to the Supreme Court), he felt that he had been used, and that he had done his job too well. "I believed

that the administration was corrupt. I believed they were trying
to cover up Watergate. I believed they were lying at the White
House," said Mollenhoff in his Canadian interview.

But the Washington press did not take Clark Mollenhoff very
seriously; in a society whose ideal was "cool," he had earned a
reputation as a passionate believer, and his voice was largely
unheard. Others who were not given much credit, because they
lacked "clout" in the House of Representatives, were six Congressmen who scheduled time in June to talk about impeachment.
They were Representatives Bella Abzug of New York, Yvonne
Burke, Ronald Dellums, and Fortney Stark, all of California,
Parren Mitchell of Maryland, and Patricia Schroeder of Colorado.

These Congressmen represented the farthest left (the term is
relative; nobody gets very far left in Congress) of their colleagues,
and the exercise was not only seen as a sterile one, but was intended as no more than an educational effort. Other than this
group, augmented perhaps by four or five Congressmen, no serious thought was being given to impeachment on Capitol Hill.

In July 1973, Joseph Kraft returned to a discussion of impeachment, although from a different perspective than it finally
developed. In a powerful column, Kraft, after first apologizing
for his defense of Nixon in 1968 (although not for his attacks on
George McGovern in 1972 for pointing out the corruption of the
Nixon administration), developed the case against Nixon thus
far. He talked about the "enemies list" and the proposed use (as
described by John Dean) of the whole apparatus of government
"to screw our political enemies." Kraft pointed out that the evidence produced thus far before the Ervin Committee demonstrated the use by the Nixon administration of the Justice
Department, the Internal Revenue Service, and the FBI to
harass political opponents for none other than purely political
motives.

Kraft also described, in his July 1 column, the crucial criminal
activities in which Nixon himself was involved. He went directly
to the June 23, 1972, event in which Nixon had ordered Haldeman
and Erlichman to use the CIA to stop the FBI investigation of
Watergate, which Kraft saw as an improper use of the CIA. Thus
Kraft certainly did observe that the events of June 23 were crucial to an understanding of Nixon's role in the conspiracy to obstruct justice.

In addition, Kraft completed the up-to-date indictment of Nixon with a comment on Nixon's false statements as to when he had learned of the Ellsberg burglary, and he also described an attempt by White House staff men, encouraged by Nixon, to pressure Congressmen and Senators, including Senator Lowell Weicker and Representative Wright Patman.

But in this first major discussion of the possibility of impeachment, Kraft saw correctly the *direction* from which it would come if not the *ground* upon which it would be based. After describing the evidence which had been developed by Senator Ervin's committee, he concluded with this prophetic paragraph:

The questions raised by that defiance of the Constitution cannot be answered by mere presidential press conferences. They can probably not even be answered, as I recently suggested, in a separate set of committee hearings. It may well be that these emerging questions can only be answered—and it now seems to me that this is where Chairman Ervin in his canniness is taking the country—in an impeachment proceeding.

There was very little talk of impeachment elsewhere in the press, as the Watergate hearings moved through June and July, highlighted by the devastating testimony of John Dean, followed in July by the revelations of Alexander Butterfield that tapes of almost all presidential conversations existed which could test the veracity of Dean as well as Nixon's involvement in the cover-up. At the end of July, one of the editors of the Washington *Star* (now the *Star-News*) pointed for the first time to the impetus toward impeachment which the controversy between Archibald Cox and the White House over the tapes might yield. Crosby Noyes found it unlikely that a court would order Nixon to give up the tapes to Cox, and that Nixon would refuse but, as Noyes pointed out, "if things should reach that point—which still seems somewhat unlikely—the pressure to bring impeachment proceedings against the President would be much stronger than it is today and the outcome extremely uncertain."

There was more impeachment talk in August, but not much. *The New York Times* began an educational process about impeachment, which would continue intermittently with articles on its "op-ed" page (the page opposite the editorial page), discussing the legal precedents and in particular the case of Andrew Johnson.

Johnson was the only American President ever to be impeached—his conviction failed in the Senate by one vote. At the time Richard Nixon left office to avoid impeachment and conviction, it is likely that more words had been written about the case of Andrew Johnson than at the time he was impeached.

The first *Times* article was on August 26, by Michael Lee Benedict, an assistant professor at Ohio State, who had written a book about the Johnson case. Benedict defended the Johnson proceedings against the common argument that they had been a travesty. He pointed out that Johnson had offered his opponents plenty of grounds for impeachment and that he might even have been convicted had the articles been more carefully drawn. Benedict also made the point that the actual Senate trial of Andrew Johnson had not been conducted in a spirit of carnival and political vendetta but, on the contrary, that the trial had proceeded with "remarkable fairness," and that the majority of the Senators appeared to have entered the proceedings with an open mind and had made their decision on the basis of the weight of the evidence.

At the time the Benedict article appeared—and there is no indication that it swayed very many people—it was commonly accepted on all sides that an impeachment proceeding would be drawn-out, divisive, traumatic, and agonizing. (It was not until the actual proceedings began that the word "awesome" became the cliché used to describe them.)

A diversionary approach to the impeachment question developed in August, once it became clear that an investigation was under way of Vice-President Spiro Agnew, for taking kick-backs from contractors in Maryland over a period of years. The charges, as they developed against Agnew, included bribery and extortion not only before his term as Vice-President but during it as well, and Agnew, perhaps sensing that the House of Representatives might take a friendlier view of bribery and extortion than a Grand Jury, had tentatively raised the constitutional argument that he could not be indicted and tried until he had been impeached and convicted. It was an argument which Leon Jaworski was later to find persuasive with respect to the President, but as far as the Vice-President was concerned it did not convince either Speaker of the House Carl Albert, or Attorney-General Elliot Richardson.

However, a federal judge in Illinois had already been indicted, tried, convicted, and sentenced for bribery, and on his appeal to the Supreme Court the judge (former Illinois Governor Otto Kerner) raised precisely that constitutional question. The effort was particularly noted in Chicago, and in August, Glen Elasser in the Chicago *Tribune* discussed the matter and cited the authorities on both sides. He concluded that only the Supreme Court could settle the "riddle of impeachment," but made it clear that Kerner and Agnew were the immediate areas for decision. As it turned out, Agnew resigned rather than face the massive evidence prepared by the Justice Department which would have made public his offenses, and Kerner's appeal was rejected by the Supreme Court without reaching the question of whether even a federal judge, let alone a Vice-President or President, could be indicted before he was impeached.

On August 20, 1973, Senator George McGovern, appearing on a network television interview, said that by denying the tapes to the Special Prosecutor the President had made it very hard to accept the argument that he had nothing to hide, and that while it was "premature for any of us in the Congress to be advocating impeachment at this point, if the President remains steadfast in his refusal to turn over the tapes even if the courts hold that he has an obligation to do so, then the Congress will have no other recourse except to give serious consideration to impeachment."

A Nixon loyalist, Richard Wilson, writing for United Features, said five days later that the McGovern view was essentially shared by Nixon's special tapes counsel, Charles Alan Wright, of the University of Texas. It was Wright who had written the brief setting forth Nixon's legal reasons for not yielding the tapes, and it embraced a broad—indeed, the broadest ever asserted—view of executive privilege. It contained, incidentally, probably the goofiest argument ever seriously advanced in a federal court in defense of executive privilege; in answer to Cox's reasonable argument that since both he and the President were in the executive branch, there could hardly be a question of "separation of powers," which always protected, if at all, one branch of government from encroachments by the other. Wright, whose reputation as a constitutional scholar suffered mightily in the course of the few months he was associated with Nixon, responded that since Cox wanted the tapes to use before Grand Juries and in trials, then the doctrine of "separation of powers" applied, since Cox would, in effect, be turning over executive documents to the judicial branch. (The absurdity of this argument was, of course, clear, when one considered that what Wright was saying was that Cox could have the tapes without constitutional impediment if all he intended to do was listen to them himself, or perhaps make them available to radio and television stations at prime time.)

In any event, Wilson took note of the tape controversy and argued that McGovern and Wright shared the view that the only remedy for the President's refusal to turn over the tapes would be impeachment. Unlike McGovern, however, Wilson was using this as an argument *against* impeachment.

After running through the standard historical view of the impeachment of Andrew Johnson, that it was "pure politics" and conducted in an atmosphere of "hatred" and that the case against Johnson was "purely political and judicially ridiculous," Wilson concluded that while the tapes issue was probably as explosive as the issue which had brought Johnson to the brink of removal from office, "the nation does not wish the trauma of an impeachment and trial which would forever more subject the tenure of the presidency to the will of Congress. And perhaps Thaddeus Stevens [the radical Republican leader who had brought the case against Johnson] was right that the impeachment process is unworkable, certainly in the absence of stronger evidence than exists today."

Wilson's conclusion was to be the standard White House brief for some time—an impeachment proceeding would be an intolerable "trauma" to the nation, and that no evidence to support such an effort existed. This line was steadily promoted by the White House and found more journalistic takers than might be imagined.

On August 6, Joseph Alsop turned his attention, for the first time, to the question of impeachment. He took a line that he was to take with only slight variations almost until the day of the President's resignation. That was, that no case had really been made, that the advocates of impeachment were an isolated left-wing group, that the facts which had been brought out were perhaps "shocking," and showed some of the White House people to be "sleazy," but that any talk of impeachment was practically unthinkable because it would "cripple" the President and, as Alsop said for the first time on August 6, 1973 (but certainly not for the last time), "it is always bad for this country to have a crippled President."

The Alsop line also included delightfully savage attacks on the proponents of impeachment and the enemies of Nixon. In this first column Representative Robert F. Drinan of Massachusetts was referred to as the "left-wing priest member" of the House. This was going rather easy on Father Drinan. John Dean was regularly referred to as a "bottom-dwelling slug," and the White House aides who were dismissed and some of whom were later indicted, convicted, and jailed were referred to as "brown-nosers," quite possibly because Alsop—a fastidious man—did not know the origin or meaning of that particular insult. But it was enough for Alsop on August 6 to say that "the President is not going to be impeached. He is not going to resign or be destroyed, either. He is going to continue to be President." He also predicted that "a lot of people who ought to go to jail are also going to avoid jail as a delightful consequence of the Senate committee hearings," a theory which he probably obtained from Charles Alan Wright at the White House, who believed that the Ervin hearings would make it impossible for the witnesses later to obtain a fair trial.

Alsop had one curious disclaimer in this first anti-impeachment column; he said that all of these good things would happen to Nixon "unless the courts hold against the President in the matter of the famous tapes." This was not as great a disclaimer as it seemed to be; it was, first of all, obvious that the courts *would* hold against the President "in the matter of the famous tapes," and Alsop stuck with his predictions of no impeachment, no resignation, long after "the courts" had held against Nixon.

On August 7, in an op-ed article by historian Barbara Tuchman, *The New York Times* returned to its educational task. Tuchman developed the very proper thesis that the Democratic party, "fearing the advantage that incumbency would give Agnew in 1976, shrinks from the idea of impeachment," and added that "so do the Republicans, fearing the blow to their party. All of us," she continued, "shrink from the tensions and antagonisms that a trial of the President would generate. *Yet this is the only means of terminating a misconducted presidency that our system provides."* (Emphasis added.)

Tuchman continued in this vein, urging that "political expediency not take precedence over decency in government." She went on to point out that the tapes were assuming too major a role, and that "what we are dealing with here is fundamental immorality." Almost alone among analysts of the situation in mid-summer, 1973, Tuchman saw that "enough illegal, unconstitutional, and immoral acts have already been revealed and even acknowledged to constitute impeachable grounds." She pointed out, quite correctly, that the so-called Huston Plan of 1970, which the President had authorized, and which called for wholesale and deliberate violations of citizens' rights by agents of the White House, would be sufficient to disqualify Nixon from office. She went on to catalog the "dirty tricks," the forgeries, the burglaries, and the proposed fire bombings which operated out of the White House under the supervision of Nixon's appointees and she wondered, "Is he separable from them?" She went on to talk of the selling of government favors to big business as the "normal habit" of the administration and wondered whether Nixon was separable from that, "or from the use of taxpayers' money to improve his private homes?"

Along with Joseph Kraft, Barbara Tuchman saw a possible role for the Ervin Committee in pointing out the impeachable offenses that would lead to a later constitutional process in the House and Senate. She concluded:

> At this time in world history when totalitarian government is in command of the two other largest powers, it is imperative for the United States to preserve and restore to original principles our constitutional structure. The necessary step is for Congress and the American public to grasp the nettle of impeachment if we must.

By September 1973, when Senator Edward Kennedy stated the obvious—"if President Nixon defied a Supreme Court order to turn over the tapes, a responsible Congress would be left with no recourse but to exercise its power of impeachment"—columnist

William Buckley agreed. It was the first serious discussion by Buckley of Watergate and of possible impeachment, and it must have come as a surprise to the Nixon hard-liners. Senator John Tower of Texas, for example, took the hard White House line after Kennedy's speech, saying, "We get into the shadowy area of separation of powers, but so far the refusal to obey a court order has never been grounds for impeachment."

Tower, of course, was talking nonsense—as he and other Nixon partisans would do frequently before the ordeal was over. No President had ever defied a court order before, and there was, thus, no precedent.

But Buckley, foreshadowing the general weakness with which he and his Senator brother (James Buckley, Conservative of New York) supported Nixon, pointed out that Kennedy was quite right. Buckley pointed out that Kennedy was proposing an essentially "political" solution to a historical constitutional problem and agreed that only political solutions are possible in such a case. Buckley concluded—after pointing out that the constitutional lawyers on both sides of the Supreme Court argument, as well as the members of the court themselves, were probably all sincere and in any event without precedents as a basis for decision—that Kennedy had "suggested the only means of breaking the *impasse* widely projected."

In September, a new voice was heard. William Raspberry had been working for a few years as a columnist on the Washington *Post*, although he generally stuck to writing about matters of concern to blacks, particularly local issues touching the District of Columbia. But as Watergate moved along, Raspberry began to discuss the larger national issues as well, and since he was in no way a member of the "inner club" of syndicated columnists, and had never picked up the conventional wisdom which they provide each other at dinner parties and governors' conferences, he was the classic "outsider," and thus able to say from time to time, "the emperor has no clothes." This he did frequently, with telling effect. His first Watergate column went straight to the question of impeachment, and particularly to the conventional belief that "the public would never stand for it," because of the great "trauma" it would cause the nation and the damage it would do to the presidency. Raspberry thought quite the opposite would be true, that "the percentage of people supporting impeachment would grow dramatically as the case started to be made and the facts organized."

Raspberry even went on to put the blame where he thought it belonged, and where none of the conventional liberal or conservative writers had assigned it—to the leadership in Congress who did not want an impeachment proceeding because they would have to vote. "The problem," said Raspberry, "is the absence of leaders in the House of Representatives with enough guts to stand up and do their duty. Most of them enjoy the Congress's clubby atmosphere too much and many of the rest fear being dismissed as merely personally ambitious."

As for the "grave damage" that would be done to the presidency by an impeachment proceeding, Raspberry was short and direct: "And none of that nonsense about damaging the *presidency*. It may well be that the biggest threat to the presidency today is—the President."

The Press:
The Establishment
and the Outsiders

By November, once the Saturday Night Massacre was over and the firestorm had abated, only to be fanned again by the revelations that some of the tapes the President had been forced to yield were either missing or had been manually altered, the talk in the columns turned, not to impeachment but to resignation. Resignation was always a preferable alternative to the Congress, and to some journalists, who thought that somehow Nixon could escape with some measure of dignity and spare the country the awesome or traumatic ordeal of impeachment and trial.

Thus Anthony Lewis of *The New York Times*, as hard an anti-Nixon commentator as there was in the country, spoke on November 8 of the problem of "legitimacy" which Nixon's conduct had created. Lewis argued persuasively that the legitimacy of Mr. Nixon's successor required a legal proceeding and that the Constitution provided only one, impeachment. He concluded that the President's resignation would "heal his country's wounds more speedily," and that if Nixon were to resign "no true consideration of legitimacy would demand that the United States go through the further trial of impeachment. Begin the process, yes; go on if we must. But to insist on impeachment would seem less like statemanship than masochism."

Earlier, Lewis's colleague at *The New York Times*, James Reston, had straddled the impeachment–resignation question. He pointed out that the best advice for President Nixon would be the Eisenhower rule of "get all the facts and all the good counsel you can, and then do what's best for America." Ignoring the fact that Nixon probably believed he was doing just that, Reston concluded that Nixon would not do that, quoted the *Wall Street Journal* approvingly to the effect that Nixon had become "a pitiful helpless giant" with no one to blame but himself, and then concluded that "the time for self-deception is past and that the time has come [for the nation] to get all the facts and do what's best for America." The main thrust of the Reston column was that the ordeal of the presidency was weakening America abroad, but he came out finally on neither side of the impeachment–resignation argument.

William Safire, a former Nixon speechwriter taken on in 1973 as a columnist by *The New York Times* to achieve "balance" in its editorial pages, was in a difficult situation. Safire over the years had shown himself to be a genuine conservative, and could have been expected, in the pages of *The Times,* to have espoused a generally pro-Nixon and conservative view *on the issues* through Nixon's second term. Alas, no sooner was he formally ensconced on *The Times*'s op-ed page for two essays a week when the Watergate case blew wide open and Safire, *faute de mieux*, found himself as the leading Nixon apologist in the major American press organ.

Thus on November 8, 1973, Safire took on the resignation forces and said that the advocates of resignation would amend the Constitution so as to read:

> The President shall hold office for a term of four years, or until such time as his rating in the two leading national public opinion polls falls below 30 percent for three consecutive months, at which time it can be assumed the President has lost the ability to govern and he must then resign.

Safire was heading off—or attempting to head off—the resignation talk which had acquired a considerable number of adherents after the Saturday Night Massacre and the revelations that the White House had tampered with the tapes. But his argument was correct, and was in fact an argument for impeachment, although Safire probably did not see it that way. But he did deflate for a time the argument that Nixon should resign, an argument which was coming not only from people who did not understand either the constitutional strength of the country or the ability of its people to understand that strength, but also from public officials who would have welcomed resignation as an opportunity for them not to have to take a stand.

In another column, Safire made his point explicit. "Some politicians," he wrote, "are trying to transfer their own wrist-to-forehead public suffering to the people at large; because some Washington denizens cannot stand the gaff, they assume the country cannot."

It was essentially the same argument William Raspberry had made one month before, but Raspberry had made it in the course of urging a serious consideration of impeachment; Safire made it from a pro-Nixon stance in an effort to point out to some previous Nixon supporters that their calls for resignation were not only premature, but probably, in the long pro-Nixon view, unnecessary.

But the strongest blow struck for a serious consideration of impeachment was made in November 1973, by a respected conservative columnist, James J. Kilpatrick:

"The time has come, much as a long-time admirer regrets to say it, to proceed with the impeachment and trial of Richard Nixon. Nothing else will clear the poisonous air and restore a sense of domestic tranquillity," he began a very widely read column.

He wrote, said Kilpatrick, as a supporter and defender of Nixon who had praised his general philosophy for twenty-five years and who liked him as a human being. Resignation, said Kilpatrick, is not the answer and in any event it was politically inconceivable that the President would resign, either before Gerald Ford's confirmation as Vice-President or even afterward. "If the most powerful office in the free world is to change hands, under the traumatic conditions that now obtain," said Kilpatrick, "the change should reflect the solemn deliberate will of the Senate."

Kilpatrick admitted that only two weeks before he had said it was "nonsense" to suppose that the Senate would vote to convict Nixon and remove him from office. But that, said Kilpatrick, was before the firing of Archibald Cox, the resignations of Elliot Richardson and William Ruckelshaus, and the emergence of the fact that some of the tapes were missing. Now he felt nothing else could quell the national doubt and distrust but a formal trial of an impeachment resolution. Kilpatrick conceded that such a trial would tie up the Senate for months and take the Chief Justice away from the Supreme Court for the same period. (It was only to Kilpatrick among the major columnists that this latter deprivation to the country seemed unfortunate; for years Kilpatrick had been a perceptive and keen analyst of the work of the Supreme Court and he sensed that some of the major "political" history of our time was being written, not by the politicians in the legislative branch but by the politicians in the judiciary.)

But Kilpatrick saw in impeachment a "tremendous advantage: We could look to the one thing that is most desperately needed now, and that is an ending." Kilpatrick saw Nixon as "under siege," his "blunders" having cost him heavily in terms of public confidence and respect, and he concluded that only an acquittal after impeachment had a chance—and only a chance—to restore the leadership necessary to rest in the presidency.

David Broder returned to an assessment of the Watergate situation in November, and it was a curious one. Broder is probably the only journalist with a national audience who takes seriously—far too seriously—the political party structures. This is curious, because he wrote a book in the early 1970s called *The Party's Over* in which he strongly suggested that political party structures were becoming increasingly irrelevant. Nevertheless, Broder saw Watergate in November 1973 as a Republican *party* problem, since he did not believe that Nixon would disclose the facts on which a judgment of Watergate could be made, nor was he likely to "end his presidency painlessly" with a resignation once Ford had been confirmed as Vice-President.

Ignoring the obvious possible remedy of impeachment, Broder turned to the Republican party, and predicted that the increasing desire of Republican party officials and candidates to put distance between themselves and Nixon meant "the possibility of a GOP wipeout of 1958 or 1964 proportions." Broder thought the Republicans would have a bright future if they could free themselves "from the incubus of Mr. Nixon's vagaries."

Broder saw some hope—although no one else saw any significance, let alone hope—in the forthcoming meeting of a Republican Coordinating Committee representing the collective leadership of the Republican party. He thought it "a timely expression of

Republican awareness of the need to separate the party's future from Mr. Nixon's." But nowhere in the column was there a suggestion that congressional Republicans might come to believe that the best way to accomplish this might be a substantial Republican vote for impeachment.

Perhaps the most articulate and reasoned anti-Nixon voice on the Right came, steadily through the whole controversy, from columnist George Will. Will had worked on Capitol Hill as an aide to former Senator Gordon Allott, a Colorado Republican defeated in 1972, Will believed, because Nixon and the Committee to Re-elect the President had ignored Republican candidates other than the President. Will had become the Washington correspondent for Buckley's *National Review,* and before the Watergate year was over he had become a columnist, syndicated by the Washington *Post* (without abandoning any of his conservative views). On the whole, the Will experiment worked out better for the *Post* than the Safire plan had for *The New York Times,* chiefly because Will never saw his commitment to conservatism as necessarily embracing a defense of Nixon. And because Will, despite his Capitol Hill background, remained an amateur and never once tried to analyze Watergate as a political event.

Once the Saturday Night Massacre had occurred, Will saw clearly that the burden had shifted to Congress: "With Archibald Cox gone, so, too, is Congress's ability to avoid either fighting or shutting up. Congress should impeach Mr. Nixon or cooperate with his compromise."

Will was speaking of the famous Stennis compromise. Will said that it would be impossible to impeach Richard Nixon for firing Cox; he said it "would be akin to hanging John Wilkes Booth because he disrupted a theatrical performance."

Will observed that Nixon unquestionably had the *rightful power* to dismiss an employee of the executive branch, but he went on to point out that once Cox had been fired, "it is clear beyond peradventure that Mr. Nixon is guilty of not complying with a court order." Will then continued, pointing out that the compromise was merely a polite form of defiance and urged Congress, if it felt strongly about that noncompliance, to fight it out on that issue. He agreed that the issue was *political* "in the most serious and reputable sense; if Mr. Nixon is not impeached and removed from office, his view of the doctrine of separation of powers will have triumphed. If Congress does not want that to happen, it must impeach and remove him for the offense of noncompliance with a court order." Will summed up the argument thus: "Congress can rule on it either way—by fighting, with impeachment, or by shutting up."

Also in November, Washington *Star* columnist Carl Rowan turned to the resignation theme. "The odds have increased dramatically in recent days," wrote Rowan, "that within the next six months, 'for the good of the country,' Richard Nixon will resign."

Rowan cited two or three examples to prove his point that Nixon was aware that he was in desperate straits. He said it was an act "of political desperation" to fire Archibald Cox, particularly when it meant forcing the resignations of Richardson and Ruckelshaus. Rowan also thought it desperate of Nixon to name Senator William Saxbe as Attorney-General and Leon Jaworski as Special Prosecutor. Rowan pointed out that it was Saxbe who had said—at the time of the Christmas terror bombing of Hanoi—that Nixon had "taken leave of his senses," and who had once labeled as "Nazis" the President's former top aides, and who had compared Nixon's "I didn't know about it" defense in the Watergate cover-up to that of a man who played the piano in a bawdy house and claimed not to know what was going on upstairs.

Rowan was prophetic in his description of the Jaworski appointment as another act of desperation. He assumed that "perhaps John Connally or someone told the President that Jaworski has seen so much big-style political crookedness in Texas that he'll dismiss a lot of the Watergate mess as trifling stuff." But Rowan pointed out that what was at stake were reputations built over a lifetime. He noted the areas that Cox had been investigating (ITT, the dairy scandals, the White House "plumbers," misuse of the Internal Revenue Service, etc.), and observed that "Jaworski must either become a threat to the President or run the risk of being labeled the greatest whitewasher of all time." Rowan correctly perceived in the situation that "either President Nixon or Leon Jaworski is likely to lose a reputation before it is all over, and nobody knows that better than Mr. Nixon. Jaworski isn't likely to sacrifice his reputation to save Mr. Nixon's."

Rowan concluded that as public outrage grew, as the House moved closer to a genuine impeachment offer, as more Republicans began to withdraw support and as more of his former aides were indicted and went to trial, the President was likely to try "resignation with honor." Rowan noted that Nixon had often done precisely what he said he would not do, and that "while 'I will never resign' may sound as firm and final as can be, [Nixon] will learn what so many before him have learned—that 'never' is a long, long time."

Tom Wicker in *The New York Times,* at the end of October and the beginning of November, put the resignation–impeachment issue squarely. As for impeachment, he made the point—it is hard to believe now, but it was important to make it then—that impeachment did not involve removing President Nixon from office. It was, as Wicker explained, only a method to bring him to trial before the Senate. (To be sure, the reasoning seemed a bit hollow from Wicker, who clearly *wished* that the proceeding would remove Nixon from office.) Wicker then went on to describe, from evidence already adduced before the Ervin Committee and elsewhere, that ample grounds existed for impeachment. And he also raised a question which did much to agitate the commentators in the months to come: Did impeachment require proof of the commission of an indictable crime on the part of Nixon, or did "high crimes and misdemeanors" merely contemplate other kinds of behavior which were impeachable but not necessarily indictable? Wicker concluded, on the basis of some constitutional history, that impeachment need not involve only an indictable crime, but as usual history solved the argument—the Judiciary Committee of the House of Representatives referred Articles of Impeachment to the House that included *both* crimes and misbehavior perhaps not precisely forbidden by law, as constituting the grounds for impeachment.

But in a column one week later, Wicker did his best to short-circuit what he called "the clamor for Nixon's resignation" which he said had become "suddenly so deafening that it may drown out good sense and overwhelm due process." The calls for resignation, as seen by Wicker, demanded "short run therapy for a catastrophic illness." Wicker then went on to describe what he saw as the dangers of presidential resignation.

He said, for example, that while such a resignation might imply some guilt on Nixon's part, it would surely be cast by the President himself "in the patriotic terms of a wronged statesman acting only

to spare his country further embarrassment." Wicker concluded
that such a resignation "might well insure rather than prevent continuing suspicion and bitterness in American politics."

Wicker was, of course, quite right—an early resignation would
have produced just such an air of suspicion and bitterness—but
what he could not foresee was that by the time of the resignation
the question of guilt would have been clearly resolved.

But the resignation—impeachment discussion was to continue
for some time, and those arguing for impeachment included not
only those who, like Wicker, favored it, but also those who, like
James J. Kilpatrick, opposed it.

It was in November that Rowland Evans and Robert Novak
first turned their attention to Watergate and the impeachment
possibility. Evans and Novak jointly write what is probably the
most widely read column about politics in America. Their sources
are other politicians (chiefly Melvin Laird) and their point of
view, throughout the year that impeachment was in the public
mind, was that the politicians would never permit it. If Evans
and Novak become convinced that principled liberals favor something, they can be counted on to predict its demise; should it
succeed, they will point out that it was an essentially moderate
centrist position made successful through the work of what they
call "moderates."

(In the summer of 1973, Evans was speaking to an acquaintance,
himself a participant in electoral politics, and asked if the acquaintance had any suggestions or advice which Evans's friend,
Melvin Laird, might give to Nixon, whose staff he had just re-
joined. The advice was short: "Resign." Evans dismissed the advice as "the typical response of a McGovernite"; one imagines
that both he and Laird—and for that matter, Nixon—wish they
had taken it more seriously.)

In any event, Evans and Novak began their treatment of impeachment on a political basis, assigning to Chairman Peter Rodino
of the Judiciary Committee the responsibility for a transformation
of the "once congenial committee into a snarling partisan cock-
pit." The reference was to Rodino's firmness on the subpoena
power which the Committee would seek, and his desire to accommodate the wishes of all members of the Committee as to the
broadness of the scope of that power. Evans and Novak reported
that Republican moderates wanted to narrow the scope of the

Committee's inquiry so as to exclude such matters as the bombing of Cambodia, the illegal impoundment of appropriations, and other "conservative Nixon acts." Rodino got his version of the subpoena power (the broad version, pleasing the liberals) approved by a partisan vote of 21 to 17, prompting Evans and Novak to describe this act as "marvelously assisting Mr. Nixon's grand strategy."

But Evans and Novak did pinpoint one crucial shift in the impeachment fight: they noted the determination by House Speaker Carl Albert to expedite confirmation proceedings for Vice-President-designate Gerald Ford, on the theory that an impeachment proceeding could be forwarded only embarrassingly while there was no Vice-President and the Speaker himself was next in the line of succession.

Evans and Novak returned to the impeachment problem in January, and probably succeeded in convincing some Nixon partisans that there was hope the Grand Jury evidence would not get to the Judiciary Committee. Evans and Novak accomplished this, evidently, by misunderstanding what they were told in an interview with Leon Jaworski.

Jaworski apparently told the columnists that the renewal of the interrogation of John Dean by the Special Prosecutor was a strong indication that they believed Dean and, by inference, disbelieved Nixon. So far, so good. He then told them, so the column reported, that he had not made up his mind whether the President could be indicted, even if the Grand Jury thought there was sufficient evidence to warrant it. He indicated that he would probably decide that a President could not be indicted and he referred to the fact that his predecessor, Archibald Cox, as well as other legal scholars, had held the same view. Keener legal analysts than Evans and Novak might have picked up the hint from Jaworski at that point that the Grand Jury did indeed have enough evidence to indict Richard Nixon, but the column blandly treated the question as an abstract legal proposition, because the columnists were emphasizing what Jaworski had told them—not about Dean or Nixon—but about his belief that it would be difficult to transfer the evidence developed by the Grand Jury into the hands of the Judiciary Committee.

Evans and Novak described the White House as "mightily pleased" by the "refusal" of Jaworski to turn over the potentially incriminating material to the Committee, and in doing so ignored a plain statement of Jaworski's—which they even reported, without noting its significance—that "evidence presented to a Grand Jury cannot go to the House *unless the judge consents*" (emphasis added). It seemed reasonable at the time, although the columnists did not draw the inference, that Jaworski planned—either alone or in concert with Judiciary Committee counsel John Doar—to ask Judge Sirica for precisely such a ruling, and that he was reasonably confident that such a ruling would be forthcoming.

The net effect of the column was indeed to please the White House, and to cause some muttering among supporters of impeachment to the effect that Jaworski was being too much a lawyer and too little an advocate, but in fact what Jaworski had told the columnists was precisely the opposite of the message their column carried—he would indeed try, and with considerable expectation of success, to get the evidence to the Judiciary Committee.

Once the congressional recess over Christmas and New Years was over, and the Congressmen had returned to Washington early in 1974, Joseph Alsop returned to the impeachment discussion. He had evidently spoken to Wilbur Mills (then known as "the powerful Chairman of the Ways and Means Committee"; later referred to as "the Chairman of the powerful Ways and Means Committee"; and now as the "once powerful Wilbur Mills"), and what Mills had told him made Alsop conclude that Nixon had somewhat less support in Congress, or could count on less support in Congress, than he had previously had. Actually, Alsop himself had vastly overrated Nixon's strength before the recess, and his column in January was somewhat out of joint with the time. What had in fact happened over the recess was that many Congressmen, expecting to find strong anti-Nixon and pro-impeachment sentiment at home, had not found it. The result is that the expected impetus for impeachment would have to wait until the full impact of Nixon's tax returns and other evidence against him had been developed.

Alsop reported the pro-impeachment sentiment in Mills's district at 50 percent, and concluded that "for the President, then, the political outlook now seems to be measurably more bleak than it appeared at the end of the last congressional session." But ever the optimist where the "long-headed" Nixon was concerned, Alsop also reported that almost all Senators and Representatives "have found strong sentiment at the grass roots that there are more important things to do than to impeach the President." Until the very end, Alsop believed that there were more important things to do than to impeach the President, almost all of them involved with Pentagon strategy. Finally, he saw that "a vote on the President's impeachment, whether for or against, will be the most dangerous single vote every Senator and Representative has ever cast. That will not make for haste." This was fairly orthodox doctrine in the press at the time; it was not until later that most observers of Capitol Hill began to see that a pro-impeachment vote—particularly for Republicans—would be a relatively easy vote to cast, since they could take the position they were merely sending the matter to the Senate for trial and final determination.

The news that someone at the White House, almost certainly Nixon himself or someone under his direction, had manually erased 18½ minutes of a tape of a conversation between Nixon and Haldeman about Watergate three days after the burglary, brought Alsop back to the subject four days later. This time he was remarkably more gloomy. He pointed to the near-defection of House Republican Leader John Rhodes, who had just delivered a speech pointing out that Republican candidates in 1974 would conduct their own campaigns—independent of Nixon—and he also cited news that members of the Joint Committee on Taxation, then investigating Mr. Nixon's tax returns, had urged the President to pay up before the Committee issued its report in April.

Alsop scorned the "technicality"—it turned out the "technicality" was a fraudulently back-dated deed—on which he presumed the Nixon back-tax assessment would be made. He ignored, to be sure, all the other areas of tax evasion which were looming so clearly and on which the Joint Committee would focus as well. But even Alsop conceded in January that the Judiciary Committee probably already had a majority for impeachment, and that it was doubtful whether the Committee would heed its counsel, John Doar, "even if he advised strongly against a pro-impeachment vote," a possibility hardly anyone else had even considered.

Alsop correctly defined, as of January 1974, the almost schizophrenic mood of the House, when he pointed out that public opinion seemed to include a substantial number of people with a genuine horror of impeachment, but whose number included many people who would be "both pleased and relieved by the President's voluntary resignation." Alsop concluded: "The truth seems to be that a majority of the voters would much like the President to resign, whereas nothing like a grass roots pro-impeachment majority has emerged as yet. The dilemma to the House is obvious."

In mid-January George Will came up with a powerful column on the question of the erasure of the 18½ minutes of tape, and pronounced that "the end of the Nixon administration is predictable" and that the unanimous report by the experts appointed by the court that the erasure had been manual and repeated "should give an irresistible momentum to the drive for impeachment."

Will, who always did more in connection with Watergate than talk either to Melvin Laird or to a few elders in the House of Representatives, filed in his column of January 18 a masterful brief on the question of Nixon's involvement in the cover-up. He pointed first of all to the report of the electronics experts, and commented how fitting it was that the "fatal blow" came in a "dry-as-dust technical report utterly lacking political coloration."

He then described the conversation which had been erased, and he referred to the "grinding logic" of the report that the repeated manual erasures could not have been an accident. From White House logs he adduced that only Nixon and four close aides had access to the tape and said that Americans now had "an inescapable conclusion: that sometime on or after October 1st, 1973, someone at or near the top of the White House, someone among five people with access to the tapes, destroyed subpoenaed evidence . . . another crime on behalf of a continuing cover-up." Will then argued that this dictated "a second common sense conclusion: whoever did this did it because he or she—or they—believed that it was better to commit the crime than to let Judge John Sirica hear what Mr. Nixon and Mr. Haldeman said about Watergate just three days after the break-in."

Will then wrote that the Watergate drama had moved into what he called a "deadly third stage." The first, he said, had been the "presumption of innocence" stage, where the question was whether Nixon was personally involved in the cover-up. The second stage, according to Will, had been the "White Queen" stage, referring to the passage in *Alice in Wonderland* in which the queen declared that she could believe "six impossible things before breakfast." Will pointed out there were many more impossible things to believe in order to find Mr. Nixon innocent.

At first, said Will, "one just had to believe that Mr. Nixon ran the most slipshod White House imaginable, and that some of his campaign employees and funds got involved in a 'third-rate burglary.'" Later, he pointed out, one had to believe that Nixon's two most trusted aides, "including two of his few close personal friends," had kept him totally in the dark. Then, Will went on, one had to believe that Nixon was refusing to release the tapes because he cared more about the abstract principle of confidentiality than about clearing his name and sparing the nation further agony, something Will obviously found very hard to believe.

"But now, thanks to six anonymous electronics experts, we know too much. We *know* that there is corruption in the precincts of the Oval Office."

And then Will finished with these devastating lines:

> We know who was operating in and around the White House when the cover-up began nineteen months ago. And we know that Haldeman, Ehrlichman, Colson, Dean, Strachan, Porter, Caulfield, Ulasewicz, Mitchell, Stans, Hunt, Mardian, Segretti, Liddy, Kalmbach, McCord, Chapin, Gray, and Magruder are gone now.
>
> So now we are in the impeachment stage and the question is: Of all the significant men who were around the White House when the cover-up began, who are still there providing the continuity in this on-going cover-up?
>
> One name springs to mind.

At this point, roughly one year after the Watergate cover-up began to come apart and a year and a half after McGovern and others began to talk about Watergate and related corruption in the White House, it was still only the "outsiders," George Will and William Raspberry, who were talking seriously about impeachment because the evidence was so overwhelming; the Establishment journalists (with the significant exception of Joseph Kraft) were still "touching the important bases," giving the pre-

dictions of White House authorities and old-time leaders of the
Congress and other old Washington hands, and not bothering to
immerse themselves in the evidence at all.

Thus, David Broder in mid-January was talking about the impeachment proceedings as "the priority business of this Congress,"
but felt that the Judiciary Committee, because it was "in awkward
transition for the old system of imperious rule by the chairman
and ranking minority member to a newer, more open, undisciplined and unpredictable style of decision-making," would be
unable to marshall the authority to do the job. "Like so many
other major questions in the newly democratized House, impeachment will be settled on the floor," Broder concluded. He was, of
course, spectacularly wrong—impeachment, in the larger sense of
a final determination of Nixon's guilt, was achieved by the
splendidly disciplined performance of the "newly democratized"
Committee—but he was not alone. Broder thought that the responsibility in the impeachment proceeding lay upon the Speaker,
the Majority Leader, and the Minority Leader, "if the outcome of
this process—whatever it may be—is to be seen as just." But it
was, of course, none of those three who finally made the process
be seen as just; it was the "undisciplined" (that is to say, unpredictable to people who speak only to the leadership) Judiciary
Committee and the good sense of the American people who were,
after all, absorbing the evidence along with everybody else, who
finally made that determination.

An editorial in the Washington *Post* on January 20 proved to
be critical. Clearly reflecting a long conversation with Leon
Jaworski—perhaps dissatisfied with the inability of Evans and
Novak to understand the direction in which he was going—the
editorial discussed the "Watergate impasse" facing the Special
Prosecutor. Although the editorial was scrupulously careful to
state that the Prosecutor had indicated in no way whether he
had come up with evidence implicating the President, it seemed
clear from a close reading that Jaworski had done just that, and
was now confronted with a real dilemma: whether to press for
an indictment of Nixon, which would undoubtedly be appealed
all the way to the Supreme Court before a trial could begin, or
to agree that a President could not be indicted until he had been
first impeached and convicted.

The editorial pointed out, quite correctly, that Jaworski's dilemma was heightened by the fact that he could not see how on his own, under any reasonable reading of his charter, he could make Grand Jury material available to the House Judiciary Committee.

But we recall that Jaworski had told Evans and Novak that Judge Sirica could give the Grand Jury material—including that on which they might base an indictment of Nixon—to the Judiciary Committee. And Jaworski had hinted to Evans and Novak as strongly as he could that he thought Judge Sirica would grant such a motion if the Judiciary Committe lawyers joined him in making it. Evans and Novak had missed the point though, so he probably told the same thing to the Washington *Post* editorial board, because the editorial concluded that Judge Sirica did have the power to, in effect, amend Jaworski's mandate, and hand over the material to the Judiciary Committee in response to such a motion.

A joint application by Mr. Jaworski and by the majority and minority counsels to the Judiciary Committee's impeachment inquiry would give Judge Sirica the opportunity to assess the scope of Mr. Jaworski's charter and to free him of the ethical restraints and inhibitions he now feels. Moreover, he could also enter an order freeing the Special Prosecutor of any lingering questions about whether his duties under the Federal Rules of Criminal Procedure diminish—or conflict with—his duty to the nation under the mandate setting up his office.

That last was a clear indication of Jaworski's concern over the federal procedural rules which seemed to require Grand Jury material to remain sealed. But as Jaworski and the *Post* correctly surmised, Judge Sirica had the power to waive those rules particularly where the national interest so clearly required it. The whole episode—Jaworski's expression of concern to Evans and Novak, and to the *Post*, and the *Post*'s measured "suggestions" to the court, demonstrates as well as anything could the interplay in Washington among the various institutions which were involved in the removal of Richard Nixon.

On January 20, Evans and Novak, relying heavily on information from within the White House—probably provided by old reliable Melvin Laird—came up with a prediction that President Nixon would "beat his tax inquisitors to the punch" by paying back the taxes he might owe, before the Joint Congressional Committee's findings required him to do so. The prediction was wrong, and so was their estimate of the amount of taxes. The Evans and Novak column predicted, correctly, that the Committee would disallow the $482,019 in deductions based on an appraisal of the presidential papers which Mr. Nixon claimed—falsely—to have given the government in 1969. They also thought that the Committee might find that Nixon had erroneously failed to pay capital gains tax on the sale of his New York apartment in 1969, as well as on the alleged sale of part of the San Clemente property, and they concluded that his total tax debt could exceed $300,000. In fact, it exceeded $475,000, and he did not agree to pay it until after the Committee had made its report, and he has yet to pay some $175,000 of it at this writing.

The Evans–Novak column reflected a split in the advice Nixon was receiving. Some "political advisers in and around the President's Oval Office are fearful," the columnists wrote, "that taxpayer reaction to any findings that Mr. Nixon is in serious tax arrears could set off another presidential crisis, perhaps rivaling even the Saturday Night Massacre and the 18-minute buzz mystery." These advisers, they said, were advising Nixon that even if he took his tax case to court and won, the political risk would be unacceptably high. They were advising him, according to Evans and Novak, to pay up in advance.

But other White House advisers, they said, pointed to "the Niagara of criticism which descended on the White House after the release of Mr. Nixon's tax figures to support their view that Mr. Nixon should yield nothing, ever, anywhere."

But "despite that Niagara of criticism" (once Evans and Novak get hold of a cliché they are loath to leave it alone), they reported a White House consensus that the earlier financial statement was essential and that while early payment of the deficiency might create some criticism (perhaps only a Yosemite in magnitude), the alternative of waiting until nailed by the Committee would be even worse.

The next day Joseph Alsop returned to the fray with a striking lead paragraph:

" 'You murder one President. You harass a second until he lays down his office. You submit to a third President being destroyed politically, not long after he's won re-election by a huge majority. And after that, you have a new kind of political system.' "

That argument, probably obtained verbatim from Alexander Haig, was described by Alsop as one that "is being energetically used by the leaders of his beleaguered White House." Alsop thought it an argument deserving extremely careful consideration, particularly by House members who would have to vote on impeachment.

Alsop then went through what he saw as the "immense" risks involved in impeaching a President, risks which he felt should not be underestimated. In the first place, he thought that the "mere process of impeachment" would be "deeply embittering and bound to take a fearful amount of time." He implied, from a reference to the Yom Kippur war, that grave dangers existed in the world and that the U.S. would be unable to meet those dangers "for a couple of years on end," evidently Alsop's estimate of the time that would be required for impeachment. "Paralysis-for-the-duration" was, he thought, the "minimum price of impeachment."

He also indicated that the White House argument quoted at the beginning of the column was a valid one in terms of the long-term risk. In support of that, he went back to Wilbur Mills, still "the powerful Chairman," who had called for Nixon's resignation but who, Alsop told us, was prepared to vote against impeachment, "because it's a damned dangerous business and because no high crime has been proved against the President."

Assuming that the Mills quote was accuate (and there is every reason to assume so, since Alsop—however wrong his estimates of the political situation might have proved to be—has always been a superb reporter), it stated a view which, if not current in January 1974, in the Congress, at least was widely believed to be current. Any number of people were calling for Nixon's resignation, ostensibly for the good of the country but on close examination more likely to be for the good of the caller's political future. Any number of Congressmen were plainly scared of the political impact in November of an impeachment vote in July or August, and Alsop correctly identified this fear. He could have paraphrased an old vaudeville joke: "How do you keep from voting to impeach a President in August?" "Get him to resign in July."

But he then went on to describe the "viewpoint of the House of Representatives as a whole" as not much different from those views of Wilbur Mills, and from that to conclude, "whatever the final verdict of the House Judiciary Committee—unless it is also against impeachment—it will not affect the House greatly." This was a view to which the White House—and Alsop whenever he had talked to anyone at the White House—clung with great strength. But it had become clear in the House of Representatives, not at the level of the leadership or the Establishment committee chairmen to whom most pundits talked, but to the great bulk of Congressmen seriously concerned with doing their job and with getting re-elected, that great weight would be attached to the verdict of the Judiciary Committee, as indeed it was. One tends to forget that, even without the final collapse of Nixon's position with the release of the June 23 tape, something close to 300 votes (out of 435) would have been cast for impeachment after the Judiciary Committee had referred its three articles.

Alsop could not, in the same column, resist a few more shots at the Judiciary Committee (Chairman Peter Rodino, for some reason, was not one of Alsop's key elders in the House), and he called it "a kind of dumping ground for left-wing Democrats of the more far-out type." According to Alsop, "everyone in the House knows this. Everyone in the House therefore discounts the Committee's opinion in advance." It is hard, in examining all of the comment about the impeachment remedy for the Watergate scandal, to find a judgment more in error.

Alsop concluded that "it still seems highly doubtful that the House of Representatives will even produce the necessary bare majority for a bill of impeachment," but hedged his bet by adding, "if most weeks continue to bring news deeply damaging to President Nixon, the present situation will surely change for the worse from the President's standpoint," which is about as bold as saying that if pigs grow wings, they will be more likely to fly.

On the same day as the Alsop column about the left-wing Judiciary Committee and its lack of influence, William Raspberry offered a perfect contrast between Establishment and non-Establishment journalism. Continuing to hammer away at the evidence, and ignoring what the insiders at the White House or on the Hill were telling their friends, Raspberry once again demolished the Nixon defense argument. He went through the long list of the President's men who had been indicted, convicted, or who had pleaded guilty, and pointed out the absurdity of the Nixon argument that the President had somehow been betrayed by "a few overzealous men." And he went on to say, with the common sense that was becoming characteristic of most Americans who watched Watergate, that Nixon's refusal to turn over evidence indicated that he must have something to hide.

Evans and Novak, meanwhile, were out with their pollsters in a "weathervane" precinct in Newark, Ohio. Evans and Novak never go to any other kind of precinct; except that the "weathervane" sometimes became a "barometer" of national trends. This one in Newark turned out to be both, and they discovered that "an overwhelming majority of these voters regard Mr. Nixon as a liar, a tax chiseler, and a poor President. Yet, they oppose even the start of impeachment proceedings, much less removal from office." Evans and Novak seemed astonished by a large vote in the precinct indicating a belief that Mr. Nixon was well aware of the Watergate cover-up (and many believed that he knew about the burglary in advance) and that either he or someone under his control had erased the key 18½-minute segment of the June 20 tape. Their astonishment came from the fact that a majority, nevertheless, believed that impeachment would weaken the country and that Nixon should finish his term. Their conclusion was that "futility, cynicism, and skepticism are the barriers, then, that may protect Mr. Nixon against future revelations," and that "if their present mood holds, however, even new disclosures will not make the impeachment case against the President." What they failed to take into account was that new disclosures, and even a thoughtful consideration of existing disclosures, would make it impossible for the "present mood" to hold. The present mood, by definition, never does hold, but that fact does not seem to deter the people who live by polls from assuming that it will.

By the end of January, Jack Anderson (America's most widely read columnist, by far) concluded that although the evidence against Nixon was "tightening the vice" on the President, "the inquiry into his impeachment is floundering."

Anderson thought the staff of the Committee had maintained tight secrecy and security only to hide its own inaction and lack of direction, that the Committee could not possibly meet its April 18 deadline, that no witnesses had been interviewed, that the Committee was concentrating its efforts not on turning up evidence but on researching "what offenses might constitute grounds for impeachment," and that in general the Committee staff was more concerned about security than about making the case.

The charges were probably all, in one way or another, true, but in retrospect it is easy to see that what John Doar and his colleagues were putting together for Chairman Rodino and *his* colleagues was the foundation upon which the evidentiary case could then painfully, brick by brick, be built. But the Anderson view was a fairly common one at the time, journalistic experience in these matters being so keyed to daily revelation and quick judgments that the careful efforts of the Committee were easily confused with inactivity and floundering.

Another common error about the progress of impeachment was advanced on the same day in *The New York Times* by James Reston. Commenting on the "widely held view here that President Nixon is now taped and trapped, that the courts and the Congress are closing in on him, and that it is only a question of time before the evidence forces his resignation or impeachment," Reston felt this was too simple, premature, and misjudged the power of the President, the weakness of the Congress, the patience of the people, and the President's capacity to act faster than the Congress, the courts, or the press.

Reston reads the traditional Washington themes better than most, but in the case of impeachment he did not look beyond the traditional themes. In the column, he talked about Nixon's ability to "dominate the news," and spoke of the forthcoming State of the Union Address, the Budget Message, and Nixon's "power to address the world on trade, energy, monetary reform, arms control, and peace in the Middle East." Reston also attached considerable importance to the power of the President to direct the attention of the nation "to his thought, lead the front pages and the TV network news broadcasts and thus, paradoxically, use what he regards as his 'enemies' to dramatize his cause."

What Reston missed, of course, was that this was not a *political* proceeding in the sense that most Washington events are, and therefore could not be measured by the customary political standards. What was happening—in the prosecutor's office, in the Judiciary Committee, and in the courts—was a series of *legal* proceedings, and legal proceedings are finite. Grand Juries eventually indict, cases come to trial, juries reach verdicts, indictments and prosecutions proceed, appeals are heard. And what was going on in the winter and spring of 1974 was that a great number of these things were coming to a head. The Grand Jury was to come up with indictments of Nixon's key aides; some of them would go to trial and be convicted. John Ehrlichman would be charged and go to trial for the Ellsberg burglary; he would be convicted. Other Nixon aides would plead guilty and incriminate others; and all the while the Judiciary Committee would be taking note of these legal events, and going over the hard evidence as well, which would lead inevitably to a vote.

Richard Nixon saw Washington the same way as Reston and some of the other Establishment editorialists. Even in the last month of his presidency, Nixon thought that a trip to Moscow and to Egypt would somehow distract public attention from the mounting evidence of his criminal involvement in Watergate. It did for a few days, as we noted the ability of Anwar Sadat to put a million Egyptians into the streets to cheer the American President who came bearing the potential for nuclear arms.

But the legal proceedings went on, and when Nixon resumed the Oval Office life it was to find that John Ehrlichman had been convicted and sentenced, that the Supreme Court would rule unanimously that he must yield the tapes to Leon Jaworski, and that the Judiciary Committee was about to vote Articles of Impeachment on three separate charges.

Toward the end of January, William Raspberry once again put the case against Nixon about as well as it could have been put, in the course of discussing the argument that there was somehow a "liberal conspiracy" to get rid of Nixon. Much of the column, written totally without any inside information from members of the Judiciary Committee or the leadership of the House or the Senate (or indeed, any of the other sources to which Watergate commentators were increasingly looking), follows here:

Columnist William Buckley, Jr. said it again the other day, alleging a politically motivated attempt on the part of Mr. Nixon's "enemies" to "formulate a high crime or misdemeanor on which he can be judged guilty."

These enemies, [Buckley] said, begin with the conclusion the incumbent must be removed from office and then look for a crime to hang him on.

Buckley was right, to a degree I suppose, but he makes it sound a good deal more sinister than it strikes me. What I see is that some of us (not all of us either liberals or conspirators) have concluded that the President ought to be removed from office, and some are working to make it happen.

And not because he wasn't our choice for President in the first place, either. For his entire first term, even while he was shilly-shallying over school integration, killing off the poverty program and offering us G. Harrold Carswell for the Supreme Court, there was not the slightest hint of a move to remove him from office.

There was political opposition, to be sure, and some of us wondered about the sanity of a people who would elect a man to office, but no one that I am aware of questioned his right to occupy the office.

But what some of us slowly came to see were not just improprieties and repugnant policies, but an attempt to transform the system into something alien to the American tradition—an attack on the country, from the inside. We were truly frightened by the mind set of a national government willing to deal in enemies lists and secret police forces and subversion of official agencies.

It is easy to forget how slowly the conclusion was reached that Richard Nixon was a danger to the country. For most of last year, for instance, it was widely suspected that the President was lying when he denied knowing about the Watergate cover-up but the general tone, among the liberals and non-liberals alike, was that the President should come clean, get rid of the worst members of his staff and apologize to the people. Impeachment was scarcely mentioned.

Since that time, Mr. Nixon has been pursued not by liberal Democrats and "enemies" but by facts and events, more often than not of his own making. His secretly recorded tapes, for instance, might have been a way to have it solidly established whether the President was lying; but he wouldn't let the tapes go.

And when he finally had to relinquish the tapes anyhow, two of them turned out not to exist and a third was discovered to contain an 18½ minute erasure that experts indicate was deliberately made.

And as a result, some of us concluded that he no longer was fit to be President. The reason we keep waving each new bit of evidence about is that we are sure we've seen the light and want everybody to see it, too.

But that is no liberal conspiracy. It isn't the Kennedys and Humphreys who have been in the forefront of those calling for Mr. Nixon to step down. It is voices like the Detroit *News* and *Time* magazine and Wilbur Mills of Arkansas.

Oh, yes, and the AFL-CIO, which has been generally credited with making possible Richard Nixon's landslide victory.

On the last Sunday of January, Joseph Kraft weighed in with a very solid prediction of what would come to pass, based on some conversations with Judiciary Committee people and House leaders, but based mostly on plain analysis of what the evidence had already demonstrated. Kraft pointed out that the toll on Nixon, his party, and the country would be "terrific" if he carried through his threat to "hang in there all the way." Kraft correctly said that "the present White House tactic is to stampede the Congress into an up or down vote on impeachment," and he predicted that the State of the Union Address set for the following week would be, in effect, a dare to the Democrats to produce that vote. But Kraft observed that the Majority Leader of the House was holding back any "extreme liberals who wanted to rush to judgment," and he correctly predicted that the Congress "will handle the impeachment issues as it handles everything else—in a deliberate fashion." Then Kraft went on the offensive. "A thorough airing of the charges against Mr. Nixon is apt to be devastating," he wrote. "Already any number of illegal acts—tax fraud, wiretapping, obstruction of justice through an

erasure of a tape, illegal contributions, attempted use of the CIA
to cover up the Watergate investigation—seem to have originated
in the Oval Office."

Kraft was only warming up: "Savvy officials here are betting
that direct evidence of criminal action by Mr. Nixon is going
to emerge. They believe that in time, the President would rather
quit than run the risk of prosecution by a Democratic administration after his term expires. That is the logic of the repeated offer
by Wilbur Mills to grant Mr. Nixon immunity from prosecution
upon resignation." What Kraft was referring to was a plan advanced from time to time by Mills, whereby the House and
Senate would pass, in effect, an immunity bill for *all* ex-Presidents,
after which Mr. Nixon would resign. The idea never went very
far.

Kraft went on to point to the troubles which overwhelmed
Nixon's associates. He singled out Vice-President Gerald Ford
and the way in which he was "beginning to seem like a dumb
Agnew" by making public statements exculpating Nixon and
blaming others. And the column was good forecasting in other
ways; in discussing the November elections, Kraft quoted some
Democrats as believing that they could raise their number in the
House to 300 seats (they wound up with 293).

Toward the last days of January, it appeared that Special
Prosecutor Jaworski was leaving no stone unturned (or at least no
columnist uninformed) of his plans with respect to the Grand
Jury evidence which would back up the indictments that would
be handed up a month later. This time it was Joseph Alsop who
had evidently been made privy to Jaworski's ideas, and unlike
the editors of the Washington *Post* but very much like his colleagues Evans and Novak, Alsop did not quite understand what
he had been told. Jaworski, of course, knew that the Federal Rules
of Criminal Procedure forbade the public dissemination of evidence presented to a federal Grand Jury, and Alsop was so informed. There was also at least one court decision which was
relevant, which held generally that the Department of Justice
cannot bring a prosecution if the defendant has previously been
before a legislative committee attended by "excessive pretrial
publicity."

But Jaworski was really talking about the possibility of Judge
Sirica's responding to a *joint* motion from him and from the

Judiciary Committee to transfer the material on which the Grand Jury would have based its indictment. Alsop assumed that because Chairman Rodino had not yet requested the material from Judge Sirica, that he would not do so, and that Jaworski was somehow displeased at this failure. But Jaworski understood very well that no material could possibly flow to the Judiciary Committee until after indictments had been handed up, and once that happened, he and Committee counsel John Doar cooperated very quickly in the motion before Judge Sirica, which was granted. But Alsop interpreted the delay as somehow a deficiency on the part of the Judiciary Committee (probably bedeviled by its left-wing members), or as he put it, "in fact, it looks very much as though the predominant left-wing group among the Democrats of Chairman Rodino's Committee are pushing harder and harder for their known desire, which is a protracted proceeding." What was happening, in fact, was that the Judiciary Committee was proceeding at its own pace, waiting for the indictments so that it could examine the material presented originally before the Grand Jury.

Alsop saw "great risks for Chairman Rodino and his attendant left-wing Democrats, if they seemed to be unduly dragging out their task. It is quite conceivable," he thought, "that the House would then vote for a motion discharging the committee by April 10, which would be later than the original Rodino target date." Such a motion in fact had been discussed from time to time by the House Republican leadership, but it was abandoned before it was seriously undertaken, because it was clear that such a motion would lose by a substantial margin.

By February 18, Alsop had shifted his focus of "futility" from the Judiciary Committee to the whole House. He came up with a suggestion for "the leaders of all factions of both parties, plus the much-involved leaders of the media, to conspire together to get the Watergate mess out of the way as soon as possible." Alsop referred to his own suggestion as "meaningless," since it came from a reporter, much, he thought, like his earlier suggestion that Nixon resign "because he simply could not work."

(The resignation suggestion a few months before from Alsop, Nixon's stoutest defender among the "intellectuals," had attracted so much interest that he was asked and agreed to say it on television. It was the first time Alsop had been on television; some people who knew him said they thought it was the first time he had ever *watched* television.)

Alsop's argument in February on behalf of a new conspiracy to get Watergate out of the way, was based on two theories. The first was that "the impeachment process is a mere exercise in futility—barring another unforeseen bombshell that will blow the President straight out of the water. What the House of Representatives does is of little consequence. Without another bombshell, there is not the remotest possibility of the needed 67 Senate votes to impeach Richard M. Nixon. So much is common knowledge." It was, of course, far from "common knowledge" that the Senate would not convict Nixon after impeachment. Anyone who had taken the trouble carefully to count the "hard" support Nixon had in the Senate would come up with anywhere from 25 to 35 Senators, some of whom had to be considered doubtful. But what had happened between January and February, as Alsop's column makes clear, was a shift in White House thinking and in the White House defense. The line had become a more flexible one and what had originally been a reliance on a solid Republican phalanx to combine with a few southern Democrats to beat impeachment in the Judiciary Committee, had become a belief that Republicans and southern Democrats on the House floor could defeat impeachment even if the Committee voted it, and was now conceding the likelihood of an impeachment vote in the House but counting on at least 34 hard-line Nixon supporters in the Senate. The walls were crumbling, at least in the view of those who read closely and were not tied to a Washington orthodoxy.

Alsop's second argument for getting impeachment out of the way one way or the other, including a remarkable assertion that "the rights and wrongs of the case do not matter all that much either," was that the times were dangerous for the United States, and a strong President was needed to deal with those dangers. Alsop believed so strongly that "the rights and wrongs of the case do not matter" that he compared Watergate and the Nixon impeachment to a "break in a sewer main," while "a holocaust of flame [the Soviet Union's penetration of the Middle East] races through the suburbs toward the inner city." It was an argument he had used before, and both he and General Haig would use again, but to diminishing effect, chiefly because outside of the Washington Establishment the country did not believe either that "the rights and wrongs of the case do not matter" or that the external danger to the nation was so great that criminal behavior could be tolerated in the White House. This prevalence of the Washington view—that impeachment was so traumatic and the need for a strong President so great—demonstrated through this whole proceeding the inability of most Washington commentators to grasp the mood of the country. Evans and Novak hinted at it with their occasional polls of weathervane precincts, but even they failed to understand, even after Nixon's resignation, how the revelations of Nixon's actions affected his 1972 supporters. Many of them, as the election returns of 1974 indicated, bore a deeper hatred for Nixon than any of the celebrated "Nixon haters" who had been "out to get him" for 25 years. After all, *none of us* felt betrayed.

By mid-February, Evans and Novak had turned gloomy on impeachment, and revealed with great fanfare a "new" White House strategy which had been apparent to almost every outside observer for months. The new strategy, according to the columnists, would be to refuse evidence to the Judiciary Committee, on the grounds that the only evidence which should be made available would be that "relevant" to the new definition of impeachable offenses advanced by the President's lawyer, James St. Clair. St. Clair's argument had always been that only an "indictable crime" would constitute an impeachable offense (although it had no constitutional support at all).

Since Nixon had been denying evidence to every other institution concerned with Watergate for months, it did not come as a great surprise that the White House had adopted what the columnists quoted one committee Republican as calling " 'a blocking, stalling, delaying action' in the most blatant tradition of a smart lawyer's play for time." Evans and Novak concluded that down the road he had chosen lay "potential disaster" for Nixon but "beleaguered in his White House redoubt and surrounded by fanatic loyalists, the President obviously hopes that during the long delays, obfuscations, and possible court battles ahead, he can recover his political power by brilliant successes in Moscow, the Middle East, and other exotic climes and ride out the impeachment storm." Evans and Novak thought, however, that if Nixon's previously "aborted dreams of recovery" were any guide, he was once again playing "the worst kind of politics."

The next day (February 19) Joseph Kraft, in the course of laying out some more of the evidence and concluding that even the tapes might show that Nixon had cleverly "laid off" his guilt on others in the White House, made one of his few miscalculations in assessing the impeachment path. Kraft gave up, at least temporarily, on John Doar, the counsel for the Judiciary Committee, who had cut himself off entirely from public contact, and who was building his case too slowly for most pro-impeachment observers. Kraft said that the advance toward impeachment was "gingerly," and said that it was becoming clear that "a role is going searching for a man . . . the role played by Edmund Burke in the impeachment of Warren Hastings—the role of laying out the broad outlines of the case." Kraft felt that someone had to act as a prosecutor and that neither Rodino nor Doar would do it because they were determined "to do everything right" and "avoid the slightest tinge of partisanship and to be fairness itself." Kraft showed some testiness toward John Doar, perhaps because he would not talk to Kraft—or for that matter, to anyone, even his old friends. Doar "is what some people call a man of the highest rectitude and what others call a bit of a Christer," wrote Kraft, suggesting that Doar's notion that "the facts should speak for themselves" might not yield the intended result. In despair over Doar and Rodino, Kraft suggested some other members of the Judiciary Committee as possibilities to play the role of formal prosecutor. He suggested the name of four Committee members —Jack Brooks of Texas, Don Edwards of California, John Seiberling of Ohio, and Robert Kastenmeier of Wisconsin—and called for one of them "to step forward." None of them did because they knew, as only the Committee members did, that Doar was proceeding inexorably toward the day when the evidence—and not his personality—would enable, indeed force him to assume that leadership role.

On February 20, *The New York Times* contributed a solid editorial analysis beginning, "The nation is moving inexorably toward an impeachment trial of Richard Nixon. His conviction by two-thirds vote of the Senate is by no means certain but his indictment by the House of Representatives sitting as a Grand Jury for the nation appears increasingly likely."

The *Times* went on to point out the obvious—that the President and his lawyer, James St. Clair, were acting in such a way as to make impeachment even more probable, by refusing to cooperate either with the House Judiciary Committee or the Special Prosecutor. The *Times* also noted that Leon Jaworski would wisely wait to test the question of confidentiality of presidential conversations until the Grand Jury had indicted the main conspirators in the cover-up, at which time he would move—assuming defense counsel did not—to subpoena the pertinent White House material and allow the matter to be settled in the courts. That is exactly what Jaworski did, and the resulting unanimous decision of the Supreme Court probably did more than anything else to convince the country—if it needed any further convincing—that Nixon's refusal to yield the evidence was not based on any constitutional ground at all but simply on the natural desire of a guilty defendant not to hand over incriminating evidence to his prosecutors.

The *Times* editorial also went a long way to demolish the argument that "specific criminal acts" would have to be proved in order for the President even to be subject to impeachment. The *Times* set forth succinctly the argument of Alexander Hamilton in the *Federalist Papers* that "impeachment is to be used against those offenses which proceed from the misconduct of public men, or in other words from the abuse or violation of some public trust. They are of the nature which may with peculiar propriety be denoted political, as they relate chiefly to injuries done immediately to the society itself." (Conservative columnist George Will had pointed to these words earlier and had suggested that perhaps Hamilton's name might appear on the next White House "enemies list.")

The *Times* concluded by suggesting that one ground for impeachment might be the President's refusal to perform his constitutional responsibility "to take care that the laws are faithfully executed," and also indicated that the use of the doctrine of executive privilege "to shield his own acts and those of his former subordinates from a searching inquiry by the Special Prosecutor" was also an offense against the Constitution. This *Times* editorial fairly accurately summed up the grounds the Judiciary Committee would later find—by a substantial majority—constituted impeachable offenses.

Later in the month, Tom Wicker in the *Times* commented on the growing trend in special elections for House seats for the voters to replace Republicans with Democrats, specifically those who were calling for Nixon's removal from office. Wicker outlined correctly the dilemma for a Republican Congressman campaigning for re-election but also correctly pointed out that—particularly in view of the special election results—the "safe" vote for a Republican incumbent was a vote for impeachment so that he could clear himself of any charge that he was participating in the cover-up, and at the same time explain to his hard-line pro-Nixon supporters that his vote merely gave Nixon an opportunity to clear himself in the trial forum of the Senate.

In the last week of February, the Washington *Post* returned to an analysis of the impeachment issues and concluded that it would have been a mistake for the Committee to accept a narrow definition of indictable crime as an impeachable offense—the one advanced by Nixon and St. Clair. The *Post* exhaustively analyzed the possible abuses of power, and defined with great particularity those presidential powers which might have been abused. The editorial spoke of the "power to share power"—to name subordinates to act in the President's name. They spoke as well of the "power to set a standard of conduct" for those he had chosen and finally the "presumption that neither the office of the presidency nor the extraordinary powers conferred upon it (by the people) will be grossly, persistently, and cynically misused."

Then, going only through the President's knowledge of and encouragement of the Ellsberg burglary, even though Egil Krogh's testimony was that he had received no direct order from Nixon to carry it out, the *Post* concluded that while that testimony might exonerate Nixon of a crime in the ordinary sense, it had hardly exonerated him for the "abuse of powers which only a President possessed." It must have made powerful reading for the members of the House that morning.

On February 28, Joseph Kraft, discussing a Nixon press conference and anticipating the forthcoming indictments of Nixon's close associates—they were to come the next day—reviewed some more of the evidence, and made the common sense observation that "had [Nixon] been a Mafia associate, he would have been long since tried and convicted and jailed just on the basis of the circumstantial evidence."

But because he was not a Mafia associate, but only the President of the United States, Kraft correctly reported that "everybody is reluctant to believe the worst." But Kraft concluded that "as the guilty pleas of his former associates add up, as the indictments of his most intimate co-workers are handed down, as his own excuses wear thinner and thinner, it becomes harder and harder to believe that Mr. Nixon is innocent [and] thus becomes more and more likely that he will be made to pay for his actions in the impeachment proceeding which the Constitution prescribes."

After seven Nixon aides had been indicted on March 1, 1974, and the ruling of Judge Sirica became imminent on whether to pass the evidence supporting those indictments along to the House Judiciary Committee, decisive action by the Judiciary Committee itself drew closer. Columnist Marquis Childs, on March 5, reported that "the odds on President Nixon's impeachment have risen [a frequent misunderstanding of gambling terms —for "risen" read "declined"] sharply since the indictment of seven of his former close aides on a wide variety of criminal charges." Childs, strangely enough, then went back to defend his own (and others') suggestion months before that Nixon's great error was not "to have faced the facts when he learned them, dismissing his principal aides and asking for public understanding of his failure to have held to account men once enjoying his complete trust." "At one stroke," said Childs, "that would have drawn the sting of Watergate and the public would have accepted this act of contrition."

Childs also cited an interview he had once had with Vice-President Ford, who had expressed "his puzzlement over why the President had not followed that course." Childs wrote that Ford "could not understand the failure to make a clean breast of the involvement of Haldeman, Ehrlichman, and company and have done with it."

It is hard to understand how Childs (and, to be sure, Gerald Ford) did not grasp as late as March 1974 that this course had always been an impossible one for Nixon to follow, since to have told the truth about the involvement of others in the cover-up would have meant involving himself. With all of the evidence at hand, it still seemed possible for some to describe Nixon's predicament in terms merely of an earlier failure to "come clean." What never seemed to be understood widely enough, until the end, was that Nixon could never have "come clean," because he, more than anyone else, knew that he was not clean.

But Childs saw in March that while the judicial process in

trying the Nixon associates stretched "a long way into the future," that the narrow view of impeachment—the "criminal act" argument—was unlikely to prevail. Childs saw that the findings of the Grand Jury, whether or not Judge Sirica forwarded the record to the Judiciary Committee, was a long step on the road to impeachment.

George Will, who had always seen the Nixon involvement in Watergate steadily and whole, returned to that analysis after the indictments. He took a hard look at the St. Clair argument and pointed out that "the White House did not just respond that a President can only be impeached for criminal acts," but quoted the White House argument to the effect that the words of the Constitution not only required a criminal offense "but one of a very serious nature committed in one's governmental capacity."

Will suggested that this argument by St. Clair had been delivered to the Judiciary Committee *in anticipation* of the indictments of Haldeman, Ehrlichman, and the others, and he based his belief on two reasons. The first, said Will, was that by defining an indictable crime (and therefore an impeachable offense) in terms of "a very serious one committed in one's governmental capacity" the White House was trying to exclude the possibility that Nixon could be impeached for tax fraud, on the grounds that the nonpayment of taxes was done in Mr. Nixon's "personal" rather than "governmental" capacity. Second, Will argued that the Grand Jury indictments made it "reasonable to infer that Mr. Nixon is guilty of participating in a criminal conspiracy to obstruct justice," and that it was therefore reasonable to infer from "the careful wording of the White House essay on the grounds for impeachment (and from what we know of Mr. Nixon's character)," that the new Nixon tactic would be to argue that he could not be impeached for *that* because it was not a "serious" crime.

Will's conclusion was obvious: "So Mr. Nixon's final argument is: 'I'm not a *serious* crook.'"

In commenting on the indictments, Nixon loyalist Richard Wilson showed that at least one count against Bob Haldeman had shaken even his loyalty. Haldeman had testified before the Ervin Committee that on March 21, 1973, Nixon had said to John Dean: "There's no problem in raising a million dollars [in hush money], we can do that, *but it would be wrong.*" One of the counts in the indictment against Haldeman alleged that he had committed perjury when he so recited Nixon's statement to John Dean. Wilson quite correctly saw that since the Grand Jury had listened to the tape of the conversation in question, the members of the Grand Jury at the very least had concluded that Nixon had not said what Haldeman reported he had said. Since Nixon had relied on Haldeman's testimony in a press conference the previous summer, in which he had re-recited Haldeman's words, the inference was strong in Wilson's mind that a "severe and damaging test of Nixon's credibility had emerged," and "that a vote on his impeachment could hang on it." Wilson concluded that "if Haldeman lied and the tapes do not record what the President's chief assistant so emphatically insisted, then the sole most persuasive evidence of Nixon's good intent begins to crumble."

That statement of Wilson's points up one problem that the impeachment proceeding posed—every Nixon defender had his own "sole most persuasive evidence of good intent" and that these individual bastions hardly began to crumble until the particular argument upon which each had relied was attacked by a particular finding of evidence. In general, the Nixon defenders in the press throughout the whole proceeding chose to deal with particular questions rather than the overall avalanche of evidence which was being painstakingly marshalled by John Doar and his associates.

As the impact of the indictments began to sink in, Anthony Lewis in *The New York Times* drew an interesting analogy:

Imagine a large corporation with a powerful president, one who makes it company policy to keep ultimate control of operations in his own hands. Over a year, sixteen of this president's close associates are charged with serious crimes.

His personal lawyer, the company's former counsel and two members of the president's staff plead guilty. So does the vice-president. Two other staff members are tried and convicted. Nine more are indicted, among them his top personal assistants and the heads of two major subsidiaries.

At a stockholders' meeting the president says he knew nothing of these affairs. He deplores them, he says, but his duty is to get on with the company's business; legal questions are for the courts. When a group of stockholders asks to see the records of his own corporate dealings, he says no: that might prejudice the trial of his associates; and besides, such disclosure is against company policy.

When there is evidence that a corporation has been in the hands of a criminal gang, we see easily enough that its president cannot escape personal responsibiltiy. We understand that he must make an acocunting to the shareholders.

And then Lewis asked a devastating question: "Is democracy more important in a corporation than in a country?"

Lewis continued in the column to shred the notion that a President is not responsible for his conduct in managing the affairs of his subordinates, and quoted James Madison that the power of a President to dismiss subordinate officials made him "responsible for their conduct, and subjected him to impeachment himself, if he suffers them to perpetrate with impunity high crimes or misdemeanors against the United States, or neglects to superintend their conduct so as to check their excesses."

Lewis also proceeded to shred the St. Clair argument that impeachment must be limited to criminal offenses "of a very serious nature committed in one's governmental capacity." Lewis found it sad "to see a lawyer who knows better make so shoddy an argument, one so devoid of support in history or logic." He summed up the St. Clair view as requiring that "nothing could be done about a President who commited murder in broad daylight on the Capitol steps." Lewis concluded that what "Richard Nixon and his lawyers really argue for is a four-year absolute monarchy—the power of kings before they were made subject to constitutions," and in that argument he prefigured the arguments in the Judiciary Committee which would find widespread support for Article II of the Articles of Impeachment that were ultimately reported to the House, and which would have passed overwhelmingly had Nixon not first resigned.

Joseph Kraft referred to the criminal indictments as similar to what Doctor Johnson once said about the prospect of hanging: "It tends to concentrate the mind."

Kraft pointed to the new mood in Congress, in which Republicans were running pell-mell to create distance between themselves and Nixon, and that Democrats had suddenly realized that "going hard at the President can pay big dividends." Kraft observed that Majority Leader O'Neill was talking confidently of impeachment, and that Chairman Rodino of the Judiciary Committee was "through playing softball with the White House in the matter of getting evidence for the impeachment inquiry." What Kraft observed, and what had not been observable to many other journalists, was that the Watergate case, for the first time, was "now coming before the Congress on the merits of the case," and that "the merits of the case are so overwhelming that the House is going to find it very difficult to avoid voting articles of impeachment." Throughout the whole course of the impeachment proceedings, writers and observers like Kraft, Will, and Raspberry, as opposed to the Establishmentarians like Alsop, Evans and Novak, Reston, and Wilson, kept a steady focus on "the merits of the case." They thus saw, long before the event, that the case—being primarily a legal proceeding—would have to be resolved on the basis of the preponderance of the *evidence*.

The day after the indictments the Washington *Star-News*, a staunch Nixon supporter during the campaign of 1972, entered what may have been an important footnote to that campaign. Commenting on the indictments, the *Star-News* said: "it comes as a shock to have a group of men indicted who held some of the most powerful offices in the land." Although conceding that the seven men indicted were clearly to be presumed innocent until proven guilty, the editorial went on to say that "the final judgment on these seven will not change the inescapable conclusion that the Nixon administration of the Watergate period was shot through with a moral corruption that may indeed qualify it for George McGovern's description as the 'most corrupt in the history of the United States.'"

The Chicago *Tribune*, in commenting on the March 1 indictments, thought that "the ripples from Watergate" were "lapping closer and closer to the doors of President Nixon's Oval Office." But the *Tribune* found that "these indictments, explosive as they are, pale in importance before a sealed envelope which the jury gave to Judge Sirica. After reading it, he announced that it would be held 'in a safe place' until further order of this court."

The Jaworski strategy was beginning to bear fruit. It now seemed clear that the Prosecutor and the Judiciary Committee would move before Judge Sirica to give the evidence—widely believed to be incriminating to the President—to the Committee, and the *Tribune* thought that the evidence had therefore made

the "sealed envelope [take] on an over-riding importance," and
that "Haldeman and company have been relegated to minor roles
in their own trials." The *Tribune,* noting the possibility that it
might be urged that the trials take place before the impeachment
proceeding went on, urged that that order be reversed, because
"for the sake of the country it may be wiser to give priority to the
Judiciary Committee."

On March 19, Senator James Buckley, the New York Conservative, gave a short statement in which he indicated his belief that
President Nixon, although not guilty of any of "the hundreds of
charges brought against him by those sections of the media that
have appointed themselves permanent grand juries and public
prosecutors," should nevertheless resign. Buckley's reasons for the
resignation were that it would spare the nation the agony of a trial
in the Senate, which might disgrace us in the outside world. The
Washington *Post* the following day pretty much demolished Buckley's arguments in an editorial. Summed up, what the *Post* said
was that if it were true that Nixon was not guilty of any of the
charges brought against him, "then why the hell should he resign?"

The *Post* pointed out that a resignation before guilt or innocence
had been determined would lead precisely to that poisonous atmosphere which Senator Buckley sought to avoid. Then, according
to the *Post,* Nixon could leave office claiming that he had been
"hounded out" by "the media," and that there would never be a
way to determine his guilt or innocence, and the great national
sore that Nixon had inflicted upon his country would continue to
fester. The *Post* called on Senator Buckley "and his like-minded
colleagues to see the constitutionally precribed process of impeachment through. That way—whatever the verdict on the President and whatever the strain on the legislators themselves—seems
to us to have overriding advantages: it can give the American
people reassurance that justice has been done, and it can give
Mr. Nixon a fair shake."

By March 20, Joseph Alsop said that while "the betting a short
two weeks ago was still against the House of Representatives
voting a bill of impeachment" (but only the betting that might
have taken place in his office), "today it is a reasonable bet that
a bill of impeachment will be voted and sent to the Senate."

Alsop found this shift of sentiment in the fact that none of the

House Republican leadership was prepared to support the White House argument that new requests for tapes and evidence by the Judiciary Committee amounted to "a fishing expedition." Alsop referred to a warning to the White House by some of that leadership that the President should yield the information to the Committee or suffer for the failure to do so, and he reported that the warning reflected a widespread view "not restricted to Republicans; for it is common among the more conservative Democrats who used to hate the whole idea of impeachment" (in other words, Wilbur Mills).

Alsop concluded that "a House majority for a bill of impeachment has begun to be a reasonable bet." But, still unwilling to analyze the evidence or the impact of the evidence, not only in the country but on Capitol Hill, he decided that "there still seems to be no possibility of the needed two-thirds of the Senate to vote against the President."

One more entry by William Raspberry deserves inclusion. In mid-March, Nixon went to Houston for a press conference with publishers. (During this time, the President always preferred to answer the questions of journalism *executives* rather than *employees*, for understandable reasons.) At the meeting in Houston, Nixon struck to his line about "defending the presidency," and talked of the horrors which would ensue if a President had to abdicate whenever his standing in the polls had dropped. Raspberry quoted the President's defense:

"You recall I found it necessary in December 1972," Nixon had said, "because of the breakdown in negotiations in Paris with the North Vietnamese, to order the bombing on military targets in North Vietnam.

"And at that time, I can assure that not only my friends but many others who had supported the actions that I had taken to attempt to bring the war in Vietnam to an honorable conclusion criticized, and criticized very strongly, what I had done.

"The day after Christmas, some of my closest advisers felt that because a poll that they had taken privately indicated that I had dropped twenty points in the polls since the bombing began, that I should consider stopping it."

Raspberry pointed out that "naturally he didn't stop it, and naturally the result was, as he tells it, dramatic success." Raspberry then returned to the denouement of the Nixon argument:

"Now, I want future Presidents to be able to make hard decisions, even though they think they may be unpopular, even though they think they may bring them down in the polls, even though they may think they may bring them criticism from the Congress which could result in demands that he resign or be impeached.

"I want future Presidents to be able to take the strong right decisions that he [sic] believes are right. That's what I did then and that's what I intend to do in the future."

But Raspberry—still operating as a writer dealing with public opinion and public events, rather than an insider translating arcane matters to a non-elitist audience—pointed out that what Nixon had been talking about had nothing to do with his present situation. "Surely," according to Raspberry, it could not be suggested "that he faced impeachment now because of his tough unpopular decisions. Even in the wake of the precipitous twenty-point drop in the popularity that he alluded to, the most drastic thing anybody proposed was that he stop the bombing that produced the drop." And Raspberry punctured the Nixon argument by stressing that no one—at that time of the terror-bombing—had even mentioned the words "resignation" or "impeachment," as even his hard-core supporters were by now doing. As Raspberry said, "he had made a tough unpopular decision, and he paid for it in the polls." But then Raspberry went to the heavy ammunition:

"Now try to make the analogy to 1974. He's down in the polls, all right, but as a result of what controversial policy? What principled determination? What tough unpopular decision?"

And Raspberry then listed the following decisions by Nixon that had him down in the polls and "quivering on the brink of impeachment":

—The decision that it is better to continue to cover up high-level involvement in the Watergate scandals than to let the truth come out;

—The decision that it is better to collect an enormous campaign war chest in laundered cash than to disclose who, and how generous, his principal supporters were;

—The decision to time the milk producers' pricing break in such a way as to raise suspicions of a political pay-off for political contributions;

—The decision to play funny games with his real estate transactions and taxes;

—The decision to justify a half-million-dollar personal income tax deduction with a back-dated deed;

—The decision to fire his Special Prosecutor, Archibald Cox, when Cox showed signs of getting too close to the center of the Watergate conspiracy;

—The decision to withhold tape recordings and other evidence of possible White House wrongdoing, followed by the decision to render up incomplete recordings with convenient gaps, followed by the decision to show not even the faintest outrage when a panel of experts declared the gaps to be deliberate erasures;

—The decision even now to frustrate the Congressional impeachment inquiry while pretending cooperation.

That done, Raspberry pointed out that "these are hardly the sort of tough decisions that need to be preserved for future Presidents."

"For it is the incumbent, not the office, who is in trouble," concluded Raspberry. "The trouble comes not from the polls but from the fact that he has presided over an administration of unprecedented corruption and because the American people didn't believe him when he said 'I am not a crook.'"

As March and April went on, the battle lines were relatively firm. Even after the April 30 release of the presidential tapes (itself a fraud, as we shall see, not only in that the amount of tapes released were less than Nixon wanted us to believe, but that they were edited and altered in such a way as to conceal his guilt), the insiders were still finding doubt that the President could or would be impeached, and the "simple-minded" outsiders were only measuring the time until the event took place. Thus, hard as it is to believe, Evans and Novak were predicting as late as the middle of June that because of "a perceptible decline

in impeachment momentum" (perceptible to whom?) they saw a
Republican vote on the Judiciary Committee of 16 to 1 as more
likely than the 10 to 7 split which less "political" observers had
predicted and which turned out to be precisely accurate. Evans
and Novak stated flatly that "polarization has occurred [on the
Judiciary Committee], to the immense satisfaction of the White
House," and this led them to the conclusion that a straight party-
line vote would be forthcoming in the Committee. This, they said,
would close Republican ranks on the floor, which would then,
including a coalition with conservative southern Democrats, defeat the Articles of Impeachment. Not since the *Literary Digest*
predicted victory over FDR for Alfred M. Landon in 1936 (Landon carried two states), had a political prediction been more
spectacularly wrong.

And Joseph Alsop, in the very month Nixon went down, quoted
"a moderate Democrat with a reputation for cool and astute
judgment of the ways of the House of Representatives" to the
effect that "as of today, the drift of opinion among House members plainly favors the President. So if I were a betting man, I
guess I'd have to bet that impeachment wouldn't be voted."

Alsop believed that "plain proof of criminality" had become
the impeachment test for "more than one Democratic Committee
member." In fact, it had *never* become the impeachment test for
any Democratic Committee member, and for only slightly more
than half of the Republican Committee members, as would have
been easy to determine by asking the members.

Alsop even thought that if St. Clair—who was probably the
source for the column—could "solidly prove the final payment of
hush-money was made without the President's knowledge," that
development "might even turn around the Committee as a whole."
That was probably true; if St. Clair had been able to convince the
Judiciary Committee that Nixon had been out of the country and
incommunicado for all of 1971, 1972, and 1973, that might also
have "turned the Committee around," and it was about as likely
an offer of proof.

Alsop even found *in July* "some surprising liberal Democratic
defections"; nothing could have better demonstrated how out of
touch with the impeachment reality he was.

There is enough here to demonstrate the clear split in the
vaunted "media" which was out to "get Nixon." The insiders who

knew a lot about politics—Alsop, Evans and Novak, Wilson, etc.— could not believe that their usual informants were wrong, and that an event without precedent in history was about to take place. The outsiders who knew a lot about the evidence—Kraft, Raspberry, Braden, Will—could not believe that a President against whom the evidence was so strong and so public could fail to be impeached and removed from office.

It remained for George Will to sum up the case in a column appearing in the Washington *Post* the day Nixon decided to resign—having himself delivered to the public what Will called "the smoking howitzer," the June 23, 1972, tape—rather than face an overwhelming vote in the House and Senate against him. Will called for impeachment, not resignation, and properly forecast a Nixon resignation speech in which "he would say, with a sincerity at once grotesque and pathetic, that he had done no serious wrong." Will urged Congress "instead of egging Mr. Nixon on to resignation, to do its duty, which involves more than just prying Mr. Nixon loose from his desk." Will saw Congress's duty as "to pronounce formal judgment against Mr. Nixon's conduct," adding that "only that will cleanse the stain of Mr. Nixon and his men from our government." It was the only slight misjudgment Will was to make through the whole long year; the actions of the other institutions of government—the Special Prosecutor, the Judiciary Committee, at least a portion of the press, the Ervin Committee, and the White House itself—had already cleansed that stain.

•

The White House:
"Will it Play in Peoria?"

•

The date was November 17, 1973, the place was Orlando, Florida, the audience was the Associated Press Managing Editors' Association, and the time was prime. President Richard Nixon had selected this forum, had asked for—and got, as always—time on all television networks to present his Watergate defense. He needed one badly; the Saturday Night Massacre was less than a month behind him, and the news had just been made public that two of the tapes he had finally been forced by court order to yield to the Special Prosecutor, were "missing." It was the beginning of what the White House called "Operation Candor."

Some people wondered what kind of a presidency we had, if a time of candor had to be part of an "operation"—there had been times in our history when Presidents were merely candid—but the announced intent of Nixon to answer all questions about Watergate had drawn an unusually large audience. A protracted discussion follows of that Orlando press conference, since in the course of it the major deceits of the Nixon defense became apparent, and the desperation of his position—to those who had paid attention to the mounting evidence—became clear. In retrospect, it is now possible to determine that the Orlando press conference, which included unquestionably the best defense Nixon was able to muster as of that date, made the proceedings in the House of Representatives inevitable, and the only question unanswered remained that of whether Nixon would resign, as the saying goes, "one jump ahead of the sheriff" in order to preserve the financial perquisites of an ex-President, or would "tough it out," as he had been advised by Senator Stennis, and suffer impeachment, conviction, and worse, a loss of his pension and other financial guarantees which Congress had previously voted ex-Presidents.

1. The first real question to which Nixon responded was one asking when he discovered that two of the nine tapes subpoenaed by Archibald Cox did not exist, and why he had apparently delayed for a matter of weeks disclosing that fact to the courts and to the public. The Nixon response was that he had discovered that the two tapes were missing late in September, about three weeks before the firing of Archibald Cox. Nixon claimed that the tapes were still being searched for and so he had his secretary listen to the ones that were available. But then we got a bit of typical Nixon:

"I should point out incidentally that the two which did not exist and which there were no tape recordings of the conversations were not ones that were requested by the Senate Committee, and consequently we felt that we should go forward with the ones that were requested by both the Senate Committee and the others." Later in the same answer, he said,

the White House counsel reported to Judge Sirica that the two tapes did not exist and gave him the reason for it. The Judge decided, and I think quite properly, that the reasons for the tape not existing should be made public and those involved with access to the tapes and those who operated the machines should be questioned so that there would be no question of the White House, someone around the President, or even the President himself, having destroyed evidence that was important, *even though the Senate Committee had not, as I have already pointed out, subpoenaed either of these two tapes.* (Emphasis added.)

Now there are two things wrong with that answer. First of all, Nixon knew when he said it that in addition to the two tapes which were missing, a third of the nine which had been subpoenaed by Cox and which he had agreed to deliver, had the famous 18½-minute gap, and that the gap had been manually produced. The second thing wrong with the answer is the double comment that the two tapes which were missing had not been asked for by the Senate Committee. The Senate (Ervin)

Committee, of course, was not even involved in the question. The subpoena which Mr. Nixon had defied was not from the Senate Committee (which never did succeed in its effort to have a subpoena sustained in the courts) but from the Special Prosecutor. At all times, the question had been whether Nixon would comply with Judge Sirica's subpoena on behalf of the Special Prosecutor, and not of the Senate. It was the Cox subpoena which Charles Alan Wright had argued through the Court of Appeals and was prepared to argue in the Supreme Court, it was the Cox subpoena which had been the subject of the "Stennis compromise," and it was the Cox subpoena which Nixon had finally ceased to defy and which had yielded the information that of nine tapes, two could not be delivered. So the argument advanced by Nixon, that the White House concentrated on tapes which had been subpoenaed by the Senate Committee was simply, as were so many other White House arguments, a deliberate deceit.

2. In a further discussion of the missing tapes, Nixon involved himself in another contradiction. He was explaining why the second of the two missing tapes did not exist. This was a conversation with John Dean late on the night of April 15, 1973. The White House explanation was that the tape had run out, due to the large number of conversations held that day, and that a new tape had not been installed until the following morning. Apart from the fact that the Secret Service, which was in charge of the taping apparatus, doubted strongly that this had happened, there were other suspicious circumstances, and Nixon's answer at Orlando did nothing to dispel them.

After describing conversations he had held that day including "a long conversation with Dr. Kissinger on foreign policy matters," and a conversation with Attorney-General Kleindienst in the middle of the afternoon, Nixon went on to say, "so I tried to find whatever recordings, whatever record that would help the Prosecutor in this instance to reconstruct the evidence because it was the evidence that he was after and not just the tapes. What I found was not a Dictabelt. What I found was my handwritten notes made at the time of the conversation. I have turned those over to, or have authorized my counsel to turn those notes over to the judge so that he can have them checked for authenticity, and I understand there are ways that he can tell that they were written at that time."

Now the reference to a "Dictabelt" is interesting because of early testimony by Henry Petersen. Petersen had testified that after April 15, he had had a conversation with Nixon in which Nixon inquired whether John Dean had been granted immunity. Petersen replied that Dean had not, but Nixon responded by saying that John Dean had told him (Nixon) on April 15, that he had been granted immunity. Petersen assured Nixon—according to Petersen—that if Dean had said that, it was not true. Nixon then told Petersen, "I have the conversation on tape, if you'd like to hear it." Petersen declined the offer.

The next day, Petersen testified, Nixon called him back to explain that he did not really have the conversation on tape, but that he had a Dictabelt which he (Nixon) had dictated after the conversation with Dean, describing the conversation, and it was there that Dean's statement that he had immunity was described. Petersen declined, he said, to hear the Dictabelt.

Now that was very instructive testimony by Petersen, because it showed, first of all, that Nixon had inadvertently told Petersen that he was recording conversations in the White House, which was doubtless the reason for the next-day call denying that the conversation was taped and offering the Dictabelt instead. Aware of this testimony by Petersen, Nixon now denied to the Associated Press Managing Editors that there was a Dictabelt either, and offered his own handwritten notes—or as columnist Mary McGrory described them, "some old dance programs"—in answer to a subpoena for the original tape. From the Petersen testimony alone, it seems quite reasonable to believe that there *was* a tape of the Dean conversation, or at the very least a Dictabelt summary of it dictated promptly afterward. But both were now missing.

3. Now Nixon turned to the recording system itself, and in the course of it raised other suspicions about the White House defense line. He offered to "explain for one moment what the system was":

This is no Apollo system. I found that it cost, and I just learned this, $2,500. I found that instead of having the kind of equipment that was there when President Johnson was there, which was incidentally, much better equipment, but I found that as far—and I'm not saying that critically—but I found in this instance it was a Sony, a little Sony that they had, and that what they had are these little lapel mikes in my desk.

That whole explanation has a lot in it. In the first place, there is the implication—more than an implication, an accusation—that Lyndon Johnson had the same kind of recording system set up at the White House. He did not; all the evidence produced so far, including that from loyal Nixon men, is that Johnson had the capability at his desk, of turning on a recording machine depending on whether he wanted to transcribe a particular conversation. And since it had to be manually operated, it was obvious to his visitor when Johnson was and was not recording their conversation.

Furthermore, $2,500—assuming the figure to be correct—buys a lot of pretty good recording equipment; even from Sony it buys a lot better system than the two Dixie cups and a taut string that Nixon wanted us to believe he used.

4. Nixon next turned to a theme he was to use many times before the end: his "cooperative" stance with respect to all of the investigating authorities. This would reach its peak, of course, on April 30, 1974, when in a televised speech he delivered what appeared to be roughly one half the contents of the Library of Congress to the Judiciary Committee—which turned out, upon receipt, to be roughly the contents of a generous size paperback book—containing the edited transcripts of a number of White House conversations. But before the editors in Orlando, it was enough to *appear* to be cooperative and to refer to his own generosity in self-deprecating terms:

> I don't mean to suggest by that [the system itself was not a sophisticated system] that the judge by listening to them will not be able to get the facts, and I would simply conclude by saying this: I think I know what is on these tapes from having listened to some, those before March 21st, and also from having seen from my secretary's notes the highlights of others, and I can assure you that those tapes when they are presented to the judge—*and I hope eventually to the Grand Jury*—and I trust in some way *we can find a way at least to get the substance to the American people* they will prove these things without question. . . . [Emphasis added.]

Further on in the same answer we have this gem:

"Testimony had been given before the Senate Committee that I was told that before the 21st of March, actually told it on the 13th of March. I know I heard it for the first time on the 21st of March, and I will reveal this much of the conversation; *I'm sure the judge wouldn't mind.*" (Emphasis added.)

This is more quintessential Richard Nixon. He hopes "eventually" the tapes can be presented to the Grand Jury; but when he spoke these words it had been four months since Archibald Cox had requested the tapes for use before the Grand Jury, and Nixon had resisted that request every step of the way. In addition, his attorneys were at that moment arguing before Judge Sirica that even though the tapes had been given to him, "national security" required that much of their contents be kept from the Grand Jury.

As for his hope that "in some way we can find a way at least to get the substance to the American people," that would have presented no difficulty; all Nixon had to do was make the tapes available, since they were—at least for the time being—his property and he was under no restriction of any kind which would have prevented it.

Finally, there was the shy "I'm sure the judge wouldn't mind" addition to his explanation of the tape of March 21. In the first place, of course the judge wouldn't mind; for four months Nixon had been under the judge's order to do just that. In the second place, the judge probably would have minded the description of the March 21 conversation which Nixon then proceeded to offer, since it was a false one. But here we have two instances of what would also be a recurring White House theme; namely, that the President was leaning over backward to cooperate with the authorities, and that anyone—prosecutor or judge or Judiciary Committee—who wanted more was unquestionably making excessive demands.

5. Now he turned to substance. Among the things that Nixon hoped would eventually come to the attention of the Grand Jury, in connection with the March 21st conversation, were, in his words at Orlando:

(1) That I had no knowledge whatever of the Watergate break-in before it occurred;

(2) That I never authorized the offer of clemency to any-body and as a matter of fact turned it down whenever it was suggested. *It was not recommended by any member of my staff, but it was on occasion suggested as a result of news reports that clemency might become a factor.* [Emphasis added.]

And third, that as far as any knowledge with regard to the payment of blackmail money, which as you recall was the charge that was made that Mr. Hunt's attorney had asked for $120,000, in money to be paid to him or he would tell things about members of the White House staff—not about Watergate—that might be embarrassing. . . . I recall very well Mr. Dean after the conversation began telling me, "Mr. President, there are some things about this I haven't told you. I think you should know them." And then he proceeded then for the first time to tell me about that money.

Now these three lines of defense, which were to be frequently played upon in varying degrees of emphasis, when examined after the press conference by people who knew the evidence, turned out to be very damaging. As to the first statement, that Nixon had "no knowledge whatever of the Watergate break-in before it occurred," it may well have been the only true state-ment of the entire press conference. But no one had *ever claimed* that he had knowledge of the break-in before it occurred; it was somewhat as though Nixon had denied emphatically any role in the sinking of the *Lusitania* (although there were people over-heated enough, had he made such a claim, to look more closely at the records of that disaster).

But the second defense, that Nixon "never authorized the offer of clemency to anybody and as a matter of fact turned it down whenever it was suggested," raised more questions than it an-swered. This took on added emphasis when Nixon followed that sentence by saying "it [clemency] was not recommended by any member of my staff, but it was on occasion suggested as a result of news reports that clemency might become a factor." What did that mean? If it was not recommended by any member of his staff, then who was it who "suggested" clemency so that Nixon could turn it down whenever that occurred? The statement that clemency had been suggested "on occasion as a result of news reports" didn't begin to answer the question; "news reports" had never suggested clemency, and if they had, it is hard to imagine the President calling the editor or reporter of the newspaper which had suggested it, in order to turn it down. John Dean, after all, had testified that Nixon had told him that "it was a mistake" to talk to Charles Colson (surely a member of the staff) about clemency for Howard Hunt, and that was how the situation arose so that Nixon felt compelled to talk about it in public at all.

As the tapes began to emerge, the suspicion aroused by this goofy answer turned into reality. What had happened in fact was that clemency had been suggested on more than one occasion by members of Nixon's staff, and that he had not turned it down but had accepted and recommended it. And later, to John Ehrlichman, he had flatly *ordered* clemency for all the burglars. Here, then, was not mere obfuscation or an obsequious pretense at cooperation to hide a generalized stance of defiance; here was the outright lie as to facts peculiarly within Nixon's knowledge of the truth.

The third defense which the President claimed would be revealed by the tapes was not as direct a lie, but only because he did not get to the substance. What he was telling the editors was that on March 21 John Dean told him for the first time about the payment of blackmail or "hush money." That may indeed have been the case, but what he did not tell the editors was that once he learned of the demand for hush money, he not only did not refuse to pay it but urged, insisted and then demanded ("for Christ's sake, get it!") that Dean and Haldeman see that the money was paid. And he expressed a feeling of satisfaction later when he was told it had indeed been paid.

So the three areas in which the tape, as Nixon told the editors, would clear him turned out to be one area in which he needed no clearance and two which he knew, while he was delivering the answer, would not only implicate him but which drove him from office.

6. Nixon was asked by one of the editors if he had told Archibald Cox to stay out of the Ellsberg burglary case and if so, why he thought the new prosecutor should stay out of it as well. It was a poorly phrased question, since there was at that time no indication that either Cox or Jaworski had been told (or if they

had been told, that they would comply) to "stay out" of investigating the Ellsberg burglary, but the answer was as revealing as if the question had been on the mark:

"I have never spoken to Mr. Cox at all. As a matter of fact, I did talk to [Henry] Petersen about it before Mr. Cox took over. And I told Mr. Petersen that the job that he had—and I would have said the same thing to Cox—was to investigate the Watergate matter, that national security matters were not matters that should be investigated because there were some very highly sensitive matters involved, not only in Ellsberg but also another matter so sensitive that even Senator Ervin and Senator Baker have decided that they should not delve further into it."

This was the standard defense of the action of White House employees in burglarizing the office of Daniel Ellsberg's psychiatrist, that it was somehow involved with "national security." It was to be the argument until two developments blew that defense out of the water. The first was Egil Krogh's abandonment of that defense at his own trial for the burglary, and his confession that the burglary had nothing to do with national defense but instead related to an attempt by the White House to smear Ellsberg. That was buttressed by Charles Colson's guilty plea to obstruction of justice in the Ellsberg case, in which he said that the effort involved was to smear Ellsberg in the eyes of the American public. The "national security" defense which Nixon used before the editors was further demolished by the release of tape transcripts on which appeared a conversation in which Haldeman, Ehrlichman, and Nixon agreed that one way to keep people from learning about the burglary was to claim that it was a "national security" matter, when in fact all three knew perfectly well that it was not.

(The "other matter so sensitive" that Senators Baker and Ervin agreed it should not be investigated turned out to be an investigation by the "plumbers" of a spy ring which Admiral Thomas Moorer, the Chairman of the Joint Chiefs of Staff, had been operating in the White House office of national security, by which Admiral Moorer was able to examine secret documents from Henry Kissinger's brief case and presumably inform the Joint Chiefs of what the President and Dr. Kissinger did not want them to know. The episode was a seamy one, and seemed to reveal that not all of Nixon's "enemies" were at large in the population; some of them—unknown for a while even to him—were in key posts at the Pentagon.)

7. The next statement worth noting in the press conference is a small one, but it shows where people familiar with the Nixon style were gathering their inferences. In answer to a question about establishing his own "credibility," Nixon responded:

> Well first, with regard to whether the investigation is complete. As you know, there is now a new Special Prosecutor, Mr. Jaworski. He is a Democrat. He has always supported the Democratic ticket. He is a highly respected lawyer, a former president of ABA in the year 1971. I may have met him. I have never talked to him personally and certainly have never talked to him about this matter, I refuse to because I want him to be completely independent.

Here was the first evidence for trained Nixon-watchers that Nixon was counting on Jaworski because he believed him to have been a "Democrat for Nixon" in 1972. When Archibald Cox was the Special Prosecutor, the White House publicity men would point out, from time to time, that Cox had said at the time of his appointment that he had voted in 1972 for George McGovern (it was not an uncommon thing to have done in Massachusetts). But no such statement was ever made about Jaworski, and Nixon's careful "he had always supported the Democratic ticket," suggested strongly that Nixon had at a minimum been informed that Jaworski had jumped the ticket at least once, to support Nixon in 1972. It is true that the only evidence to support this conclusion was that Nixon had suggested the contrary, but in the days of "Operation Candor" that was often evidence enough.

Attention also should be paid to the statement that Nixon had refused to talk to Jaworski "because I want him to be completely independent." But Jaworski has said that when he came to Washington to talk to Alexander Haig about becoming the Special Prosecutor, Haig and Nixon wanted very much that he talk to Nixon, but that *Jaworski* refused because he thought it would be improper.

8. Now Nixon went back to procedural matters, to reinforce the notion of his cooperative spirit, and his eagerness to "put Watergate behind him." In the same answer in which he talked about

Jaworski's status, he talked about the necessity "to let the Grand
Jury proceed as quickly as possible to a conclusion" and then
made this special argument:

> And I should point out to you, as you may recall, Mr.
> Petersen testified before the Ervin Committee that when he
> was removed from his position—you recall he was removed
> in April when the Special Prosecutor was put in—that the
> case was 90 percent ready. For six months, under the Special
> Prosecutor who was then appointed, the case has not been
> brought to a conclusion. And I think that now, *after six
> months of delay*, it's time that the case be brought to a con-
> clusion. [Emphasis added.]

That was an astonishing statement, and if any of the editors
were aware of the reasons for the "six months of delay" they did
not demonstrate it by a follow-up question. What was clear to
every lawyer who had looked at the proceeding, and surely to
the leaders of the White House defense (in which Nixon was
certainly at least *primus inter pares*), was that the White House
refusal to yield the tapes was not the primary, but the *sole* cause
of that delay.

Cox had made it quite plain that he was proceeding toward
indictments in the cover-up case, along with investigating other
aspects of the proceeding that were not so well advanced, but
that he had delayed indictments precisely because of the existence
of the tapes and their nondelivery. It is a well recognized principle of criminal law—particularly in the federal jurisdiction—
that if a defendant is indicted and evidence which might have
exculpated him exists in the hands of the government and is not
presented to the Grand Jury, then the indictment and any subsequent conviction is irreparably tainted and must be reversed.
So Cox was, in effect, holding Grand Jury action in abeyance
while he subpoenaed the tapes which might exculpate some of
the defendants (or, as it turned out, implicate them further),
and the responsibility for the six-month delay was squarely that
of the White House refusal to yield the tapes which might have
ended the delay. Under those circumstances, for Nixon to attack
the *prosecutor* for delay was unconscionable.

9. Now we find Nixon, in his eagerness for self-exculpation, turning back upon himself with an interesting contradiction. He was asked whether, at the time he gave Egil Krogh "approval for the Dr. Ellsberg project," there was any discussion of the illegality of that "operation," which turned out to be a burglary. Nixon's answer pointed out, correctly, that the question involved an assumption as to which there had been no testimony, namely that he, Nixon, had approved the project. Indeed there is no such evidence, although some members of the prosecution staff feel that Krogh might have such knowledge. In any event, Nixon said quite directly that "he learned for the first time on March 17, 1973," of the burglary.

However, he was unable to leave the matter alone, probably because thinking about it triggered his memory about March 17. It was on that date, as the transcripts of his tapes were to show, that John Dean discussed the Ellsberg burglary with him, a matter of which Mr. Nixon seemed very well aware on that date.

And so Nixon went on: "With regard to such activities, *I personally thought it was a stupid thing to do, apart from being an illegal thing to do.*" (Emphasis added.)

If that is so—if Nixon believed when he heard about it for the first time that it was "stupid" and, more important, "illegal," then why did he describe it to Henry Petersen as a "national security matter" which neither he nor, subsequently, the Special Prosecutor's office had any business investigating? One would think that a burglary which had received so much attention at the White House would be either a "national security" matter or "stupid and illegal," but hardly both. Perhaps sensing this contradiction, Nixon followed the "stupid and illegal" portion of the answer with a rambling attempt to return to "national security," by saying that "the reason that Mr. Krogh and others were engaged in what we call the plumbers operation, was because of our concern at that time about leaks out of our government—the Pentagon Papers which was, as you recall, what Ellsberg was all about—as well as other leaks which were seriously damaging to the national security . . . and that's what they were working on."

In other words, the Ellsberg burglary was a "national security" matter which was "stupid and illegal," but which was a "national security" matter. This part of the performance was embarrassing, but it did shed some light on the subsequent conversations with Dean and others about how to develop a cover story for the burglary in Dr. Fielding's office.

10. The Providence *Journal-Bulletin* had reported in October that Nixon had paid only $792 in federal income tax in 1970 (on income earned in 1969) and only $878 in 1971 (on income earned in 1970). Now the managing editor of the *Journal-Bulletin* asked Nixon if those figures were accurate.

The answer was a long one and full of self-pity and, as it turned out, more lies. Nixon was obviously ready for the question. He neither confirmed nor denied that the precise amounts quoted by the *Journal* were correct, but he described the taxes paid in those two years as "nominal," thus confirming at least the basic *Journal* story that on income in excess of $200,000 (his presidential salary) each year, he had paid less in taxes than people working at the White House as gardeners or busboys. The reason, said Nixon, was that he had received some expert advice and had acted upon it:

Lyndon Johnson came in to see me shortly after I became President. He told me that he had given his presidential papers, or at least most of them, to the government. He told me that under the law, up until 1969, presidential or vice-presidential papers given to the government were a deduction and should be taken and could be taken as a deduction from the tax.

And he said, "You, Mr. President, ought to do the same thing." "I don't have any presidential papers." He said, "You've got your vice-presidential papers." And I thought of that a moment, and I said, "All right, I'll turn them over to the tax people." I turned them over. They found they were— they appraised them at $500,000.

. . . And so the tax people who prepared it, prepared the return and took that as a deduction. Now no question has been raised by the Internal Revenue Service about it, but if they do, let me tell you this, I'll be glad to have the papers back and I'll pay the tax, because I think they're worth more than that.

I can only say that we did what we were told was the right thing to do and of course what President Johnson had done before and that doesn't prove certainly that it was wrong because he had done exactly what the law required.

Since 1969, of course, I should point out, Presidents can't do that, so I'm stuck with a lot of papers now that I've got to find a way to give away or otherwise my heirs will have a terrible time trying to pay the taxes on things people are going to want to buy.

And all of this was preceded by the statement that he had paid a low amount of taxes, not "because of the deductions for shall we say a cattle ranch or interest or—you know—all these gimmicks that you've got where you deduct from—which most of you know about, I'm sure."

Now this defense of the Nixon tax returns, three weeks before they were to be published, is a landmark in the Age of Nixon. Even twenty-five years of this kind of statement had not prepared Americans for the mass of lies it contained. It is difficult—it was difficult even then—to know where to start. But a good place might be the gratuitous comment of Nixon that the low payment "wasn't because of the deductions for shall we say a cattle ranch or interest or all these gimmicks." An examination of Nixon's tax return shows that virtually the only "gimmick" he did not use to reduce his taxes—even including the legal ones—was a cattle ranch. There were thousands of dollars of deductions for interest (including $1.48 paid as a service charge on a charge account at a Washington department store). There were deductions for a portion of the cost of laundering a rug in Mrs. Nixon's bathroom at San Clemente. There was even a deduction for depreciation on a Cabinet table which White House tour books said had been "given to the nation" by Nixon. There was a deduction for the cost of a "Masked Ball" given to entertain young Tricia Nixon and her friends, and for depreciation on a house Nixon owned in Whittier, which depreciation accounted for many times the rent on the house he reported as income. So much for the gimmicks.

But the major untruth told to the editors that night, of course, involved the role of Lyndon Johnson in the major fraud—the gift of the Nixon pre-presidential papers to the National Archives. Richard Nixon needed Lyndon Johnson's advice on the tax advantages of donating papers about as much as Bernard Berenson needed a guide at the Uffizi. Nixon in 1969, "shortly after assuming the presidency," was well aware of the advantages of donating papers, presidential or otherwise, to the National Archives, *since he had done so in the previous year and claimed a deduction of nearly $100,000.* The conversation with Lyndon Johnson—Johnson was dead by this time and thus a reliable source for Nixon to use —almost certainly never took place. If there was any conversation at all, it could not have been the one described. In the first place, Nixon had already given papers to the government and had taken deductions. In the second place, Johnson knew—as did Nixon— that Congress was about to close this loophole in 1969, and Johnson decided it would be improper for an ex-President to rush to claim a deduction ahead of the cut-off date. Nixon, on the other hand, knowing that Congress was going to set a date sometime in 1969 after which such deductions would no longer be permitted, had his legislative lobbyists devote a major share of their time to urging Congress to set the date as late as possible so that he could complete his gift and claim the deduction. It was and is totally unbelievable that Nixon would have first heard of this idea from Johnson under the circumstances he described.

For a lawyer, the rest of the language was also strange. Nixon said that if the IRS were to disallow the deduction, he would be happy to take the papers back because he thought he could sell them. But if he had truly made a *gift*, sufficient to qualify for the deduction, then he would be unable to take the papers back—and his thinking that he could take them back probably betrayed the less than total donation that even his back-dated deed had provided. The deed, of course, thus had two defects. In the first place, it had been given a date prior to the cut-off date when in fact the deed was not even prepared until almost a year later. And in the second place, the deed had so many restrictions that it would not have qualified as a *gift* even if it had been made in a timely manner. Nixon then compounded the confusion—probably deliberately—by suggesting that his heirs would have trouble paying taxes on the papers, suggesting that he intended to keep them in his estate rather than sell them, as he had indicated he would do one sentence earlier. All in all, it was a statement designed to obfuscate the true question, which was whether the President of the United States could accomplish by a clumsily back-dated deed the evasion of all but a "nominal" amount of taxes on a sizable income. Put another way, could a poor boy from

Whittier achieve wealth simply by paying no taxes over two years on more than half a million dollars of income? As of the time Nixon spoke to the editors in Orlando, the answer to both questions was in the affirmative.

11. Nixon then turned, of all things, to a discussion of campaign financing:

"Neither party was without fault with regard to the financing. They [Democrats] raised $36 million, and some of that, like some of ours, came from corporate sources and was illegal because the law had been changed and apparently people didn't know it. . . ."

The statement is close to the truth only in that portion which recites the total amount raised by the Democratic campaign of Senator McGovern through the primaries and the general election. The rest of it is a splendid example of a Nixon statement. In the first place, the General Accounting Office never alleged, after the most minute and scrupulous examination, that so much as one dollar of Senator McGovern's contributions had come from corporate sources, whereas 16 corporation and 18 corporate executives had been indicted or had pleaded guilty to giving illegal contributions to the Nixon campaign. Second, there is the misrepresentation that "the law had been changed and apparently people didn't know it." The law *had* been changed, but some fifty years before the press conference in Orlando—the Corrupt Practices Act, passed in 1925, had always forbidden corporate contributions to a campaign. When Maurice Stans and Herbert Kalmbach and the other Nixon fund-raisers were out talking to corporate executives about the advantages that would flow to their companies from "four more years," they were not confused by any late change in the law; they knew corporate contributions were illegal even as they were being solicited.

12. Nixon next turned, in his pursuit of candor, to a discussion of "executive privilege." The general question he was asked was whether, in his opinion, "executive privilege is absolute." The Nixon reply is worth quoting *in extenso:*

I, of course, don't. I have waived executive privilege with regard to all of the members of my staff who have any knowledge of or who have any charges against have been made against in the Watergate matter. I have of course voluntarily waived privilege with regard to turning over the tapes and so forth. Let me point out, it was voluntary on my part and deliberately so to avoid a precedent that might destroy the principle of confidentiality for future Presidents, which is terribly important.

If it had gone to the Supreme Court—and I know many of my friends argued, why not carry it to the Supreme Court and let them decide it—that would first have had a confrontation with the Supreme Court between the Supreme Court and the President, and second, it would have established very possibly a precedent, a precedent breaking down constitutionality that would plague future presidencies, not just Presidents. I could just say in that respect, too, that I referred to what I call the Jefferson rule. It is the rule, I think, that we should generally follow, a President should follow, with the courts when they want information and a President should also follow with committees of Congress when they want information in his personal files.

Jefferson, as you know, in that very, very famous case had correspondence which, it was felt, might bear upon the guilt or innocence of Aaron Burr. Chief Justice Marshall, sitting as a trial judge, said that—held that Jefferson as President had to turn over the correspondence. Jefferson refused.

What he did was to turn over a summary of the correspondence—all that he considered was proper to be turned over for the purposes of the trial—and then Marshall sitting as Chief Justice ruled for the President. Now why did Jefferson do that?

Jefferson didn't do that to protect Jefferson. He did that to protect the presidency. And that's exactly what I will do in these cases. It isn't for the purpose of protecting the President. It is for the purpose of seeing that the presidency, where great decisions have to be made and great decisions can't be made unless there is very free flow of conversation and that means confidentiality—I have a responsibility to protect the presidency.

At the same time I will do everything I can to cooperate where there is a need for presidential participation.

Here was the emergence of the great "presidency" defense; the notion that somehow there was an entity called "the presidency," or sometimes "the office of the presidency," which had to be defended selflessly by Richard Nixon, who was never merely defending himself. This was a public relations operation, begun at the same time as Operation Candor, and which had found its public face with the formation of a "Committee to Defend the Presidency," formed by Nixon's friend and Pepsi-Cola executive Don Kendall (who had helped secure Nixon's profitable law firm connection in 1962, and who had been rewarded by the President with a profitable Pepsi-Cola franchise in Russia as a result of the Summit Conference in 1972).

But almost all of the discussion involving the concept of "the presidency" was the sheerest kind of nonsense, historically and constitutionally. To start with, Nixon had not "waived executive privilege" with respect to White House staff members against whom Watergate charges had been lodged. On the contrary, he had instructed them all in how to deceive investigators, committees, and grand juries by sly statements like "I have no knowledge of that," and in other cases had merely ordered them to "stonewall" the questioners.

As to his statement that he had "of course voluntarily waived privilege with regard to turning over the tapes and so forth," it had the virtue of being totally opposite to the truth, and not, as many Nixon statements were to be, ambiguous. He had never waived privilege with regard to the tapes, he had not turned them over voluntarily, he had in fact been forced—on pain of being held in contempt of court—to turn over to Archibald Cox the six tapes and the one manually altered tape of the nine which Judge Sirica had ordered him to yield.

As for the failure to go to the Supreme Court, Nixon was probably correct that he decided to defy the Court of Appeals rather than go to the Supreme Court because he knew that he would lose in the high court. That would have established a precedent, one which was to be established six months later when he did decide to go to the Supreme Court on the principle of executive privilege, only to lose unanimously.

The reference to "what I call the Jefferson rule" is a fascinating one. Nixon has it all wrong, and it could not be by accident, since he had previously referred to the Jefferson case and it had been widely reported that he had misstated the facts. No matter, he misstated them again, on national television, before the Associated Press editors.

The *facts* of the case were correct as far as Nixon stated them. That is to say, Jefferson had correspondence which Aaron Burr felt might demonstrate his innocence. Burr had subpoenaed President Jefferson to appear personally at his trial and produce the evidence. Jefferson declined to *appear personally*, but voluntarily submitted all of the correspondence. Nixon's statement that "Jefferson refused," implying that he had refused to turn over the correspondence, was simply wrong.

Nixon then has Jefferson "turning over a summary of the correspondence"—evidently he thought Jefferson might have used some nineteenth-century equivalent of Senator Stennis for the purpose —but what Jefferson did was not to turn over a *summary* of the correspondence, but the *correspondence*. So the rest of Nixon's assumptions about "what I call the Jefferson rule" are all wrong, as well. Jefferson may have done what he did to protect the presidency—feeling that the presidency is well protected if the President obeys the same laws that govern other citizens—but if that was Jefferson's protection then Nixon would have done well to emulate it.

All the metaphysical talk about "the presidency" as a place where "great decisions" are made, suggests that someone other than the President is making those decisions at that place. It was this kind of cloudiness which was to leave the President and his attorney James St. Clair in legal shreds before the Supreme Court.

Finally, we have Nixon saying here, "I will do everything I can to cooperate" which was also to be a continuing theme, a statement of cooperation accompanying each refusal to cooperate.

13. Nixon was eager to get in an answer to a question about the milk price increase scandal, and when he announced at the end of the press conference that he was ready to answer it, his hosts informed him that his television time of one hour had run out. Nixon waved imperiously to the cameras and said "television, keep me on just a minute yet," and then turned to the Chairman of the Managing Editors and said "I'll tell you the time." Nixon then started his answer, after first telling the television audience "it's a lousy movie anyway tonight," surely a graceless way to bite the hand of the network chiefs who had fed him so well.

The answer to the milk question was a foreshadowing of the White Paper on the matter Nixon was to release a few weeks later. He discussed the charge that milk producers had contributed enormous amounts to his campaign in return for an increase in the support price of milk in 1971, a presidential action which overruled a recommendation against the increase by the Secretary of Agriculture. The Nixon defense of this move was that after the announcement had been made that prices would not be increased, "Congress put a gun to our head."

Nixon then proceeded to define the "gun." He described it thus: "102 members of Congress signed a petition demanding not 85 percent of parity but a 90 percent support price. And 28 members of the Senate—most of them Democrats, including Senator Mc-Govern—signed the petition demanding—the petition or signed the bill—which would have made the milk support price between 85 and 90 percent."

That is not much of a gun. One hundred and two members of the House out of 435, and 28 Senators out of 100 is hardly lethal force. Nixon went on to say that his advisers told him that there was no way that he could avoid the price increase, because the House and Senate would not only vote for a bill calling for the increase, but would be able to override his veto. This was too much of a gun even for the White House staff, which later prepared the White Paper on the milk price. There it was said that the President had received advice that even if a bill were passed, his veto would be sustained, but that the veto would hurt Nixon badly in the dairy states. But thinking now about the President, rather than the presidency, Nixon went ahead and granted the price increase anyway—at least so far as his claims to the editors were concerned.

That Orlando press conference sounded just about all the themes of the Nixon defense. But it was to play out for nine months, and over that period a number of other activities and defenses were to be presented. The rest of Operation Candor went on until the release of the Nixon tax returns on December 8. Whoever it was in the White House who was responsible for Operation Candor was probably in disgrace thereafter; the tax returns hastened the end rather than postponed it. After the Orlando press conference, there followed preliminary and then final White Papers on the ITT case and the milk price increase case. Very little was gained by either.

From the general recitals in the ITT White Paper, it appeared that Nixon's solicitude on behalf of ITT was only because of his generalized concern about enforcement of the antitrust laws. He felt that they should not be used against "mere bigness," and that translated into opposition to the efforts by the antitrust division of the Department of Justice to test the use of the antitrust laws to break up enormous conglomerates. Nixon maintained that he favored vigorous enforcement of the antitrust laws. It is an axiom of American politics that a politician who begins a statement with strong support of a particular policy, is about to announce his support of an exception to that policy—usually to help a supporter or group of supporters. Thus, "no one believes more than I in the free enterprise system, particularly as applied to agriculture, but the farmers in my district need this subsidy." But neither in the White Paper nor at any other time during his administration did Nixon ever indicate his support for any use of the antitrust laws against anyone, except perhaps against some labor unions.

It was hard to believe Nixon's claim that he was concerned about an attack on "mere bigness," as an abstract philosophical principle, when the country already knew that he ordered Kleindienst to drop the ITT appeal; his comment, on the basis of Nixon's presumably strong feeling about antitrust policy, was preceded by the phrase, "you dumb son-of-a-bitch, don't you understand the English language?" Devotion to principles of government had never been known in the past to stir such a strong response from Richard Nixon, and the strong inference remained that some special relationship with ITT—such as the company's reported offer to contribute $400,000—may perhaps have prompted his feelings.

If the ITT White Paper was vague, the milk price White Paper was an exercise in overkill—and simultaneously in underkill. Many pages of the document were taken up with a recital of the legislation which more than 100 Congresmen and more than 25 Senators had introduced in an effort to raise the support price for milk, collectively constituting the "gun at the head" Nixon had spoken of before the editors in Orlando. Each bill was set forth at some length and the net effect, unless the reader kept the numbers of sponsors in mind, was to create the impression that the President's decision to keep down the price of milk was a lonely one, unshared by anyone on Capitol Hill—whereas the reality was that only something like 25 percent of both Houses of Congress opposed him. What was understated, however, was any relationship to the basis for the milk price change—namely, that the President had raised the price in response to a pledge to his campaign, (later redeemed) of a sum of money anywhere from $400,000 to $2,000,000 to be paid by the various political arms of the milk producers' organizations.

One passage will suffice. In describing the key meeting between the President and the dairy leaders on March 23, 1971, the White Paper has the President opening the meeting "by thanking the dairy leaders for the support they had given to administration policies and praised them for their activism in pursuing goals which were important to them. The remainder of the meeting was taken up with the dairy leaders pleading their case for higher supports and with other administration officials expressing concern about overproduction and higher retail prices."

But a tape of that meeting in the Cabinet Room does not quite tell the same story. It quotes Nixon as follows:

I first want to say that I am very grateful for the support that we have had [inaudible word] in this group. . . . I know too that you are a group that are politically very conscious not in any party sense but you realize that what happens in Washington not only affects your business success but affects the economy, our foreign policy [inaudible word] affects you. And you are willing to do something about it. And I must say a lot of businessmen and others I get around this table, they yammer and talk a lot but they don't do anything about it. *But you do and I appreciate that. I don't need to spell it out. Friends talk, and others keep me posted as to what you do.* [Emphasis added.]

The White Paper says that at that meeting "there was no mention whatsoever of campaign contributions." Given the President's language, there was no need for it.

The timing of the President's decision to raise the price and the announcement of that decision is also interesting. Forty-eight hours intervened, during which long-time Nixon associates Murray Chotiner and Charles Colson, talked to the milk producers about their pledged contribution. The implication is strong that they were told that the public announcement of the price increase depended upon immediate delivery of at least some of the pledged money. The Washington *Post* spelled it out pretty clearly in an editorial:

> The President had been told that the milk producers were pledging $2 million to his re-election campaign. On March 23, 1971, he met a group of dairy representatives and congratulated them on their political consciousness. "And," he added, "I don't have to spell it out." That afternoon he decided to overrule his Secretary of Agriculture and give the milk lobby a major increase in support prices. Later that afternoon his assistant, Charles Colson, told the AMPI [the milk producers' association] to reaffirm its contribution pledge. AMPI did so and actually made the first token delivery of money before the administration publicly announced the new price support level.

Much has been made of the decision, during Operation Candor, to release copies of Nixon's federal income tax returns for 1969, 1970, and 1971. The literature on the matters involved therein, and the reason why the Joint Committee on Internal Revenue Taxation found that the President had understated his taxes by nearly half a million dollars (a figure reluctantly agreed to by the Internal Revenue Service, which had routinely approved Nixon's tax return the first time around) have been gone into at length and are summarized in detail in the Joint Committee's report. What is interesting in tracing the White House defense activity, is to look back at the events which made it necessary for Nixon to reveal his tax returns at all.

Throughout 1973, rumors persisted about the source of funds for the purchase of Mr. Nixon's lavish estate at San Clemente. One line of defense was to sell the press—an effort which was largely succesful—on the idea that this estate was a "Western White House," when in fact it was a private villa owned by Mr. and Mrs. Richard Nixon. Still, the question continued to be posed: Where did Nixon get the money to pay off a million dollar mortgage on the property, and why had he and his spokesmen told two different stories as to how the property was acquired?

This speculation, plus reports in California newspapers that there was reason to believe the funds for the purchase of San Clemente came either from the Teamsters' Union or from leftover 1968 campaign funds, prompted the White House to put out a third story, buttressed by a firm of accountants (two of whose former associates had been pardoned in the previous year by Mr. Nixon), as to how the property had been purchased. This time, it was said to involve a transaction with an entity formed by Nixon's good friends, Robert Abplanalp and Charles "Bebe" Rebozo.

Along with the release of financial information about the purchase of the San Clemente property, a financial net worth statement was also released by the accounting firm. For a while, the financial statement eased some of the pressure which had arisen with respect to the possible sources of funds for the purchase of San Clemente. But then people began to look at the financial statement itself and several things were readily apparent.

First of all, it was clear that a capital gains tax must have been owed by Nixon when he sold his New York City apartment, unless he claimed that San Clemente was now his principal residence. This would be a difficult position to maintain, not only because San Clemente was *not* his principal residence, but also because Nixon had specifically stated that it was not his principal residence in order to avoid paying any California state income tax.

It was also apparent from looking at his net worth statement that Nixon owed a substantial capital gains tax on the sale—if indeed there ever was a sale—of a portion of his San Clemente estate to Abplanalp and Rebozo in 1970. Nixon claimed to have received a substantial amount for that "sale," the proceeds of which he used to pay off the mortgage while he kept the dwelling and the ocean-front real estate. And since he had sold that portion of the property for more than its share of the original purchase price, it was clear he had made a profit on the sale and should have paid a capital gains tax.

But the net worth statement also seemed to show that either Nixon had paid practically no income tax at all, or else he had a substantial flow of funds from somewhere else. It was clear that he could not have sustained the standard of living he did, and have acquired and maintained large estates in both California and Florida, without either an infusion of cash from the outside or by not paying taxes and thus keeping a substantial cash flow inside.

As questions of this kind began to arise about the net worth statement, the Providence *Bulletin-Journal* broke the story, which had been leaked to it by an Internal Revenue Service employee, that Nixon had paid less than $1,000 in federal income tax for both 1969 and 1970.

All of this forced him—as a part of Operation Candor, to be sure—to release his tax returns, and refer them to the Joint Committee on Internal Revenue Taxation for a determination of whether and by how much he had underpaid his taxes for the years in question.

Typical of the loyalty which Nixon felt toward his employees, aides, and advisers was the closing sentence in the presidential statement releasing the tax returns:

"Any errors which may have been made in the preparation of the President's return were made by those to whom he delegated the responsibility for preparing his returns and were made without his knowledge and without his approval."

But it would not wash. If it had been found, for example, that an error had been made in adding up a column of figures, or that an insignificant tax deficiency had resulted from an error in claiming a deduction, then the disclaimer might have made some sense. A busy man, after all, leaves accounting matters to assistants. But these tax returns had made Mr. Nixon rich; they were the central financial event in his life, and no one "to whom he delegated the responsibility for preparing his returns" would have taken on the task either of failing to report nearly a quarter of a million dollars in capital gains tax which was clearly due, nor could they have taken on alone the job of claiming a deduction for a half million dollars worth of "pre-presidential papers" for which no deduction could be made unless a wholly fictitious deed were prepared, back-dated, signed, and notarized. *The New York Times* summed it up thus:

"Mr. Nixon is disclaiming knowledge that common sense indicates he must have known and disclaiming responsibility that cannot be disclaimed. This eagerness to disavow his own acts is as disturbing as the acts themselves."

In any event, nothing probably damaged Nixon in terms of public opinion more than the end of Operation Candor—the release of his tax returns. Senators and Representatives, some of whom might have been counted on to support him for a while, reported angry comments from their constituents, some of them at low economic levels, complaining that they had paid more taxes than the wealthy President. It constituted, in the eyes of most people, an admission of guilt that he had indeed evaded substantial amounts of income tax. And the timing of the Joint Committee report was significant: it was issued early in April, just as Nixon's countrymen were sitting down to the distasteful task of paying what the law required of them, without being able to take the benefit of substantial deductions.

Another White House effort, during this time of decline, was to try to involve Secretary of State Henry Kissinger as much as possible in the Nixon defense. Much of the use of Kissinger was beyond his control, as when Ron Ziegler from time to time would announce that the President had spent his day giving instructions to Kissinger during Kissinger's days of shuttle diplomacy in the Middle East. By this time most people guessed or knew— and the tapes confirmed—that Nixon was spending all of his time devising new scenarios to get out of accountability for Watergate. On one such occasion, Kissinger was required on a weekend to fly from Washington to San Clemente for no other purpose than to share a "photo opportunity" with Nixon; it was felt important at the time that the two men be seen on the nation's front pages, presumably discussing matters of high foreign policy.

Kissinger participated in this ruse on a few occasions, and it hurt him with his once almost-impregnable group of supporters in the press. Richard Wilson referred to it as "the decanonization of Henry A. Kissinger," which he said had to come sooner or later, but said it was unfortunate for some American foreign policy objectives that it came when it did.

Kissinger's first political involvement, perhaps inadvertently, came on October 26, 1972. The day before, the Washington *Post* and other newspapers which ran the *Post* story, had broken the fact that a $350,000 secret fund existed in the White House and that H. R. Haldeman was one of the paymasters. The *Post* had been hitting the Watergate corruption story hard prior to that time, and some polls around the country were beginning to show that the corruption issue was having an impact in the election. In retrospect, the election results make it clear that the distance between the candidates was too great for McGovern to have made up, but if the momentum that had begun to develop on the corruption issue had continued, it is likely that the result would have been closer, and that Nixon's vaunted "mandate" would have been somewhat less sweeping.

But the next day, Kissinger drew every reporter in Washington to a press conference at which he announced that "peace is at hand." He was talking, of course, about Vietnam, and the story stayed on Page One for the week which remained until Election Day, and no subsequent Watergate story ever received any prominence at all until the election was safely over. Peace was clearly not "at hand," on October 26; Kissinger must have known that fairly substantial negotiations remained ahead, chiefly with Saigon, and it has never been satisfactorily explained why the emphasis was made on October 26 unless it was to distract attention from Watergate.

At the time, the nation had very little experience with an ongoing Nixon effort to distract attention from the scandal, and it was hard to believe a week before the election that that is what was happening.

It was not so hard, in the week following the Saturday Night Massacre, to detect this technique in the sudden calling of a worldwide "alert" of American forces, in response to some kind of Soviet threat in the Middle East. At the time, the Soviet Union had already announced its intention to vote in the UN for a cease-fire commission in Egypt which would not include either Americans or Russians, and yet Kissinger and his allies in the press explained the necessity for the alert as the insistence by the Russians that they participate in the peace-keeping force.

When the question was raised following the alert, Kissinger was unconvincing. He said that it was "inconceivable that America would ever conduct its foreign policy with a view to domestic political considerations," ignoring the fact that a substantial and growing number of Americans believed that the Vietnam war had been conducted for four years for precisely those reasons. Further-more, by the time of the Saturday Night Massacre, the duplicity of the White House was so evident that there was a predisposition to believe that the alert was fake, even if there had been evidence to show that it was justifiable. Ron Ziegler said at the time, using the Leninist phrases that were in vogue at the White House, that those who questioned the legitimacy of the alert would be "anni-hilated by history," and Kissinger himself promised that "within a week" evidence would be presented to demonstrate beyond a doubt that Nixon and the Secretary of Defense had ample reason to mobilize American troops around the world. At this writing, it has been more than 52 weeks, none of that evidence has been forthcoming, and Kissinger has indicated that it will not be. The conclusion with which one is left—and it seems clear just who has been "annihilated by history"—is that the alert was called in order to draw some public attention away from Nixon's defiance of the law, the impending announcements that two of the tapes were missing and a third mutilated, and it was an unfortunate event for a man of Kissinger's independent status.

In March 1974, some Congressmen traveling with Kissinger by plane, reported that he had told them that if Nixon were im-peached and replaced by Gerald Ford, he (Kissinger) would almost certainly resign. The story attracted some halfhearted denials, but there seemed good reason to believe Kissinger had said it. It was pretty clearly an example of "impeachment poli-tics," an attempt to raise doubts that the grand design of Ameri-can foreign policy could continue after a Nixon presidency. It probably caused a few Congressmen to think harder for a few days about impeachment, but its more lasting effect was to make Kissinger closer to Nixon and thus further damage his own effec-tiveness as an independent force in American foreign policy.

On April 11, 1974, after weeks of negotiation with Nixon at-torney James St. Clair, the House Judiciary Committee finally determined that Nixon would not yield any evidence voluntarily, and issued a subpoena for some 42 White House tapes. St. Clair asked for and got two delays, but the subpoena was finally return-able on April 30. Even the Republican leadership was making it very clear to the White House during this time that the refusal of the President to honor the subpoena would unquestionably become in itself a grounds for impeachment, and one that would carry by a handsome majority.

So on the night of April 29, the grand White House strategy became apparent in a prime-time television address, in which Nixon announced that he was releasing to the Judiciary Committee and to the public, hundreds of transcripts—1,200 pages in all of presidential conversations—which he maintained would make it possible "to settle the matter once and for all."

It proved to be, along with the release of Nixon's tax returns, the major blunder of the White House defense. It is true that a refusal to have yielded the tapes to the Committee would have cost Nixon dearly—and certainly guaranteed his impeachment—and it is equally true that if he had yielded *tapes*, which he finally was required to do anyway, it would also have done him in. But the release on April 30 of all of the transcripts which he had carefully edited and from which most of his foul language was deleted, proved to be a body blow to his own chances for regaining any measure of confidence with the American people.

In the furor caused by the substance of the summarized conversations released on April 30, 1974, an important procedural question went unanswered: Who had prepared the transcripts? Who had listened to *all* the conversations, and written down an accurate transcription of them? Who had then edited them, deciding which conversations were to be shortened, which edited, and which deleted? Who had wielded the pencil?

These questions became even more important during the Watergate cover-up trial, in which some of the tapes were played, and the transcripts proved to have been heavily edited, with whole passages incriminating Nixon omitted. In addition, tapes were played of presidential conversations about the cover-up, which had been omitted entirely from the transcripts which had been made public, some on the public grounds that they were "irrelevant" to Watergate.

Who had made those decisions—that is to say, who in the White House had the authority to doctor the transcripts and, in the process, falsify the evidence? It could have been Nixon himself, but it would have been more in character for him to have delegated that job to someone else, and that "someone else" could hardly have been anyone but Ziegler or General Haig. As of this writing, no questions—at least no public questions—have been asked of either of them.

The release of the documents and the speech describing them represented a typical Nixon performance. The speech was full of partial and outright lies about what the transcripts contained.

The speech was a solemn one, lasting thirty-six minutes. Nixon sat at his desk and behind him were two stacks, each several feet high, of huge notebooks embossed with the presidential seal and a description of the dates of the conversations they contained. As he spoke, the transcripts were revealed by the cameras and it must have seemed to the television audience that Nixon was turning over enough volumes to have filled at least half of a normal-size public library. But when the material was delivered to the Committee the next day, it all fitted within a large mimeographed report (made larger by the fact that the lines of conversation were triple spaced), and when it was finally boiled down into print it proved to be about the size of (but more racy than) a Jacqueline Susann novel.

The speech contained some gems:

"The full resources of the FBI and the Justice Department were used to investigate the incident thoroughly. I instructed my staff and campaign aides to cooperate fully with the investigation." The truth: a later tape would show that Nixon ordered his aides to obstruct the FBI investigation and ordered other close associates to "stonewall it."

"For nine months—until March 1973—I was assured by those charged with conducting and monitoring the investigation that no one in the White House was involved." The truth: from the day of the burglary, Nixon was fully informed of all the people in and formerly in the White House who were involved, and he cooperated actively in covering up their involvement.

"[The transcripts] include all the relevant portions of all the subpoenaed conversations that were recorded—that is, all portions that relate to the question of what I knew about Watergate or the cover-up, and what I did about it." The truth: many highly relevant portions were deleted from the transcripts, precisely because they *did* relate to the question of what Nixon knew about Watergate or the cover-up, and what he knew was a great deal.

"As far as what the President personally knew and did with

regard to Watergate and the cover-up is concerned, these materials—together with those already made available—will tell it
all." The truth: "these materials" were a last ditch effort, through
clever and not-so-clever editing and deletions, to *conceal* what
"the President personally knew and did with regard to Watergate
and the cover-up."

"Parts [of the transcripts] will seem to be contradictory with
one another, and parts will be in conflict with some of the testi-
money given in the Senate Watergate Committee hearings." The
truth: here was Nixon's loyalty at work again, flatly stating that
some of his comrades who had testified before the Watergate
Committee, in a manner designed to protect him, had perjured
themselves.

"John Dean charged in sworn Senate testimony that I was 'fully
aware of the cover-up' at the time of our first meeting on September 15, 1972. These transcripts show clearly that I first learned
of it when Mr. Dean, himself, told me about it in this office on
March 21—some six months later." The truth: deleted portions of
the transcripts and other tapes showed clearly that John Dean
was telling the truth and that Nixon was "fully aware of the
cover-up" from the day it began, which was a few days after the
burglary itself.

"Now, how [the 18½-minute gap in a June 20 tape] was caused
is still a mystery to me and I think to many of the experts, as
well. But I am absolutely certain, however, of one thing: that it
was not caused intentionally by my secretary, Rose Mary Woods,
or any of my White House assistants." The truth: this is as close
to an admission of guilt as we ever got. Since only Rose Mary
Woods and two White House assistants had access to the tapes,
in addition to Nixon, what he is telling us here is that since the
gap was caused by repeated manual erasures, they must have
been done by Nixon himself.

"I was particularly concerned by [Dean's March 21] report that
one of the Watergate defendants, Howard Hunt, was threatening blackmail unless he and his lawyer were immediately given
$120,000 for legal fees and family support, and that he was at-
tempting to blackmail the White House, not by threatening exposure on the Watergate matter, but by threatening to reveal
activities that would expose extremely sensitive, highly secret
national security matters that he had worked on before Water-

gate." The truth: five months before, Mr. Nixon had referred to these "extremely sensitive highly secret national security matters" as "stupid and illegal." Furthermore, even the edited transcripts revealed that the "national security" cloak thrown over the Ellsberg burglary was a "scenario" devised by Nixon, Haldeman, and Ehrlichman to prevent testimony about it.

"If read with an open and a fair mind, and if read together with the record of the actions I took these transcripts will show . . . that I never offered clemency for the defendants, and that after March 21 my actions were directed toward finding the facts and seeing that justice was done fairly and according to the law." The truth: the transcripts and the deleted portions of the transcripts showed and were to show that Nixon not only *offered* but *ordered* clemency for the defendants at an early date, and that after March 21 his actions were directed toward concealing the facts and seeing that whatever was done, it was not justice.

The next morning, April 30 (the anniversary of the first Nixon speech on Watergate, in which he announced the departure of Haldeman, Ehrlichman, Kleindienst, and Dean), the public relations machine began to operate. Copies of the transcripts in mimeographed form were delivered with great fanfare to the Judiciary Committee and passed along to the members. In spite of the Nixon pledge of the night before that the transcripts would be simultaneously released to the public, they were not to be given to the press until so late in the day that it would be impossible—or so the White House thought—to summarize them on the evening television news or in the afternoon newspapers.

What *was* released to the press, however, was a 50-page "summary" of the transcripts prepared by, of all people, James St. Clair. It was a long tendentious argument to the effect that the transcripts exonerated Nixon from some of the charges that had been made against him, and some that had not. It worked, as far as the afternoon newspapers were concerned, and St. Clair's arguments were prominently featured. They were never to surface again, once people had the opportunity to read the transcripts and discover that St. Clair was relying on five or six lines wrenched out of context.

But the public relations move did *not* work as far as the evening television news was concerned, because the correspondents found a few Congressmen who were willing to let them sit in the

office and read the by-now public transcripts. The result is that
a number of the highlights were reported verbatim on the evening
television news, and a strong anti-Nixon reaction began from the
public which saw the television summaries.

Over the days that followed, even Senator Hugh Scott of
Pennsylvania, the Republican Majority leader who, it had been
thought, would swallow anything he had been told by Nixon and
turn it somehow into exculpatory material, was horrified. Newspapers around the country which had previously been solidly
pro-Nixon turned against him, and his support in public—already
badly eroded—sank almost out of sight.

The reason was the kind of man the transcripts revealed Nixon
to be, as well as the illegal acts in which they showed him to be
involved. As for the latter, the transcript of March 21 was quite
enough, although there was a great deal more.

That transcript showed that John Dean had discussed Howard
Hunt's demand for hush money. Nixon showed in that conversation that he knew all about the Ellsberg burglary and that he
recognized its illegality and the need to cover it up, and he repeatedly urged and finally ordered ("For Christ's sake, get it")
Dean to pay the money.

But it was not so much the specifics that appalled people who
took some time, any time, to read the transcripts. Newspapers
vied with each other to produce all or a significant portion of the
transcripts, a race that was won by the Chicago *Tribune,* which
began printing them when they were first distributed and was
out by the following morning with a supplement carrying all of
the conversations.

What emerged from the totality of the conversations was a
devious, profane, shallow man in the presidency, incapable of
making the simplest decision and growing more and more conscious with each passing day of the necessity to conceal the
evidence of his own misdeeds. Many people commented on the
dreadful paucity of language; the Nixon men spoke in what must
surely be the most circumscribed vocabulary of anyone holding
the office; it was as though they had determined to spend
months in the White House speaking only in Basic English.

They proved in their conversations to be ignorant of the
simplest concepts of law, and to treat not only Watergate but
other high domestic and foreign policy questions totally in terms

of how it would look, or how it would appear, and in all of the pages there was no indication that anyone was concerned with what the impact of any of their actions might be upon the public or the country or the political system. If anyone had ever suspected that Richard Nixon had entered public life to get rich and to accumulate power and that he had no other goals for his country or his people, these transcripts confirmed that suspicion.

In addition, it was clear from the frequent use of the device "(expletive deleted)" that Nixon's language was profane and scatological. He was undoubtedly not the first President to use the four-letter words that have become, in skilled hands, an earthy addition to American speech, but two things were apparent from Nixon's use of the words. First, he used them in a sort of artificial way, as though he sensed that to use these words made him seem more manly, so that the conversations seemed to have taken place in the locker room of a high school football team rather than in the highest office of state in the world. Second, other Presidents who used these words had not spent a lifetime hypocritically developing an image of decency and abhorrence of profanity and obscenity. It had been Nixon, after all, who had during his campaign in 1960 made much of Harry Truman's use of vulgar language, and who had lectured the American people about the need to elect him so that children could know that decent language was being used in the White House. And yet, the transcripts made it plain that had Nixon spoken the words in public that he spoke to the White House tapes, he would probably have been arrested before Lenny Bruce.

And as a final note, Nixon didn't even get any legal credit for having come up with the edited transcripts in answer to the Judiciary Committee's subpoena for the tapes. Only two or three of his loyalists on the Committee were able to bring themselves to say that they thought there had been compliance with the subpoena; an overwhelming majority agreed to write Nixon a cold, short letter, informing him that in the opinion of the Committee he had *not* complied with the subpoena.

One of the most effective devices used by the Nixon campaign for re-election in 1972 was the assignment of "surrogates" around the country to speak in Nixon's place, since the campaign "game plan" called for an aloof Nixon busy with affairs of state (if the

tapes had only been public then, it would have been clear that
the "affairs of state" with which Nixon was busying himself involved the Watergate cover-up, almost exclusively). This was a
technique to which the White House returned during the beleaguered days of late 1973 and the first six months of 1974. The
trouble was that where, in 1972, Congressmen, Senators, Cabinet
officers, and others were only too pleased to go out and defend
the administration, by late 1973 there was hardly anyone on whom
to call. Gerald Ford kept up a steady travel schedule, appearing
somewhere outside of Washington almost every day to announce
that this or that piece of evidence as yet unrevealed would clear
the President, but the act became a tiresome one and eventually
a rather comic one, once it was determined that the "evidence" of
which Ford spoke consisted of White House tapes which Ford not
only had not heard but which he resolutely refused to hear.

So the only "surrogates" available were those within the White
House, and they were widely used but to little effect. Father John
McLaughlin, a Jesuit priest who had been in and out of politics
for some years, had signed on in 1970 as a Nixon speechwriter,
and he was used in his capacity as resident priest to defend Nixon's
moral conduct. Father McLaughlin probably reached the peak
of his career as a Nixon spokesman a few days after the release
of the damning transcripts, when he used all of his Jesuit training
(but to little avail) to argue that the tapes showed Nixon to be
a truly moral man, and that the use of profanity and obscenity
was merely a necessary "catharsis." McLaughlin, dressed well as
usual, had come to the press conference from his apartment at
the Watergate, and ran into some flak, not only from the reporters but from his Jesuit superiors, for seeming to take lightly
his vows of poverty.

Patrick Buchanan, who had been the head of the White
House "attack group" during the campaign of 1972, continued
to function in that role as the Watergate tide began to engulf him and his leader. Buchanan is a literate man, which
marked him immediately as an exception in the Nixon White
House of 1974, and he made himself highly available. The result
was that he wrote a number of articles for the very newspapers
he was denouncing for their liberal bias, such as *The New York
Times* and the Washington *Post,* and on more than a few occasions
pointed out that no Nixon adherent could get a fair trial in the

District of Columbia, because it was a city a majority of whose citizens were black and whose juries, worse luck, reflected the composition of the community from which they were drawn. This kind of not-so-subtle appeal to racial prejudice did not seem to have very much impact.

Bruce Herschensohn was another White House aide out on the circuit. Herschensohn's targets were the radio and television talk shows, particularly where they had recently had a guest who seemed to be anti-Nixon. During the early months of 1974, I appeared on a number of these programs in the course of exploiting my book *Perfectly Clear—Nixon from Whittier to Watergate*, and Herschensohn was hot on my trail. Someone from the White House would phone the producer of almost every program on which I appeared, demanding "equal time" for Herschensohn.

Even Nixon's family was pressed into service. While the furor over the tapes, and the kind of man they revealed Nixon to be, had not yet abated, David and Julie Eisenhower were trotted out in the Rose Garden for a press conference. The fiction was that the press had somehow "asked" for the press conference with David and Julie, but at the outset the reporters made it clear that it was a White House press conference and that they were there to hear what Julie and David had to say. They had very little to say, as it turned out, and the suggestion by cartoonist Herb Block of the Washington *Post*, that perhaps the effort by David and Julie would be followed by similar press conferences by the White House butler and perhaps later by a few of the gardeners, was not followed.

During the 1972 campaign Charles Colson was able to put together, on rather short notice, a fictitious committee to support President Nixon at the time of the bombing and blockading of Haiphong harbor in May of that year. Those committees were not so easy to form two years later. The President's friend Don Kendall formed a group called "Committee to Defend the Presidency." Kendall's efforts in setting this up were not too successful —he asked some people to join, including former Nixon cabinet members, by telling them that others had joined, when in fact they had not. Once these people began to talk to each other, the number of possible sponsors dropped away and when Kendall began to run his ads in newspapers, urging readers to write to their Congressmen to oppose impeachment, his list was rather slim. It included only three former cabinet members, George Romney, Winston Blount, and Clifford Hardin (the Secretary of Agriculture whose decision not to raise milk prices had been overruled by Nixon under pressure from the milk producers). In addition, he had Mamie Eisenhower, John T. Connor of "Democrats for Nixon," Bob Hope, and Frank Fitzsimmons (the President of the Teamsters' Union who developed a very close relationship with Nixon over his last year and a half in office).

But Kendall's group never amounted to very much, and its failure to attract any really big names was a reflection of the growing popular mood, not only among ordinary citizens but among members of the Establishment as well, that there was very little in Nixon's cause that could be defended.

By far a more colorful and successful (in terms of fund-raising) pro-Nixon committee was that created by an obscure former rabbi from Masachusetts named Baruch Korff. Korff established a group called "The National Citizens' Committee for Fairness to the Presidency, Inc." and set off on a gigantic fund-raising effort. He raised several hundred thousand dollars, mostly in small contributions from Nixon bitter-enders. Before the impeachment proceedings reached their climax, Korff was using the money to travel around the country giving pro-Nixon speeches and holding pro-Nixon rallies, in the course of raising more money. Since Nixon's resignation, he has stayed with what still appears to be a good thing, and is paying himself and an assistant to administer the fund, which he is using to pay Nixon's legal bills and which he says he will use to pay medical bills as well. Toward the end, it must have been embarrassing to Nixon that his only public supporter seemed to be Rabbi Korff (who dismissed the rather gross anti-Semitism revealed by the transcripts, by saying he looked "at deeds, not at words"), since his was precisely the sort of ragged grass roots movement which the Nixon men had traditionally suspected and despised.

As the impeachment mill continued to grind exceeding fine, Nixon and his advisors turned to the idea of travel as perhaps a way to distract the attention of the people from what was happening before the Judiciary Committee. So in the spring of 1974, the President embarked on a travel schedule which would have seemed almost frenzied for a President not preoccupied with his own impeachment, and which, as it turned out, merely heightened the belief that the White House "at this point in time" would try anything to take people's minds off Nixon's troubles.

Domestically, perhaps the high point of the President's travel came when he went to the dedication of the new home of the Grand Ole Opry in Nashville, for generations the temple of country and western music. There, with George Wallace looking on (although it was hard to tell whether he did so approvingly), the President appeared on national television to preach the virtues of country music and country patriotism, and then— in another presidential "first" of the type he liked to compile— played with a yo-yo in the company of Country Music Hall of Fame member Roy Acuff. It was a bizarre moment, and cannot have done very much to increase respect for the presidency, but neither Don Kendall nor Rabbi Korff seemed to mind.

As for foreign travel, Nixon went to Paris in April for the funeral of Georges Pompidou. There, he created some negative comment among Frenchmen by using the occasion to hold a series of widely publicized whirlwind meetings with other heads of state who had come to Paris with the idea that they were to attend a funeral. But if Mr. Nixon's taste came into question at his use of the occasion for domestic political purposes, his mental state became a subject of some anxiety when it was learned that he had left his car while driving through the streets of Paris, in order to shake hands with some of the curious Frenchmen who lined the route, and had said to a number of them in the course of the hand-shaking, "it's certainly a great day for France." Even Premier Pompidou's political opponents found that statement a difficult one to comprehend or approve.

Finally, in June, Nixon went to the Middle East and upon his return, away again to Moscow. The Middle East trip was highlighted by the discovery that President Anwar Sadat of Egypt shared the ability of his predecessor, Gamal Abdel Nasser, to turn a million or so Egyptians into the streets of Cairo for a state occasion. With all three U.S. television networks dutifully looking on and treating the event as news rather than a political appearance directed at the public and the Judiciary Committee, Nixon enjoyed a triumphant tour of Egypt, in the course of which he promised the Egyptians the same kind of nuclear reactor which had enabled India to develop an atom bomb a few weeks earlier.

In Israel, the reception was somewhat muted but correct. One happening must have distracted Nixon; mindful that people with access to the tapes and transcripts had said that some of the deletions included reference to Jewish members of the White House staff as "Jew-boys," some Israelis prepared a plaque visible along Nixon's route in Tel Aviv, proclaiming "Mr. Nixon, we're all Jewboys here."

The summit meeting in Moscow had very little result, either in terms of foreign policy or of Watergate politics, since by the time of the visit the die had almost been cast in the House Judiciary Committee, John Ehrlichman was on trial and seemingly sure to be convicted, and the Supreme Court was nearing its unanimous declaration that Mr. Nixon's arguments about executive privilege were totally without constitutional foundation. On balance, this was probably just as well, since otherwise Nixon might have been tempted to make a bold foreign policy move as a means of distracting public opinion, and it could hardly have been an advantageous one for the country. But observers at the Moscow summit noted that Brezhnev and the other communist leaders' enthusiasm for Nixon seemed diminished; their vaunted intelligence sources in the United States had apparently finally discovered what almost every careful newspaper reader had known six months before—that Mr. Nixon's tenure was now sharply limited.

The final White House technique to avoid what had become the inevitable was the adoption of what came to be known as "impeachment politics." What this involved was a tailoring of the Nixon administration's foreign and domestic policy so as to appeal to that combination of southern Democrats and conservative Republicans who made up what the Nixon strategists were counting on—a hard 34 votes in the Senate. The Constitution calls for impeachment to be voted in the House of Representatives by a simple majority, but for a conviction and removal from office a two-thirds majority in the Senate. That meant that any 34 Senators could keep Nixon in office, and he began to change his public policies in order to try to keep the votes of 34 conservative members.

Early in the Nixon administration, at the urging of a few environmentalists attached to the Nixon team, the White House had called for a comprehensive land-use law, which would have had some impact upon the virtually unfettered rights of real estate developers to scar the land and destroy useful and potentially useful environmental resources. A bill was drafted by the administration, and as 1973 ended it began to move through the legislative mill. When it got to the House Rules Committee, however, the Nixon administration torpedoed it. At White House urging, Republican leadership, including those Congresmen responsive to Senator Barry Goldwater of Arizona, prevailed on Republicans and a few Democratic allies in the Rules Committee —aided mightily by the forces of real estate developers and the Chamber of Commerce—to kill the land-use bill in committee. But the action was so raw, and the reversal on the part of the Nixon administration so total, that much of the effect of it was lost, so clearly did it appear that Nixon policy now depended entirely on getting votes in the Senate against conviction.

Along the way, Nixon refused flatly to annoy in any way the oil companies who were reaping a bonanza from the Great Energy Shortage of the winter of 1973–1974. Thus, he threw all of his weight against any proposals to ration gasoline, and vetoed a bill passed by both Houses which would have rolled back the gasoline price and had the effect of reducing the huge windfall profits which his own administration had guaranteed to the oil companies. The White House strategists doubtless thought that by this technique they might pick up a few votes from the oil states, but it turned out to be too little and too late.

Among the other examples of "impeachment politics" could be listed the administration fight on the floor of the House of Representatives, over the opposition of almost all of the country's mayors and industrial state governors, to kill the Community Action Program, the only remaining—and smoothly functioning— element of the anti-poverty programs put into effect by Lyndon Johnson.

In 1974, after announcing its intention to nominate Paul Nitze, a former Under Secretary of Defense and a true hard-liner on arms policy, as Assistant Secretary of Defense for international security affairs, Nixon pulled back the nomination as a favor to Barry Goldwater, who had announced that he would oppose the appointment of any former aide to Robert McNamara to a post at the Department of Defense.

Along the way, Nixon announced his support for the reinstitution of the death penalty for certain crimes, stated his strong opposition to public financing of political campaigns, and appointed Goldwater's old national GOP chairman, Dean Burch, to the White House staff in an ill-defined role as "counselor."

It was not a very pleasant view of the presidency; for a man who spoke almost every day about the need to preserve the majesty and respect of the office, Nixon was acting in every way to lower his and its prestige.

The Judiciary Committee: Casting and Rehearsal

On July 24, 1974, in the high-ceilinged room which had always served as the meeting ground for the Committee on the Judiciary of the House of Representatives, the Committee had assembled to begin public debate leading to a vote on resolutions sending Articles of Impeachment of Richard Nixon to the House of Representatives. The first speaker was the Chairman, Peter W. Rodino, Jr. of New Jersey, and although he was speaking for himself and for his Committee, he could have been speaking for us all:

> We must decide whether the President abused his power in the execution of his office. The great wisdom of our founders entrusted this process to the collective wisdom of many men. Each of those chosen to toil for the people at the great forge of democracy—the House of Representatives—has a responsibility to exercise independent judgment. I pray that we will each act with the wisdom that compels us in the end to be but decent men who seek only the truth.
>
> Let us be clear about this. No official, no concerned citizen, no representative, no member of this Committee welcomes an impeachment proceeding. No one welcomes the day when there has been such a crisis of concern that he must decide whether "high crimes and misdemeanors," serious abuses of official power, or violations of public trust have in fact occurred.
>
> Our own public trust, our own commitment to the Constitution, is being put to the test. Such tests, historically, have

come to the awareness of most peoples too late—when their rights and freedoms under law were already so far in jeopardy and eroded that it was no longer in the people's power to restore constitutional government by democratic means.

Let us go forward. Let us go forward into debate in good will, with honor and decency and with respect for the views of one another. Whatever we now decide, we must have the integrity and the decency, the will and courage to decide rightly.

Let us leave the Constitution as unimpaired for our children as our predecessors left it to us.

It was to be a momentous time. On the same day as Rodino spoke, the Supreme Court unanimously ruled, in United States *v.* Nixon, that the claim of "executive privilege" must fall before the arguments of the Special Prosecutor that the evidence the President had been concealing was needed in a criminal proceeding. John Ehrlichman, one of the President's closest assistants, had been convicted a week before in federal court of complicity in the burglary of Dr. Fielding's office, and within a week he would be sentenced to five years in prison. And within ten days, previously concealed evidence would be released which would demonstrate even to the most hardened Nixon defenders that the President had been guilty of—indeed, had instigated—an obstruction of justice that began almost within hours of the Watergate burglary that had touched off the whole inquiry. And Rodino's Committee, functioning at last in front of the American people through television, would go through the evidence it had painstakingly assembled and vote Nixon's impeachment on three counts.

How had it reached this point? How had the Committee come from a position of shrinking from its constitutional duty only nine months before to the day when it was fully prepared to function as the founders of the republic had intended that it should? Who were these blacksmiths at the "great forge of democracy"?

The Judiciary Committee of the House of Representatives, over the years, had been the forum for important national debate. Most recently, during the 1960s, it had been the place where major legislation had been hammered out. Under the chairmanship of Emanuel Celler of Brooklyn, and the majority leader, William McCulloch of Ohio, the Civil Rights Act of 1964, the Voting Rights Act of 1965, and the Fair Housing Act of 1968 had all been drafted.

It had been the Judiciary Committee which had, over the years, considered America's immigration policy (and in so doing, had worked out the procedures by which some of its future members would come to these shores), and in the Nixon years it was the Judiciary Committee that had considered the "law and order" legislation of the administration. Now it was to sit in judgment on the President himself and act, in James Madison's phrase, as the "grand inquest of the nation."

Although some had called it a "dumping ground" for left-wing members of the Congress, it had never been appropriate to call it that. It *was* an activist committee, and one traditionally willing to consider new legislative departures, but its chairmen, Celler for many years and now Rodino, had always been a part of the leadership group in the House of Representatives and had always functioned according to what that leadership sensed to be a consensus in the House. In 1974 the make-up of the Committee was a reasonable cross-section of the American people in whose name it was to perform its most historic function.

—Harold D. Donohue of Massachusetts, in his last term in the House, was the ranking Majority (Democratic) member, and no one had ever called him a left-winger in the memory of man. Donohue was a leadership man, and he reflected faithfully the views of his constituents in and around Worcester. When the impeachment proceeding came along he was 73 years old, and had served in the Congress since 1947. Donohue worked closely with Rodino, and it could be safely assumed throughout the debate that his proposals were the leadership's proposals and that his amendments would have a solid majority at least among the Democrats.

—Jack Brooks of Texas had served in the House for more than twenty years, from the area around Galveston. Brooks probably will be most noted in history books as the "other man" in the celebrated photo of Lyndon Johnson taking the oath of office aboard Air Force I in Dallas on November 22, 1963. Brooks was a friend of Johnson's, and retained a populist economic philosophy, made effective by a knack of colorful speech, throughout his

years in the House. Brooks was salty, direct, and, when it came
to what he conceived early on to be the abuses of office of
Richard Nixon, hard-hitting and effective. It was a subcommittee
of Brooks's which had investigated the excessive spending at San
Clemente and at Key Biscayne, and had come up with the fact
that millions of dollars of taxpayers' money had been spent on
Nixon's personal residences.

—Robert W. Kastenmeier of Wisconsin was as firm and un-
yielding a liberal as could be found on the Committee, or for
that matter in the House. Kastenmeier represented Dane County,
whose major city is Madison—not only the capital of the state
but the site of the state university, and he reflected both
the steady commitment to progressivism which Wisconsin has
always provided in our national politics, and the concern about
injustice and reform traditionally represented by the students at
the university. He had served in the House for fifteen years.

—Don Edwards of California was probably the only man in
public life who had served as both an FBI agent and the national
chairman of Americans for Democratic Action. He represented a
largely working and middle-class district in San Jose, California,
and had been the first and leading congressional supporter of
Senator Eugene McCarthy's bid for the presidency on an anti-
war platform in 1968. Edwards had been a leader of the anti-war
forces in the House, and had acquired some seniority and considerable respectability on the Committee as the hearings began.

—William L. Hungate of Missouri represented Mark Twain
country (the area around Hannibal), and hardly a legislative
day went by that he did not remind his listeners of that fact.
Luckily, Hungate was qualified to make the connection, since he
possessed a dry wit and an ability to cite not only Twain but
other American humorists with telling effect during debate. One
had the feeling as the impeachment debate went on that while
Hungate shared his colleagues' serious view of the matter, he was
probably alone among the membership in having a good time as
well. There are not many Congressmen with a well-developed
sense of humor, and Hungate was a welcome exception.

—John Conyers, Jr., of Michigan had rapidly moved up in the
House of Representatives since his election in 1964. He was not
the senior black Congressman, but certainly he was the most
effective. Conyers was an able and thoughtful contributor to de-

bate, although it was clear his mind was made up on the question of impeachment even as the earliest consideration of the matter began in 1973. Conyers did not refer, throughout the proceedings, to the fact that he was a high-ranking member of the White House "enemies list," and that ugly racist references had accompanied his listing, but it must have contributed to his deep sense that impeachment was the appropriate remedy.

—Joshua Eilberg of suburban Philadelphia had served in the House since the election of 1966, and had generally gone along with the leadership. He was not a particularly distinguished or leading member, either of the Committee or of the House, but his experience in the Pennsylvania legislature and his close connections with the Democratic organization in Philadelphia had taught him valuable political lessons, and by 1974 he was a reliable member on the Democratic side.

—Jerome R. Waldie of California had come to Congress in 1966 from a solidly Democratic district he had previously represented in the state legislature. In his early years in Congress, Waldie had tended to follow the ancient maxim of Sam Rayburn, "if you want to get along, go along," but the Vietnam war and the slow pace of Congress had begun to radicalize him. By the early 1970s, he was convinced that the failure of the House to take any action at all against the Johnson and Nixon war policies demonstrated the uselessness of a career in that chamber, and in 1973 made his decision to leave Congress in order to seek the governorship of California. But the coming impeachment struggle occupied an enormous amount of his time, and he never got his campaign off the ground. The result was that Waldie was virtually a lame duck Congressman during all of the impeachment debate. It had the traditionally bad effect of giving his opinions slightly less weight, but it had the good effect of liberating him so that he could—and did—play a leadership role among the Congressmen on the Committee who continually pressed for a quicker pace and a sharpening of the charges against Nixon. Waldie was one of the earliest sponsors of an impeachment resolution, and—with Don Edwards of California—was a leader of the impeachment group outside of the leadership.

—Walter W. Flowers of Alabama was a confirmed supporter of George Wallace and a fairly orthodox southern conservative on domestic and foreign issues. As a result, he came to be seen as a leader of a "swing" group of southerners and conservative Republicans, by observers whose perceptions had been dulled by orthodoxy. The reasoning went as follows: if a Congresman has steadily supported Richard Nixon on his Vietnam policy, and if he has supported Richard Nixon in his attempts to exploit racism, and if he has supported Nixon on the hard-line "law and order" issues, then he will support Nixon on impeachment. That reasoning, in the case of Flowers and his southern and border colleagues on the Committee, turned out to be fatally flawed. The reason it was wrong in Flowers's case was that he really did believe in the positions he espoused in the House, and was not merely taking those positions for ignoble political reasons. Nixon prolonged the war in Vietnam and exploited racism because he believed that that was where the votes were. Flowers supported those efforts because they not only reflected the views of his constituents but his own. And when it came to impeachment, he did not approach that question with political motives, either. He looked at the evidence, saw that crimes had been committed, and resolved to vote for the constitutional remedy.

—James R. Mann of South Carolina was another southern conservative but one without the colorful Wallace attachment which made Flowers such an object of study. Mann is a thoughtful legislator who takes his responsibilities seriously, and he became convinced as the evidence mounted that a vote for impeachment was crucial. Mann helped with the drafting of articles which would please the Republican moderates and yet not seem too weak for the strong liberal wing of the Committee which wanted firm language. In addition, Mann's contribution to the debate was probably more eloquent than any one else's.

—Paul S. Sarbanes of Maryland was the final draftsman of the Articles of Impeachment, as adopted. Sarbanes had been a good lawyer, and he proved to be a skillful analyst of the evidence. It was hard for the Nixon men on the Committee to overcome Sarbanes's quiet and obviously carefully prepared analysis of the evidence and the language that would set it forth. Sarbanes appeared cautious, and he has never been a leader in the Committee's battles over legislation, but he demonstrated great political courage and considerable skill at the outset of his career in tackling, head-on, a Baltimore Congressman who had piled up enough seniority to be an important Committee chairman.

—John F. Seiberling of Ohio, from the tire family, seemed the most aristocratic and well-born member of the Committee (at least on the Democratic side; Hamilton Fish, a true country squire, played that role for the Republicans), and had come to the House primarily as an anti-war advocate. He did not play an important role in the debate, but like so many of his colleagues, was a reliable vote for impeachment.

—George E. Danielson of California was, like Don Edwards, a former FBI agent, but unlike Edwards had no prior reputation for liberal politics when he came to the House in 1970. He had served previously as a member of the California legislature, and it was thought that the district he came to represent had been created especially for him by his colleagues in Sacramento. But Danielson's record had become steadily more liberal over the years, and he was effective in the impeachment debate, his wry humor often puncturing some rather pompous argument from the other side.

—Robert F. Drinan of Massachusetts was the first priest to have been elected to Congress (his colleague on the Committee, Charles Froehlich, would yield his seat later in 1974 to the second). Father Drinan, as the dean of Boston College Law School, had led a delegation to Vietnam in the late 1960s, and had returned a passionate advocate of American withdrawal, and it was this that had first elected him to Congress in 1970. He was, in addition, the first Congressman to support the presidential candidacy in 1972 of George McGovern, and had served as the chairman of the Massachusetts delegation at the 1972 Democratic Convention. Drinan thus had a reputation—at least among the orthodox press—as a "far out" liberal, and he wisely muted what had been his early leadership on the impeachment question and permitted those of his colleagues more identified as conservatives to lead the debate. But Father Drinan had been the first Congressman to introduce an impeachment resolution, and had continued to focus the attention of the members on the "unspeakable" as early as the fall of 1973. As the unspeakable became the unavoidable, he must have taken considerable quiet pleasure in the result.

—Charles B. Rangel of New York was the only member of the Committee on either side who never once spoke of the "awesome" responsibility that had fallen upon the members. Rangel was an impeachment advocate, he thought the evidence was obvious and clear, and he felt the Committee should have got on with the job considerably earlier. He shunned hypocrisy, and his Harlem constituents—who had first elected him in 1970 in an upset over Adam Clayton Powell—probably shared his feeling that a good deal of hypocrisy was involved in the statements of a great many members that they found themselves "reluctant" to do their impeachment duty. Rangel was not only intelligent, but "street-smart" as well, and he was anything but reluctant in the course of the proceedings. He thought Nixon had committed crimes, the Constitution provided for impeachment in such a case, and he went ahead and cast his vote.

—Barbara C. Jordan of Texas was elected to the House of Representatives in 1972 and had quickly made it clear that she was a serious person, and one to be counted with in terms of lasting influence in the House of Representatives. She had served in the Texas Senate, and she had always been associated with President Johnson and his wing of the party in that state. She came to the Committee and its deliberations on impeachment without any of the ideological freight—right and left—that burdened some of the other members, she had probably studied the evidence and the constitutional precedents more carefully and thoroughly than any other member, and her contributions to the debate were outstanding.

—Ray Thornton of Arkansas was another southern member who was mistakenly thought by some observers—the ones who had observed the politics but not the evidence—to be a possible southern Democratic vote against impeachment. Thornton dashed these hopes as the debate began, with a claim that a failure to impeach "would effectively repeal the right of this body to act as a check on the abuses that we see." Thornton played a key role in the drafting of acceptable articles, and his strong pro-impeachment stand unquestionably influenced a number of House members who were not on the Committee. That influence would undoubtedly have appeared, had the full House had an opportunity to vote on the articles of impeachment.

—Elizabeth Holtzman of New York was a freshman member, whose very presence on the Committee had enormous significance. Holtzman had defeated Emanuel Celler in the primary election in 1972 (the Democratic nomination in Brooklyn is equivalent to election), and thereby had made Rodino, by operation of seniority, the Chairman of the Committee. Holtzman was a strong advocate of impeachment, and had made her campaign against Celler on the issue that the leadership of the House, and particularly the Judiciary Committee, needed renewal and re-invigoration.

—Wayne Owens of Utah had been a campaign aide to Senator Robert Kennedy and an assistant to Senator Edward Kennedy when the Senator held the office of Senate Whip. Owens was serving his first term in Congress, and was a candidate for the Senate from Utah. He found himself impaled on a dilemma from which he was unable to remove himself: he hesitated to advocate impeachment for fear of offending his prospective conservative constituents in Utah, and his own strong convictions prevented his opposing impeachment. The result was that he appeared indecisive, and it cost him—it is estimated—the Senate seat in the election of November 1974.

—Edward Mezvinsky of Iowa was another first-term Democratic Congressman, whose re-election was thought to be uncertain if he appeared to be a strong advocate of impeachment, since he had been elected in a generally Republican and conservative district. But Mezvinsky pushed ahead, appeared as a strong impeachment advocate, and won re-election handily.

The Republican members of the Committee—seventeen in all—could hardly have been considered "left-wingers." Indeed, with only one or two exceptions, they were regulars in the Republican ranks in the House of Representatives, and White House strategists and those in the press who thought like White House strategists in dealing with impeachment only as a political event, thought from the beginning that their ranks would be solid in favor of the President. But as with so many other events in the unfolding impeachment strategy, they missed assessing the legal and personal equations that were to yield doubt among these Republicans. When seven of them voted for impeachment there was genuine surprise in the press; there should not have been. It had been clear for some time that this was one issue on which Congressmen were going to make up their minds according to the evidence, and it seemed likely that any Congressman who appeared to do so would not be penalized at the polls.

—Edward Hutchinson of Michigan was a Nixon stalwart on the

Committee. In the unlikely event of a Republican majority in the House of Representatives, he would have been the chairman, and could have been counted on to cooperate with the Republican leadership.

—Robert McClory of Illinois was a more independent member, but had rarely before broken ranks with his Republican colleagues. But McClory came from the Republican suburbs of Chicago, and it was always clear that an anti-Nixon vote on the Committee would not hurt him among his constituents. From the beginning of the proceedings, McClory showed that he was in considerable doubt about the matter and his final vote for two of the three articles of impeachment was anticipated.

—Henry P. Smith, III, of upstate New York, had announced before the Committee hearings began his intention to leave the Congress, and it is doubtful if anyone would have noticed had he not made a public announcement of it. He had never deviated from the orthodox Republican line of the leadership, nor had he ever contributed in any noticeable way to debate or to legislation. He created a mild flurry of interest as the hearings began by indicating that the only conceivable ground for impeachment that he saw was in the bombing of Cambodia, which Nixon had concealed from Congress and the public. But when he had an opportunity to vote on that proposition, he went along with the President anyway.

—Charles W. Sandman, Jr. of New Jersey decided early in the hearings, for whatever reason of his own, to be the Committee clown. He performed as a kind of road company of Senator Joseph McCarthy, full of grins, grimaces, and asides to the audience, and probably contributed in a small way to the further decline of Nixon's popularity, so loud and illogical was his defense of the President. Sandman had been swamped in an attempt in 1973 to be elected governor of New Jersey; his performance before the Committee did nothing to arrest his electoral decline and he was retired from the House by the voters of his district in November 1974.

—Tom Railsback of Illinois was a leader from the beginning among the Republicans, in the search for acceptable wording of Articles of Impeachment for which they could vote. Railsback was from the tri-city area of Rock Island, the heartland of Richard Nixon's Middle America, but Railsback saw the evidence against the President as requiring a vote for impeachment, and it had no diminishing effect on his popularity among his constituents. Railsback repeatedly visited the district, and as repeatedly indicated that "his people" would be pleased with his vote no matter which way it went. (Railsback, by the way, was demonstrating a second law of politics, that when a politician announces publicly that he is going to vote "his conscience," he is about to oppose his party's leadership.

—Charles E. Wiggins of California proved to be Nixon's strongest and most effective advocate. Wiggins is a good trial lawyer, and he performed far more effectively than any of the President's own lawyers had during the whole time of Watergate. Wiggins knew the rules of evidence, and his efforts to narrow the scope of consideration to indictable crimes—indeed Wiggins tried to apply the stadard of "reasonable doubt" to the proceedings, where clearly "a preponderance of the evidence" was all that was required—worked for a while, and forced the Committee majority to sharpen the articles to demonstrate the evidence upon which they were relying.

—David W. Dennis of Indiana also took the lawyer's tack, but did it ineffectively and was to appear so shrill and obdurate in his defense of Nixon as to weaken not only the President's case but Dennis's own support for re-election. In a heavily Republican district, he was defeated in November 1974.

—Hamilton Fish, Jr. of New York had a number of distinctions as a member of the Committee. He was not only Gordon Liddy's Congressman, he had defeated Liddy in a primary election and had then persuaded the Nixon administration to hire Liddy at the Department of the Treasury so as to avoid Liddy's candidacy on the Conservative Party line in the general election. In addition, Fish was a third-generation Representative in his district, his father had served as Congressman when Franklin D. Roosevelt had lived in the district. Fish was as modern as his father had been old-fashioned, and during the Congressional debate Fish, Sr., now in his 80s and a strong member of the Committee to Defend the Presidency, publicly called upon his son to vote against impeachment. The generation gap was evident, however, in Fish's calm and reasoned participation in the debate on the side of impeachment. He was overwhelmingly re-elected.

—Wiley Mayne of Iowa, who had been narrowly re-elected in

1972, was another Republican member who faced the electoral dilemma. Mayne resolved it by a steady and colorless defense of Nixon, and lost by a substantial margin in the November election.

—Lawrence J. Hogan of Maryland was a young politician very much interested in rising in his party and his state. He had planned to leave Congress in 1974 and seek the Republican nomination for governor in his generally Democratic state. When, on the eve of the public hearings, Hogan made the surprising announcement that he was going to vote for impeachment, it was widely believed that the Congressman—who had been a hardline prosecutor before his election to Congress—had done so in order to get Democratic votes later in the year in his race for governor. Whether this was Hogan's calculation will never be known, since he lost in the Republican primary race for governor, in part because his anti-Nixon stance, and the public way in which he had announced it before the evidence was formally presented, hurt him with many voters in his own party.

—M. Caldwell Butler of Virginia was a freshman Republican from the South, and thus—by politically orthodox terms—could be counted on as a hard Nixon vote. But Butler, too, was looking at the evidence, and the more he looked at it the more he favored impeachment. He voted for all three articles, and the election returns showed that his solidly conservative district had approved his stand.

—William S. Cohen of Maine was the one Republican member always thought of as most likely to vote for impeachment. Cohen was an intellectual and a liberal among Republicans, which did not set him too far apart from his Maine constituents. He quietly played a leadership role among Republicans for impeachment, and in the process must have impressed his constituents; he won by an increased majority in the Congressional elections later in the year.

—Trent Lott of Mississippi stayed with Nixon until the end. Lott was more politician than juror; he came from one of the most pro-Nixon districts in America (in most of Mississippi, racial politics is still good politics), and he never let his constituents down.

—Harold V. Froehlich of Wisconsin was another Republican Congressman with an electoral problem. He had been narrowly elected in 1972 over a priest, who was to be his opponent in 1974. Froehlich genuinely agonized over the choice he had to make on the Committee, finally came down on the side of impeachment, but lost anyway—in the opinion of most observers in his district, the impeachment vote was not an important factor.

—Carlos J. Moorhead of California was perhaps the member of the Committee who participated least and seemed least affected by the evidence. His comments were few, but irrelevant.

—Joseph J. Maraziti of New Jersey was not only a strong Nixon defender but a strong Maraziti promoter. He always won the dash to the press after each closed Committee session, and the press enjoyed reporting his comments on the evidence, which always seemed, when the evidence finally came out, to have been at variance with the facts. Maraziti was defeated for re-election after the impeachment vote, but as much for local scandals as for his vote in favor of Nixon.

—Delbert L. Latta of Ohio had been placed on the Committee just as the impeachment proceeding began, replacing a member who had left the Congress. Latta was put on the Committee by the Republican leadership to be a strong pro-Nixon advocate; he turned out to be only a steady pro-Nixon vote. His efforts at advocacy were overshadowed by his colleagues, particularly Wiggins, and Latta's presence during the impeachment debate was little noted.

The son of a bricklayer who had come to the United States from Italy in the wave of Italian immigration in the first quarter of the twentieth century, Peter Rodino was an inspiring example of the political behavior of the sons of immigrants. He grew up, by his own account, in a neighborhood of Newark—called, naturally enough, "Little Italy"—so tough that gunfire was heard in the streets. Rodino is unquestionably aware that many sons of immigrants who grew up in the same neighborhood and had the same options as he turned to crime instead of to the law (and a few, to be sure, would turn to both).

Rodino saw the American Dream differently, and studied and worked hard, achieving a law degree from the University of Newark. In World War II, he was one of the few enlisted men who earned a commission overseas, where he served in combat with the First Armored Division, returning to Newark as a captain. Within two years he had been elected to Congress, and some measure of his emphasis in public life can be gleaned from the following account of his activities which he placed in the Congressional Directory after eighteen years of service in the Congress:

> Holds knighthood in the Sovereign Military Order of Malta; grand officer, order of merit, Italian Republic; Star of Solidarity, Italian Republic; knighted by former King Umberto of Italy; knight of the order, Crown of Italy; knight of St. Maurizio e Lazzaro; Italian Cross of Merit and other various foreign decorations; awards and citations from Veterans of Foreign Wars, Catholic War Veterans, Jewish War Veterans; AMVETS Congressional silver helmet award; recipient of 1964 Bill of Rights Award for distinguished public service in the field of Government; past national chairman, Columbus Foundation, Inc.; honorary life member of Unico . . .

Rodino became a leader of Italo-Americans in Congress and nationally (his most recent post having been as chairman of Italo-Americans for McGovern), and was the author and chief sponsor of legislation making Columbus Day a national holiday.

It would have been easy under the circumstances to dismiss him as a narrow, parochial, big-city machine Democrat, with the kind of liberal voting record his working class and increasingly black district required in order to be re-elected. And, indeed, there were many who did so dismiss him. (It is even reasonable to assume that had Rodino been a Congressman, not from Newark where the spirit of "reform" is relatively quiescent, but from Manhattan where it rages, that reform elements in the Democratic party would have defeated him in a primary election by the mid-60s, and would have replaced him, if the past is any guide, with a liberal whose speeches would have been widely quoted in the New York *Post* but whose legislative leadership would have been minimal.)

Those who counted Rodino as a minor figure had not taken the trouble to look at the record or at the man. Rodino was a frustrated novelist and poet, and a man who drew genuine emotional satisfaction from reading the classics. In addition, he felt keenly his own status as a "hyphenated American," and had played a strong role in amending the immigration laws, which had been restrictive for forty years. In addition, he was of strong assistance to Emanuel Celler during the latter's lengthy chairmanship of the Judiciary Committee, in rounding up support for the major civil rights legislation the Committee wrote and guided to passage.

Rodino became Chairman of the Judiciary Committee only at the start of the 1973 session of Congress, as the Watergate scandal began to burst from the bottle Nixon had unsuccessfully tried to cap. After less than a year in the job, he presided over the first major Watergate-connected Judiciary hearings, to pass on the qualifications of Gerald Ford, who had been nominated to replace Spiro Agnew as Vice-President. The calm and patience Rodino demonstrated at that time, and his obvious intention not only to *be* fair but to *seem* to be fair, and the way in which he managed to allow the varying ideological groupings on the Committee to have their say and to feel that the procedures had permitted them adequate opportunity, should have been a guide to the way he would conduct the impeachment inquiry.

As the Ervin Committee hearings wound to an inconclusive end in the fall of 1973, Rodino sensed that the next legislative step would have to be impeachment. Four or five resolutions of impeachment, from Drinan and Waldie of the Judiciary Committee and from other House members, had already been prepared and filed. Those resolutions were routinely assigned to the Judiciary Committee, and, with no complaints from their authors, Rodino took no action. Drinan, Waldie, and the others wanted to be on record, and wanted some attention focused on impeachment as the ultimate and appropriate procedure, but they also knew that there were probably less than fifty votes for impeachment if the matter came to the floor in September and October of 1973. But by October 23, the firestorm caused by the Saturday Night Massacre * was at its height, Congressmen and Senators were using the once-dreaded word, "impeachment," freely, and Rodino—after conferring with Carl Albert, the Speaker—announced "with a deep sense of sadness" that impeachment proceedings must begin in his Committee. The next day, he said the hearings would be "broad-scale" hearings, thus telling the other members of the Committee that its work with respect to im-

---

* The newspaper terminology is instructive; it is probably the first time a massacre has caused a fire-storm, but both phrases are too firmly in the language for logic or linguistics to get them out.

peachment would not be confined to the obvious area of the Watergate cover-up, nor would it even be limited to those areas of Nixon's wrongdoing already under fire—such as the nonpayment of income tax, the misuse of government agencies to "screw our enemies," and the approval of the so-called "Huston Plan" to permit White House agents systematically to violate the law.

A "broad-scale" impeachment inquiry would include—and did ultimately include—a thorough investigation of such charges against Nixon as the secret bombing of Cambodia, the impoundment (refusal to spend) of funds voted by Congress, and similar "political" matters, including some highly questionable pardons granted by Nixon to former Teamsters' president James Hoffa and Mafia chieftain "Gyp" DeCarlo.

In his announcement of a broad-scale investigation, Rodino said that it would be conducted by an expanded staff and that he would begin assembling the staff immediately. In addition, on a purely legal front, he referred to his Subcommittee on Criminal Justice, chaired by Congressman Hungate, legislation to extend the life of the Grand Jury which was then concluding its investigation into the Watergate cover-up. As a legal footnote, this legislation extending the term of the Grand Jury formed the basis for a challenge by H. R. Haldeman, to his subsequent indictment. Haldeman's attorneys took the line that the extension had been improperly granted. On appeal, the Haldeman argument was unanimously rejected.

Rodino also set a meeting for the full Committee to take place within a week, "to consider the granting of subpoena powers." That was an ominous statement, particularly as it was followed—with typical Rodino understatement—by the following concluding paragraph:

> I am gratified that the President has said he will release the tapes that have been a key element in the Watergate investigation to this time. Nevertheless, the Committee is charged with the responsibility of acting on the various resolutions on impeachment and to development procedures to determine whether there is a *reasonable basis* for the charges brought in the House of Representatives that the President has committed high crimes or misdemeanors.

By that paragraph, Rodino suggested not too subtly to the White House that he had observed recalcitrance in the past in delivering materials relevant to the various inquiries, and served notice that he would keep the subpoena power as a club in the locker, to be used if necessary.

He also drew an initial line in what was to become a continuing battle over the standard of proof required for impeachment. According to Rodino on October 24, the hearing was to determine if there was "a reasonable basis" to conclude that high crimes or misdemeanors had been committed. St. Clair and his allies in the Committee—led by Congressman Wiggins—would try to obliterate that line and substitute one of proof "beyond a reasonable doubt." When it was all over, Rodino's original definition survived, and received the support of all but a handful of the Committee members.

On November 15, Rodino asked the House for an initial funding of $1 million to get on with the investigation; by the end of April he was to ask for—and get—another $733,000, which he thought would take the Committee through the end of June. There has yet to be a supplementary appropriation sought, and the total cost of the extra work of the Committee is probably limited to the combined figure of $1,733,000.

On December 10, under some pressure—particularly from pro-impeachment forces—to "get on with it," Rodino said that what he called the "first stage" was well underway. He said that the existing staff of the Judiciary Committee had begun to collect evidentiary material, and that the newly acquired computer capability of the House of Representatives would be used to store and retrieve all the evidence that had been collected. Most of it, as of that date, had come over from the Ervin Committee, which had assembled a mass of data and had already programed it for computer use.

During all of this time, Rodino was still seeking a chief counsel. He had received numerous suggestions, including proposals that the Committee engage Archibald Cox for this purpose, but Rodino was determined to proceed cautiously and select a chief counsel who could command respect from the Committee and the nation. He wanted, if possible, a Republican. He had to have someone who had not "taken sides"—not only on the matter of impeachment (an obvious necessity) but also on the various Watergate questions as they had arisen. That almost required that it be someone who had taken no part in government—either in the legislative or prosecutorial branches—for the past two years. In addition, he wanted an experienced trial lawyer and someone of unimpeachable integrity who had, in addition, the proven ability to organize, discipline, and lead a substantial staff.

From the preceding qualifications, it is clear why Rodino's search took as long as it did. Finally, on December 20, Rodino announced the appointment of John Doar as chief special counsel to the Committee for the impeachment proceeding.

Doar was a Republican, and he was "an outsider" to the Congress and had been, for many years, to the executive branch as well. He had been highly recommended, not only by the law school deans, judges, prosecutors, and leading political figures (including Senator Kennedy) whom Rodino had consulted, but also by his own reputation.

Doar had come to the Department of Justice and joined the civil rights division while Dwight Eisenhower was in the White House. He stayed under President Kennedy, and was named by Attorney-General Robert Kennedy as the Deputy Assistant Attorney-General in that division, serving under Assistant Attorney-General Burke Marshall.

In the Civil Rights Division (as Deputy and later, as Assistant Attorney-General under President Johnson), Doar acquired considerable identity as a lawyer who prepared his cases carefully (if anyone had a complaint against John Doar, it was that he prepared his cases *too* carefully). In addition, during the grave and violent civil rights disturbances of the 1960s, Doar showed himself to be a man of great physical courage. On more than one occasion, he had confronted angry mobs of whites and blacks and had been able to talk both of them into awaiting a legal result for their disputes.

After leaving the Justice Department, Doar had served as the director of an experimental private community action program in the Bedford-Stuyvesant section of Brooklyn, which had been created under the inspiration and continuing supervision of Robert Kennedy, by then a United States Senator from New York. Doar later served for a year as chairman of the Board of Education of the City of New York, at a time when black–white confrontations over decentralization of authority had reached their peak.

Doar had, in short, every qualification that Rodino had set down, and over the course of the seven months that he served as special counsel to the Judiciary Committee, he enhanced an already luminous reputation. The first step he took when he came to Washington was to seal himself off from the press and, indeed, from any personal contact outside of the Committee. It made for a lonely seven months, but it effectively stopped in its tracks any possible complaint against Doar for fraternizing or—in a flap that was later to arise—for "leaking" of Committee material to the press and to the public.

Doar began at once to recruit and employ a staff. By the time the investigation and the hearings were fully under weigh, more than fifty lawyers and an equal number of supporting investigators, secretaries, and legal assistants had been assembled to work under Doar's direction.

By January 7, 1974, the minority Republicans had appointed a counsel of their own. He was Albert Jenner of Chicago, a distinguished lawyer who had served as president of the American Bar Association and as chairman of its committee to pass on the fitness of judicial appointees.

No sooner was Jenner's appointment announced than he came under attack from some of the pro-Nixon conservatives on the Committee. His "crime" was a political one; in the campaign of 1970, he had served as a co-sponsor of a dinner honoring and raising funds for Senator Adlai Stevenson, III, with whom Jenner had worked in the past and whose re-election he favored. It was hardly the kind of thing that appealed to the partisan members of the Committee, and they began a backlash against Jenner which would end shortly before the Committee began its public hearing with his "firing" by the minority.

But by that time Jenner had indicated his strong beliefs that a probable case for impeachment had been made, and Doar assigned Jenner the job of assistant chief counsel so that he remained on the Committee staff through the hearings. Jenner's trouble was that he believed the mandate of the Committee to be to make recommendations on the basis of law and evidence, and he discovered almost as soon as he was appointed that the people who had appointed him had in mind a different function:

to serve as an advocate for President Nixon. It was an honest confusion: Jenner saw himself in a judicial capacity, and the Committee Republicans (or at least most of them) wanted a trial advocate.

The Judiciary Committee: The Drama Unfolds

Doar and Jenner promptly turned most of the investigative work (which consisted mainly of collecting all available evidence either from the Ervin Committee or the Special Prosecutor) to other staff members, and turned their own attention to the threshold question which was to occupy the Committee for some time. That question was: precisely what constituted an impeachable offense? There were a number of Committee members ready to pronounce themselves expert on the question, as there were in the press and elsewhere, and Doar and Jenner began to look at the constitutional and judicial precedents.

The staff question settled and a budget voted, Rodino in late January announced that he would ask the full House of Representatives to affirm the Committee's responsibility to proceed with the inquiry, and would also seek a confirmation of the Committee's authority to issue enforceable subpoenas for the appearance of witnesses and the production of evidence. It was an indication of the thoroughness with which Rodino planned to proceed. The Committee *had* subpoena power, and the impeachment resolutions had been referred to the Committee by the Speaker. There was thus no need for an additional authorization by the full House since the matter could proceed according to traditional rules: the Committee would hold hearings, it would vote articles of impeachment, up or down, and that bill would come before the House much as any other matter cleared by a committee.

But that was not enough for Rodino. He wanted the House to be aware of the extreme importance of what it was asking the

Judiciary Committee to do, and he also wanted to send a message "downtown"—the standard reference on Capitol Hill for the White House—that the House was serious and that the Committee was deadly serious. So Rodino asked the Committee to vote—and it responded, unanimously—to recommend that the full House of Representatives adopt a resolution calling for the impeachment inquiry. It would specifically "authorize and direct" the Committee "to investigate the conduct of the President of the United States, to determine whether or not evidence exists that the President is responsible for any acts that in the contemplation of the Constitution are grounds for impeachment, and if such evidence exists, whether or not it is sufficient to require the House to exercise its constitutional powers."

As a part of the resolution, the Committee recommended that the House reenforce the power of subpoena held by the Judiciary Committee.

Rodino's speech in support of the resolution was at once powerful and revealing. It demonstrated what he was to show the House and the public throughout the hearings; namely, the sense of history which he wanted his colleagues to share, the feeling of momentum which he had sensed, and the historic importance he attached to it. He began with a quotation from Edmund Burke, whose writings on constitutionalism and impeachment Rodino had carefully studied. He had also read other historical analyses of impeachment, and had read the modern accounts of the Andrew Johnson impeachment with particular interest. But on February 6, in support of his resolution in the House, he began with Burke:

> "We stand in a situation very honorable to ourselves and very useful to our country, if we do not abuse or abandon the trust that is placed in us."
> We stand in such a position now, and—whatever the result —we are going to be just, and honorable, and worthy of the public trust.

Rodino then described the general jurisdiction and responsibility of the House. He quoted from the Constitution (Art. I, Sec. 2) that the House shall have the sole power of impeachment, and he referred to the large number of impeachment resolutions that had been introduced by members late in 1973, and which had been referred to his Committee by the Speaker. "We have reached the point," he said, "when it is important that the House explicitly confirm our responsibility under the Constitution."

He repeated his request for a reconfirmation of subpoena power. He pointed out that such a resolution had always been passed by the House, and then he turned to possible results of his inquiry.

"We are going to say little," he said, beyond the general obligation he had described. He said the Committee would seek first to understand what is contemplated in the constitutional definition of impeachment, for which purpose he said they would study the papers of the founding fathers, historical precedents, and the words of the Constitution itself.

He also said that the Committee would consider on the basis of resolutions already referred, evidence already on the public record, and other evidence which the Committee would obtain, "whether or not serious abuses of power or violations of the public trust have occurred," and "whether, in fact and under the Constitution, the President is responsible for any such offenses."

Rodino then turned, inferentially to be sure but clearly enough for those who had been listening to the political criticism of the House, and said:

> We cannot turn away, out of partisanship or convenience, from problems that are now our responsibility, our inescapable responsibility to consider. It would be a violation of our own public trust if we, as the people's representatives, chose not to inquire, not to consult, not even to deliberate, and then to pretend that we had not by default, made choices.

Rodino then turned to what was, for him, the most serious problem. "The manner in which we proceed is of historic importance," he said, "to the country, to the presidency, to the House, to the people, to our constitutional system, and unquestionably, to future generations." He said "our whole system, since the founding of the republic, rests on the principle that power itself has constitutional limits and embodies a trust. Those who govern are regularly accountable to the people, in elections, but always most highly accountable to the law and the Constitution itself. We ourselves are accountable."

He then talked of another criticism which had been leveled at the House and which, it was thought, would constitute one of Nixon's strongest weapons—weariness of crisis on the part of both the governors and the governed:

> It has been said that our country, troubled by too many crises in recent years, is too tired to consider this one. In the first year of the republic, Thomas Paine wrote: "Those who expect to reap the blessings of freedom must, like men, undergo the fatigue of supporting it." For almost 200 years, Americans have undergone the stress of preserving their freedom and the Constitution that protects it. *It is our turn now.* [Emphasis added.]

Rodino would make no promises and set no schedules. He said the Committee would do its work fairly, and that when it had completed its inquiry it would make its recommendations to the House. And he said all of this would be done "as soon as we can."

As he concluded, he spoke of honor and he spoke once again of the future generations which were so much on his mind. "Whatever the result, whatever we learn or conclude, let us now proceed with such care and decency and thoroughness and honor that the vast majority of the American people, and their children after them, will say: 'That was the right course. There was no other way.'"

When, the 1972 election safely behind him, Richard Nixon concluded an agreement with our "allies" in Saigon (and only incidentally with our enemies in Hanoi) which permitted him to bring all American combat troops out of Vietnam, he spoke of it, repeatedly, as "peace with honor," although it immediately became apparent that there was no peace, and what had gone before had guaranteed there would be no honor. With his speech on February 6, 1974, the immigrant's son from Newark had marked the beginning of the end of a process that might bring real peace, and that would surely bring real honor. The resolution passed the House the same day, by a vote of 410–4. Perhaps because the vote was so overwhelming, the event was hardly noticed, but to those who read what Rodino had to say, and who contemplated the failure of the Republican leadership to oppose the resolution, it was a strong indication that when the Committee ended its inquiry, it would be with a recommendation for impeachment that would be supported by a substantial majority—in the House, and in the country.

The next major issue to confront the Committee was one that would occupy a considerable amount of time in debate and would never be fully settled. That was the question of what constituted "an impeachable offense." Some background to the argument—particularly the political part of the argument—is necessary in order to understand how Doar and Rodino dealt with the question.

The constitutional language is spare:

"The President, Vice-President, and all Civil Officers of the United States, shall be removed from Office on Impeachment for, and Conviction of, Treason, Bribery, or other high Crimes and Misdemeanors."

The language itself was of not much assistance. What was a high crime? What was a misdemeanor? What was the significance of the use of the word *other?* It was easy to arrive at a Bill of Impeachment, if treason or bribery was the offense alleged, but treason (although it is a word used far too much in political discourse) is clearly and narrowly defined in the Constitution as giving aid and comfort to the enemy in wartime, and must be proved by the testimony of two witnesses to an overt act. It is true that H. R. Haldeman, in one of his rare public appearances, had said that those opposed to American policy in Vietnam were trying "consciously to aid and abet the enemy," but except for that vulgarism, no accusations of treason had been levied by one American against another since Richard Nixon and Joe McCarthy and their allies had used the phrase rather loosely in the 1950s.

Bribery was certainly involved in some of the charges against President Nixon, most specifically in the allegations relating to the increase in milk prices and to the leniency with which the Justice Department treated not only ITT but other potential offenders against the laws whose executives had thoughtfully contributed large sums—from their corporate treasuries to be sure, and not from their pockets—to Nixon's various campaigns. In addition, the offense to which Herbert Kalmbach pleaded guilty, that of offering an ambassadorship in return for a campaign contribution, fell within the ambit of bribery, and the Department of Justice was prepared to move against Vice-President Agnew—had he not resigned and pleaded guilty to income tax evasion—on multiple charges of bribery as well as extortion.

But Rodino and his allies on the Judiciary Committee had decided fairly early that while these "peripheral" matters would receive a fair investigation, that public opinion would not support an Article of Impeachment based solely upon any of the charges which could be subsumed under the general rubric of bribery.

So the question got back to "high crimes and misdemeanors," and a lot of legal and political jockeying went on with respect to the definition of those terms. Nixon's spokesmen, and the President himself whenever he had the chance, tried to impose a narrow construction on the language. They maintained from the beginning that in order for the House of Representatives to vote for impeachment, it would have to find clear evidence, beyond a reasonable doubt, that Nixon had committed "indictable crimes," in other words, crimes for which he could be tried in an ordinary court, convicted, and sentenced.

This line was, of course, very useful to Nixon. By narrowing the definition of impeachable acts to actual crimes, they would prevent a vote on offenses which would be considered attacks upon the Constitution, failure to faithfully execute the laws, or other presidential abuses of power that were not expressly forbidden by statute.

The question of what constituted an impeachable act should not have been confused with the degree of proof which the House Judiciary Committee was required to reach. That was a separate question, and Rodino and Doar correctly saw that it should be the subject of separate research. If the House of Representatives functioned roughly as a Grand Jury, then the standard of proof required of the members would only be that the case be proved by "a preponderance of the evidence." That is to say, since it is the function of a Grand Jury only to determine that an offense has been committed, and that there is "probable cause" to believe that a certain named individual has committed it, he may then be bound over for trial.

At a trial, of course, the standard of proof is much higher. Trial juries must determine the defendant's guilt "beyond a reasonable doubt," but since the function of the Grand Jury is only to decide whether a trial should be held, its standard of proof is lower.

Along with the effort by the Nixon forces to narrow the definition of impeachable offenses went a companion effort to raise the standard of proof to that ordinarily required of a trial jury. Rodino and Doar took the position, which was the only reasonable one under the law and the only one supported by legal precedents, that the House of Representatives in voting impeachment would be functioning in effect as a Grand Jury, and that it was the Senate which would try the case, where the standard of proof must be "beyond a reasonable doubt."

The question of "impeachable offense" remained. If it was to be required that a "crime" be alleged and established by a preponderance of the evidence, that would be easy enough. Certainly the evidence supported the existence of enough crimes, committed by Nixon even in his presidential capacity. In an earlier book *(Perfectly Clear—Nixon from Whittier to Watergate)* I set forth in an appendix a number of criminal statutes which Nixon or people acting directly under his authority and with his approval, seemed to have committed. Under the general heading of obstruction of justice, there were any number of crimes of which the mounting evidence in 1974 suggested Richard Nixon's guilt "on a preponderance of the evidence." It seemed clear—even without the conclusive evidence of the June 23 tape—that Nixon had ordered the use of the CIA to block an FBI investigation into the source of payment to the Watergate burglars. The Huston Plan, authorizing White House agents under his control to break and enter, seize mail, and plant listening devices and wiretaps, was surely another. In addition, other tapes and transcripts had revealed that Nixon set in motion plans to use government agencies—such as the Internal Revenue Service—for improper political purposes, and that was also forbidden by law. In addition, it appeared that testimony from Nixon's tax advisers might yield at least a *prima facie* case against Nixon for tax evasion, if not for fraud.

Nevertheless, Rodino felt that to accept the "indictable crime" limitation would do two things he did not want his Committee to initiate. First of all, it would constitute a far more limited inquiry than he had in mind. He was not concerned as much with "convicting" Nixon as he was with vindicating constitutional principles which he felt the evidence demonstrated that Nixon had breached.

He was also worried, and it was a concern shared by Doar, that
the natural reaction of the lawyers on the Judiciary Committee—
all the members are lawyers, by definition—might be to seek, perhaps unconsciously, the higher standard of proof required in a
criminal proceeding in court, if it were established that criminal
conduct was the sole basis for impeachment.

Furthermore, Rodino's own reading of the impeachment precedents, from the works of Edmund Burke to the modern day
"revisionist" accounts of the impeachment and trial of Andrew
Johnson, had led him to believe that the proceeding was far too
important and would have far too great a historic significance to
be limited to the question of statutory crimes. He felt, as did most
constitutional scholars, that the impeachment clause had not been
placed in the Constitution merely to provide a forum in which a
President, from time to time, might be tried as a common criminal
for breaking one or another statute of the United States. Rodino
thought that impeachment, as the only and ultimate weapon which
the people had against a President, other than the test every four
years at the polls, was designed to reach far more important and
dangerous conduct, and he assigned the Committee staff, in its
initial legal research, to determine whether or not this was correct.

It was the first document the Committee staff was to produce,
and on February 21 a lengthy report of some 60 printed pages
issued from the Committee entitled "Constitutional Grounds for
Presidential Impeachment." It was a staff report, with a careful
notation from the chairman that "it is understood that the views
and conclusions contained in the report are staff views and do
not necessarily reflect those of the committee or any of its members." It was, nevertheless, an immensely influential document;
it clearly reflected—despite the disclaimer—the views of at least
a bare majority, and perhaps a substantial majority of the Committee, and it will unquestionably take its place in the literature
of constitutional law as the definitive study of the question of
what constitutes an impeachable offense.

Although as the inquiry began, Americans tended to think of
impeachment as a remedy to be used exclusively against a President, and knew that in that way it had been used only once before, the report went into *all* the previous uses of the power. In
our history, impeachment had been invoked against—in addition

to President Andrew Johnson—one Secretary of War (William W. Belknap), in 1876; one Supreme Court Justice (Samuel Chase), in 1804; one appellate judge (Robert W. Archbald), in 1912; one Senator (William Blount), in 1797; and eight district judges (John Pickering in 1803, James H. Peck in 1830, West H. Humphreys in 1862, Mark H. Delahay in 1873, Charles Swayne in 1903, George W. English in 1925, Harold Lauderback in 1932, and Halsted L. Ritter in 1936). In addition to these cases of impeachment, and the debate which preceded and accompanied them, there were to be considered the records of the Constitutional Convention as well as a significant body of writing and legal precedents concerning the earlier English cases, from which the impeachment clause in the American Constitution had been taken.

All of this was exhaustively developed in the Committee staff report. The Committee staff went back to the earliest English times, and concluded that at the time of the American Constitutional Convention the phrase "high crimes and misdemeanors" had been in use for over 400 years in Parliament. It was first used in 1386 in the impeachment of the King's Chancellor, and while it appeared that some of the charges involved common law criminal offenses, the major allegations were that he had broken a promise made to Parliament and, curiously enough, he was also charged with failing to spend money which Parliament had directed that he spend. This was a foreshadowing of the charge against Nixon for illegal impoundment of funds, surely not a crime by any definition, and one for which no officer of government could be indicted, but which since the earliest usages had been accepted as a grounds for impeachment.

In an extended analysis of pre-revolutionary uses of impeachment, the staff study pointed out that in almost every case, while some criminal behavior was alleged, the general complaint of "high crimes and misdemeanors" involved, more often than not, charges generally phrased as "violation of duty and trust." Thus, during the first half of the seventeenth century, more than one hundred impeachments were voted by the House of Commons, and all involved either treason or "high crimes and misdemeanors." According to the study, "the latter included both statutory offenses, particularly with respect to the Crown monopolies, and non-statutory offenses." Two charges, for example, against the Royal Attorney General in 1621, under the heading of high crimes and misdemeanors, were that he failed to prosecute after beginning suits, and that he had exercised authority before it had been properly vested in him.

After the Commonwealth (1649–1660), Parliament—by now more powerful—began to enlarge the scope of high crimes and misdemeanors by including such charges as "negligent discharge of duties" and "improprieties in office." Thus, the Earl of Oxford was charged, in 1701, with "violation of his duty and trust" in taking advantage of his access to the king to secure various royal rents and revenues for his own use, thus increasing the "grievous taxes" which the people of England had to pay. He was also accused of using his official office to procure a Navy commission for Captain Kidd, even though Oxford knew him to be "a person of ill fame and reputation."

The impeachment of Warren Hastings, the first Governor-General of India, raged as a controversy in the Parliament from 1786 to 1795, and has always served as a source for determination of the meaning of impeachment and impeachable offenses in the American Constitution, since the debate in Parliament over Hastings took place during the same time as the debates in the Constitutional Convention.

Hastings was charged with "high crimes and misdemeanors" in that he had permitted "gross maladministration, corruption in office, and cruelty toward the people of India," according to the staff report. The original resolutions proposed for the impeachment of Hastings—offered by Edmund Burke—contained both indictable and non-indictable offenses. One article, for example, alleged ordinary criminal conversion, charging Hastings with having confiscated the income of certain begums, but another charge referred to the grave consequences of a revolt in a province of India, and charged Hastings with responsibility for those consequences, including many deaths, because he had "provoked" the revolt. These matters were of considerable importance to the drafters of our Constitution, as a reading of the debates on the impeachment clause make clear.

The report concluded that there were two lessons to be learned from a study of four hundred years of English experience with the phrase "high crimes and misdemeanors." The first was that the specific charges under that heading included both criminal and noncriminal matters; the second was that the phrase itself was confined solely to impeachment cases, and had no roots in the ordinary criminal law.

The study then turned to the application of the phrase intended by the drafters of our Constitution, based upon a close study of the debates and commentary of the period. As to the general consideration of the question of impeachment, the report makes clear that the founders were well aware that the Revolution had been fought against the tyranny of an absolute monarch and that there was a necessity to build in protections against the abuse of executive power. One member of the Constitutional Convention referred to this as the danger of creating "the foetus of monarchy." Alexander Hamilton was a strong advocate of including an impeachment power in the Constitution, in large part because he was simultaneously an advocate of a single executive. Hamilton argued that where responsibility was plural, it tended "to conceal faults and destroy responsibility." He said that a plural executive destroyed "the two greatest securities [the people] can have for the faithful exercise of any delegated power, responsibility . . . to censure and to punishment."

Other delegates made it clear they were placing the President under different restraints than those which applied to a monarch. Thus James Iredell, who was later to become a Justice of the Supreme Court, said that under the Constitution the President must be "personally responsible for any abuse of the great trust reposed in him." James Wilson, a delegate, later defended the Constitution at the convention in Pennsylvania called to ratify the document:

"Sir, we have a responsibility in the person of our President; he cannot act improperly, and hide either his negligence or inattention; he cannot roll upon any other person the weight of his criminality; no appointment can take place without his nomination; and he is responsible for every nomination he makes . . . yet not a *single privilege* is annexed to his character; far from being above the laws, he is amenable to them in his private character as a citizen, and in his public character by *impeachment.*"

Gouverneur Morris of Pennsylvania originally opposed at the Constitutional Convention the inclusion in the document of a provision for impeachment of the President, arguing that the executive could "do no criminal act without [assistants] who may be punished." Morris argued that since the President acted through his subordinates, and since they would be "amenable by impeachment to the public Justice," there was no need to spell out a power to impeach the President. During the debates, Morris changed his position, and became an advocate of the inclusion of an impeachment power, but before he changed his mind, he was answered by George Mason of Virginia:

"Shall any man be above justice? Above all shall that man be above it who can commit the most extensive injustice?"

And James Madison, who participated in the debate over the impeachment power to a greater degree than almost any other delegate, argued that in the single power of the executive, "loss of capacity or corruption was more within the compass of probable events, and either of them might be fatal to the Republic," and that a provision for impeachment of the President was thus necessary to defend the larger community against "the incapacity, negligence or perfidy of the Chief Magistrate."

Benjamin Franklin and Edmund Randolph carried the argument even further; Franklin supported impeachment on the grounds that it was "favorable" to the President, on the theory that where impeachment was not available and the chief executive had "rendered himself obnoxious," the only recourse of the people might be to assassination. Randolph argued for the propriety of an impeachment provision, on the grounds that since the chief executive would have enormous opportunity to abuse his power, "should no regular punishment be provided it will be irregularly inflicted by tumults & insurrections."

As for the grounds for impeachment—the phrase that ultimately came to be "high crimes and misdemeanors"—the initial draft called for the President's impeachment and removal from office only on grounds of treason or bribery. George Mason, whose own state of Virginia and five others included "maladministration" as a grounds for impeachment, offered the addition of "maladministration" on the grounds that "treason as defined in the Constitution will not reach many great and dangerous offenses. . . . Attempts to subvert the Constitution may not be treason as above defined."

James Madison thought that "maladministration" was too vague a term, and Mason then withdrew the word and substituted "high crimes and misdemeanors against the state," which language was then adopted, with eight states voting in favor and three against.

The words, "against the state" were later dropped by the Committee on Style which drafted the final document.

The Judiciary Committee report made it plain that the framers of the Constitution were familiar with the English history of impeachment proceedings, and noted that the concurrent impeachment of Warren Hastings was much in the minds of the members of the Constitutional Convention and was referred to during the debates. Alexander Hamilton later referred to Great Britain as "the model" from which the impeachment provision had been borrowed, and it was also observed that the framers of the Constitution were not only well-educated men but many were lawyers, of whom a large number had studied law in England.

Thus the phrase, "high crimes and misdemeanors," with the gloss it had acquired over 400 hundred years of English impeachments and the understandings attached to it as a legal "work of art" referring to kinds of presidential maladministration, was well understood at the time of the adoption of the Constitution. In the *Federalist Papers* Hamilton described impeachment as:

"Those offenses which proceed from the misconduct of public men, or, in other words, from the abuse or violation of some public trust. They are of a nature which may with peculiar propriety be denominated *political*, as they relate chiefly to injuries done immediately to the society itself." (Emphasis in original.) Joseph Story, later a Justice of the Supreme Court, wrote 50 years later in his "Commentaries on the Constitution," that impeachment applied to "offenses of a political character," noting from his study of the Convention and the constitutional precedents that impeachment had a "more enlarged operation" than application to crimes alone, and that it reaches "what are aptly termed political offenses, growing out of personal misconduct or gross neglect, or usurpation, or habitual disregard of the public interests, in the discharge of the duties of political office."

James Iredell, defending the Constitution at the ratification convention in North Carolina, argued that a President "must certainly be punishable for giving false information to the Senate," thus giving some historic justification for a proposed article of impeachment relative to Nixon and his chief military aides having supplied fictitious information to the Senate with respect to the bombing of Cambodia.

James Madison had argued during the debate at the Constitutional Convention that a President would be subject to impeachment for "the wanton removal of meritorious officers." This argument of Madison's found support at the time of the impeachment of Andrew Johnson, for what many Congressmen and Senators believed to be the "wanton removal" of Secretary of War Edwin Stanton, and afforded in 1974 at least a tenuous justification for an article of impeachment based on the dismissal of Special Prosecutor Archibald Cox.

But in the same portion of the debate, Madison touched upon a deeper basis for impeachment, and it came to be accepted—200 years later—by many members of the Judiciary Committee. It was referred to later as the "superintendency" ground, based on Madison's statement that a President would be subject to impeachment if he permitted his subordinates "to perpetrate with impunity high crimes or misdemeanors against the United States, *or neglects to superintend their conduct,* so as to check their excesses." (Emphasis added.) That argument of Madison's, at a time when a score of principal subordinates of President Nixon had either confessed their guilt or had been convicted of crimes, assumed great importance in the subsequent debate within the Judiciary Committee.

The Committee report included a close study of each of the American impeachment cases. It concluded that the conduct alleged in articles of impeachment which had been recommended to the House fell into three broad categories; "(1) Exceeding the constitutional bounds of the powers of the office in derogation of the powers of another branch of government; (2) behaving in a manner grossly incompatible with the proper function and purpose of the office; and (3) employing the power of the office for an improper purpose or for personal gain."

The Committee conceded that even though many of the articles —although less than one-third of the total of 83 articles of impeachment which the House of Representatives had adopted—had explicitly charged the violation of a criminal statute, the House had not even always used the technical language of the criminal law, even when the conduct alleged fell within the definition of an indictable crime. But the clear evidence as marshalled by the report demonstrated that articles of impeachment much more commonly alleged that the officer to be impeached had "violated his duties or his oath or seriously undermined public confidence in his ability to perform his official functions." The report also made the point that where criminal and noncriminal grounds were both stated as separate articles of impeachment (and sometimes within the same article), it seemed likely that the decision of the whole House to impeach had been on the basis of all of the allegations viewed as a whole, rather than on any of the particular items of misconduct charged. This section of the report concluded:

"The American impeachment cases demonstrate a common theme useful in determining whether grounds for impeachment exist—that the grounds are derived from understanding the nature, functions, and duties of the office."

The report then summarized the whole "criminality" issue, and reached some strong conclusions. "The central issue raised by these concerns," said the staff report, "is whether requiring an indictable offense as an essential element of impeachable conduct is consistent with the purposes and intent of the framers in establishing the impeachment power and in setting a constitutional standard for the exercise of that power." The report made it clear that impeachment, a constitutional remedy, was intended by the framers to reflect more than "indictable crimes," and to embrace as well "grave misconduct that allegedly injured or abused our constitutional institutions and our form of government so as to justify impeachment."

The use of the phrase "high crimes and misdemeanors," the report concluded, was confined to impeachment cases and had been used in England and in this country to charge officials with a wide range of both criminal and noncriminal offenses, and there was ample demonstration that the men who wrote the Constitution were aware of "this special, noncriminal meaning of the phrase."

"Impeachment and the criminal law serve fundamentally different purposes," the report argued. "Impeachment is the first step in a remedial process—removal from office and possible disqualification from holding future office. The purpose of impeachment is not personal punishment; its function is primarily to maintain constitutional government," said the summary of the precedents.

In summing up, the staff urged that

to limit impeachable conduct to criminal offenses would be

incompatible with the evidence concerning the constitutional meaning of the phrase "high crimes and misdemeanors" and would frustrate the purpose that the framers intended for impeachment. State and federal criminal laws are not written in order to preserve the nation against serious abuse of the presidential office. But this *is* the purpose of the constitutional provision for the impeachment of a President and that purpose gives meaning to "high crimes and misdemeanors."

The report effectively demolished the St. Clair argument that the Judiciary Committee must find evidence of an indictable crime, and must find it beyond a reasonable doubt. Some of the bitter-end Nixon defenders on the Committee, ignoring the report, continued to use that as their standard and to cite it as one to which the Committee should repair. But for the overwhelming majority of the Committee, the issue was settled when the staff report appeared. Not only did it represent exhaustive scholarship, but it had the approval not only of John Doar but also of Albert Jenner, the counsel appointed so recently by the Republican minority.

But it was clear that, outside of the Committe, hardly anyone else had bothered to read the report. One continued to read in the press comments by writers who pretended to a knowledge of the Constitution and the issue, that the meaning of "high crimes and misdemeanors" was the general meaning one might glean if the phrase had been first written in the twentieth century, and no understanding at all of the tradition and meaning it had acquired under the English common law and impeachment practice, at the Constitutional Convention and the debates which followed, and in impeachment proceedings in the American Congress ever since.

High officials of the government, who might have been expected to do their homework on an issue that so clearly involved their own tenure of office, continued to echo the St. Clair argument instead of reading the basic documents. Thus, a high aide to Henry Kissinger, with a well-earned reputation as an intellectual, could say in all seriousness that since the word "other" preceded "high crimes and misdemeanors" in the impeachment section of the constitution, it therefore must follow that St. Clair was right and that indictable crimes must be proved before the Committee beyond a reasonable doubt.

But Rodino, and the substantial majority of the Committee which had read the report, entertained no such further doubts, and as the Committee moved into the phase of listening to evidence it was clear that the standard they were to apply was the one urged by the Committee report on grounds for impeachment, and not the narrow standard urged by the President and his attorneys, however often that view was echoed by uninformed comment in the press and elsewhere.

As a matter of fact, the impact of the staff report on grounds for impeachment can be seen in the second Article of Impeachment which was finally recommended. That article charges President Nixon with using the powers of his office in violation of his constitutional oath to "faithfully execute the office of President of the United States, and . . . to the best of [his] ability, preserve, protect and defend the Constitution of the United States," and in disregard of his constitutional duty to "take care that the laws be faithfully executed."

That conduct was alleged to have included, in at least three instances, actions by Nixon "acting personally and through his subordinates," in failing to "take care that the laws be faithfully executed" by failing to act when he knew or had reason to know that his close subordinates endeavored to impede and frustrate lawful inquiries, and concluded that Nixon had "acted in a manner contrary to his trust as President and subversive of constitutional government, to the great prejudice of the cause of law and justice and to the manifest injury of the people of the United States."

In all of Article II, there is scarcely an indictable crime mentioned, yet it is the article which carried by the highest margin within the Committee. Its language depends directly upon James Madison's theory of impeachment as guaranteeing an accounting of the President's "superintendency," which was cited earlier. Article II serves as a powerful precedent for the future, informing us all that a President may indeed be impeached for failure to superintend the acts of his subordinates. As William Hungate said during the debate, "Yes, Virginia, there is a law of agency," referring to the rule of law that a principal is responsible for the acts of his agents; in this case, not only Haldeman, Ehrlichman,

Dean, Colson, etc., but also the heads of federal agencies which were misused at Nixon's direction and with his consent.

Indeed, the three Articles of Impeachment which were approved, taken together, demonstrate the aptness of the research done by the Committee on the question of grounds for impeachment. The first article describes clearly criminal acts, charging President Nixon with participation in the cover-up of the Watergate burglary and the implication in the cover-up of his chief aides and assistants, all includable in the crime called "obstruction of justice." The second article, based as it is on Madison's theory of "superintendency," charges Nixon with as many acts of omission as it does acts of commission, and demonstrates that future Presidents will be called to account in a similar manner. The third article, based on Nixon's defiance of the Committee's subpoenas for evidence, makes an impeachable offense out of the assumption by the President of "functions and judgments necessary to the exercise of the sole power of impeachment vested by the Constitution in the House of Representatives."

It was, perhaps, the final irony of these proceedings that the President who had tried so long to maintain himself in office by vain recitations of the doctrines of "separation of powers," should have been placed on the verge of impeachment precisely because he violated the clear mandate of separation laid down by the Constitution.

The next "crisis" to face the Committee was the request by James St. Clair on March 8, 1974, for leave to participate in any hearing or other process before the Committee in connection with the impeachment inquiry. St. Clair sought the right to cross-examine witnesses as well as the right to request that the Committee call designated witnesses and to introduce what he believed to be relevant and material evidence.

St. Clair's letter making the request was a cold one, and asked John Doar "to have this matter resolved by the Committee at your earliest convenience." But St. Clair understood that the question was a serious one, and that as a pure matter of law he had no right to be represented. It became clear, five days later, when he wrote to Doar complaining that his request had not yet been granted, that the request itself was less a part of the *legal* proceeding than it was a part of the larger *public relations* proceeding being conducted by the White House. In his second letter St. Clair said: "I am sure you realize that in order for me to represent the *presidency* adequately it is imperative that I be allowed to participate in any prehearing discovery, as well as at any hearing conducted by the Committee." (Emphasis added.) Doar's response was to begin promptly, and to complete within three weeks, a study for the benefit of the Committee outlining the precedents and the basis on which the Committee could make a choice.

Both Doar and Rodino knew from the research that had already been accomplished that they would be on firm legal ground to disregard and deny St. Clair's request. But Rodino wanted time to gauge whether it might not be better, in order to guarantee that "appearance of fairness" which he had early decided was so necessary, to grant St. Clair's request. But Rodino believed that even if he granted the request, it would be important to be able to demonstrate that he was doing so in spite of clear legal authority not to do so.

The Committee report made it clear that participation by Nixon or his legal representatives was a matter of grace, and not a matter of right. It began with the customary and well-settled analogy of impeachment proceedings—as distinguished from the actual trial in the Senate—to those of a Grand Jury. While conceding that "there is no doubt that an impeached official has a constitutional right to a trial in the Senate," where the proceeding is in every sense adversary, the report made it equally clear that no such right existed in the House Committee or even on the floor of the•House itself.

A Grand Jury proceeding, the Committee report noted, is an investigation to determine whether a crime has been committed and whether criminal proceedings should be instituted against named persons, and not an adversary hearing in which the guilt or innocence of the accused is to be determined. A Grand Jury traditionally, said the report, quoting a recent Supreme Court case, "has been allowed to pursue its investigative and accusatorial functions unimpeded by the evidentiary and procedural restrictions applicable to a criminal trial." The report continued, saying that "accordingly, the Supreme Court had consistently rejected claims to procedural rights by witnesses called before Grand Juries, holding that the introduction of trial-type procedures in a Grand Jury inquiry would 'assuredly impede' or 'halt the orderly progress of investigations' and transform them into 'preliminary trials on the merits. . . .' "

Witnesses before Grand Juries almost always appear without counsel, and may neither make objections to questions which are asked nor challenge the authority of the Grand Jury, the report noted, adding that Grand Juries may even hand up indictments solely on the basis of hearsay evidence. Lest this seem harsh, it should also be noted that Grand Jury proceedings are conducted in secret and the results generally made public only in the form of the indictments, if any, which result.

When the Committee report turned to the specific matter of impeachment proceedings, and the history of impeachment before the Congress, the staff report found some ambiguity. Some proceedings had permitted participation by the accused and his legal representatives; most had not. But the report made it clear that where participation had been permitted, it had been addressed by past committees "as a question of grace, not of right." And finally, the report said that "no record has been found of any impeachment inquiry in which the official under investigation (or his legal representative) participated in the investigation stage preceding commencement of committee hearings."

Thus it was clear that Rodino was entirely within his rights in refusing St. Clair's participation; it would have been totally unprecedented to permit his participation prior to the commencement of the official debate within the Committee—that is to say, while evidence was being presented to the Committee by its counsel by the use of documents, tapes, and the testimony of some witnesses.

Rodino, having finally satisfied himself that he was under no legal obligation to do so, announced permission for St. Clair to participate, to a limited degree, in the proceedings. St. Clair later did participate, and even called some witnesses and cross-examined others, but his performance was relatively ineffective, and his questioning of witnesses produced only cumulative testimony and evidence; it seemed clear that what was important to the White House was the *request* for participation and the hope that it might be declined, so that Nixon and his supporters in the press could talk about a breach of "fair play."

The episode demonstrated the care which Rodino and Doar

were taking. It must have seemed obvious to Rodino, who had been through a number of political campaigns and observed a great many more, that while the Committee was looking for evidence and had to reach a verdict, the Nixon White House was seeking bigger game—a demand from public opinion that the impeachment proceeding either cease or, in any event, come out favorably to the President. The request for St. Clair's participation in the hearings was designed to achieve a backlash of public sentiment against the "high-handed, authoritarian" way in which Rodino would then be accused of running the show.

But the careful work which Doar and his staff had compiled and the decision reached by Rodino to permit limited participation by St. Clair, effectively blunted whatever chance this public relations campaign might have had to succeed, and the hearings inexorably ground on.

The next great question to confront the Committee—and the nation—was one involving the production of evidence. Even as Rodino and Doar and his staff were doing the necessary research on the question of whether St. Clair had the right to attend the hearings and to cross-examine witnesses, the presentation and summarizing of evidence for the members had gone forward to the point where additional evidence was required.

A few days after the staff report on grounds for impeachment had been presented, John Doar wrote to James St. Clair. In the letter, Doar requested tapes of presidential conversations prior to and following the celebrated conversation of March 21, 1973. The dates were important, because John Dean had testified that it was on March 21 that he told the President of the Watergate defendants' demands for hush money, and had received what he interpreted as the President's approval.

On that day, according to Dean, President Nixon had said to Dean, "it will be no problem to raise $1 million." Haldeman had testified to the Ervin Committee that immediately following that phrase, Nixon had added "but it would be wrong." Doar sought, by the acquisition of tapes of presidential meetings during the days before March 21 and the days immediately afterward, to try to obtain evidence which might at least resolve this conflict.

The letter from Doar to St. Clair coincided with a similar written request from Rodino to Nixon, and on March 5, Nixon replied:

Dear Mr. Chairman,

Thank you for your letter of February 26, 1974.

My special counsel, Mr. St. Clair, has received requests from Mr. Doar and is responding in my behalf.

· *I want to take this opportunity to reiterate that I intend to cooperate with the Committee on the Judiciary in its investigation in a manner consistent with my constitutional responsibilities as President.*

The interests of our country and the American people require that this matter proceed as expeditiously as possible and I am sure that you and Mr. Hutchinson will see that *these proceedings are not unduly delayed.*

Sincerely, Richard Nixon.   [Emphasis added.]

The Nixon defense had entered a new phase. Still in the belief, encouraged, to be sure, by significant elements of the press, that what was at stake was a *political* contest rather than a *legal* one, Nixon was simultaneously pledging cooperation while he had already made the determination that he would not furnish any additional evidence to the Committee, as St. Clair made clear the next day. He was able to maintain this pose for some time, while he baited Rodino and the Committee in the desperate hope that they, in anger, would cite him for contempt for refusal to honor committee subpoenas, and thus pose the impeachment case in procedural rather than substantive terms.

It now seems clear that from this point on Nixon had made his decision to "stonewall." He would furnish no information to the Judiciary Committee, for the very good reason that if he did the Committee would only examine the evidence and conclude from it that he was not a *participant* in the cover-up, but its *leader.*

But by refusing information and refusing to yield evidence to the House, and by doing so in as contumacious a manner as possible, Nixon was taunting the Committee, and hoping against hope that it would "take the bait" (a phrase he had used in an earlier conversation about the employment of a similar technique on the Ervin Committee) and cite him for contempt *and close the hearings.* That would have put the grounds for impeachment on the narrow procedural question of whether Nixon had an obligation to respond to a subpoena from the House of Representatives and *that* question was still open as far as the Supreme Court was concerned. St. Clair must have seen a glimmer of hope that the issue might conceivably be resolved in the President's favor.

The strategy, then, was to withhold evidence in as defiant a manner as possible, hope for a vote for a contempt citation from the House of Representatives, and then appeal the impeachment verdict *prior to trial in the Senate.*

Nixon was undoubtedly counting on—and had every reason to imagine he would receive—the indulgence of the leadership in the House and Senate in postponing the Senate trial, or perhaps even the vote in the full House, until the constitutional and legal question of whether the President was required to respond to a subpoena could be resolved. Every step he and St. Clair took from March 5 onward reflects that determination.

But it now also seems clear from the deliberate and non-provocative way in which the Committee proceeded, and in the minimal responses it made to the enormous provocation offered by the flat refusal to convey evidence, that at least Rodino and Doar—and the inner group of Rodino's "right arms" in the Committee—perceived this danger and were determined not to fall into the trap the White House had prepared.

The day after the Nixon letter to Rodino, St. Clair responded to the request from John Doar, and announced that he would only deliver to the Committee copies of tapes which had already been subpoenaed by and turned over to the Special Prosecutor; he would not give Doar access to any further and so far unrevealed tapes or documents.

Simultaneously, a drumfire of criticism began to emerge from the White House, which was orchestrating a similar campaign among friendly sources in the press, to the effect that the initial Committee request had been a broadside one, and constituted a "fishing expedition."

As the keynote to this campaign, Nixon said at a press conference before a group of business executives in Chicago, that the request from the Committee amounted to a demand that the Committee be permitted to "back up a U-Haul trailer to the White House" and haul away what it pleased.

St. Clair complained that no specific documents or tapes had been requested, and his complaint found an immediate echo

among the band of Nixon supporters on the Committee. Two
days later, some fuel was added to the fire by St. Clair's request
that he be permitted to sit in on the preliminary hearings and
to cross-examine witnesses.

Rodino's response was muted. In a statement to the press, Rodino had reference to the White House campaign:

> During the past few days the White House has made a
> number of statements charging that the House Judiciary Com-
> mittee has requested permission to examine hundreds of thou-
> sands of White House documents and thousands of hours of
> recorded conversations covering the widest variety of sub-
> jects. It has been said that the Judiciary Committee wants to
> back a truck up to the White House and cart off boxes of
> records for examination by the impeachment inquiry staff.
> These statements are not accurate. . . .

That part of the statement out of the way, Rodino resumed
his serious mien. He said that he had promised the House that
the Committee would not abuse its trust and that it intended to
consider on the basis of evidence, on and off the public record,
whether or not serious abuses of power had occurred, and if so,
whether they were grounds for impeachment. He then made a
strong indication that he at least had resolved that the Committee would not contest the question of impeachment on ground
that Nixon himself had prepared and preferred:

"The Judiciary Committee does not view itself as being engaged in a law suit with the President. It has been authorized
and directed to conduct a thorough inquiry, and we will do that.
We expect and will continue to expect full cooperation from all
persons. The Constitution permits nothing less." Rodino then proceeded to shift the burden back to the White House, by pointing
out that the original exchange of correspondence between Doar
and St. Clair demonstrated that all Doar had asked for were
"some very specific recorded conversations of the President in
the month before and the month after March 21, 1973."

Rodino noted that the White House had said that these requests amounted to 41 separate conversations, and he stated, "so
be it."

Rodino said the Committee "hoped" that the President "will

conclude to make them available to the Committee," and stated the desire that "our lawyers secure the material without sub-poena." He then concluded:

"We will consider the advice of our counsel, but we will make the final decision as to if and when to issue a subpoena and for what material." He had refused the bait, and made it as clear as he could that the Committee would continue to conduct a legal proceeding, despite the enormous temptations offered by the White House to make the matter a political one.

There the matter stood for nearly three weeks. The Committee would meet, some of the pro-impeachment members would grumble that it was time to issue a subpoena, but Rodino would prevail—with the assistance always of Donohue, Brooks, Kastenmeier, Edwards, and Hungate and often more of the Democratic members—and take the public position that Doar and St. Clair were continuing to negotiate, and that he was "confident" that the evidence would be forthcoming.

Rodino was putting on his own pressure, and he was beginning to prevail. The more testy the White House became, the more statements of the Nixon men emerged about "fishing expeditions" and U-Haul trailers, the more columns were generated about the "attack on the power of the presidency," the more Rodino would appear reasonable and patient, without missing an opportunity to point out that the requests for evidence which the Committee had made were precise and involved specific evidence it felt it needed.

On April 4, Rodino issued a two-edged statement. He announced that, under certain restrictions consonant with the rules of the House and past impeachment precedents, St. Clair would be permitted to participate in the proceedings, not as a matter of right but because the Committee felt it would give more of an appearance of fairness. He also referred to the question of evidence:

> The patience of this Committee is now wearing thin. We have a constitutional responsibility in this inquiry. When we made our request [for evidence], we made it not out of curiosity, not because we were prosecutors, but because it is our responsibility. We have tried to pursue it in a spirit of accommodation with this President.

Rodino repeated that "a specific request for specific evidence of specific facts of specific relevance" had been made on February 25, and that that request so far had not been honored. "However, we are going forward," he said. He responded to St. Clair's dilatory request that the Committee be more specific with respect to the 41 recorded conversations by stating that "so as to avoid any possible basis for misunderstanding, we have instructed our counsel to send to Mr. St. Clair a letter setting forth specifically why the Committee has the responsibility to examine the particular conversations." He then let the rope out another notch:

"We shall not be thwarted by inappropriate legalisms or by narrow obstacles to our inquiry. We have waited patiently to get the recorded conversations. *We will subpoena them if we must.* Whether the evidence is inculpatory or exculpatory, we will scrutinize it fairly." The explanatory letter was sent, painstakingly setting forth the relevance—to a charge of obstruction of justice—of each of the requested conversations.

On April 11, the first subpoena was finally issued, Rodino having indicated that the patience of the Committee had finally worn too thin. On the same day, in an attempt to avoid any appearance of persecution, Rodino announced the guidelines for St. Clair's participation in the hearings and in the examination and cross-examination of witnesses.

The subpoena described the conversations of which the Committee wished to have tapes. There was a prophetic note on the subpoena; in the time-honored legal language, a sergeant-at-arms of the House of Representatives was "commanded to summon" the President to "produce and deliver" the documents described in the subpoena, and the orders to the sergeant-at-arms ended, "Herein fail not." The subpoena was made—in the language of the lawyers—"returnable" on April 25.

On April 19, attacking from another salient, Doar by letter requested from St. Clair more tapes and other documents with respect to Nixon's meeting with the milk producers, relative to the increase in milk price and the suggested connection between that presidential action and a pledged campaign contribution.

On April 23, two days before the documents requested by the subpoena were required to be delivered, Rodino successfully urged the Committee to extend the deadline for compliance to April 30. At the same time he stated the intention of the Committee to pursue, by subpoena if necessary, the request for materials relevant to the milk case and to the controversy with respect to ITT. The next day, Doar, again by letter, requested additional materials with respect to ITT.

The night before the extended due date of the subpoena, Nixon delivered his famous television address, posing in front of a tall stack of embossed notebooks, and announced his new version of the Stennis compromise. The edited transcripts of some of the conversations which had been subpoenaed, and many more, almost all of which were later revealed to have been sharply edited to eliminate material incriminating to the President, were to be delivered to the Committee the next day, April 30. On May 1, Rodino announced that the President's action was unsatisfactory.

He issued a statement regretting "that while we demonstrated time and time again that we were not seeking any confrontation with the President of the United States, we were only seeking evidence—the best evidence—the relevance of which under the Constitution and the resolution only *we* can determine."

Rodino said flatly that

> whatever else the President may have done or been thought to have done on Monday evening (April 29), and whatever individual members of this Committee may think of the merits of that action, the President has not complied with our subpoena. We did not subpoena an edited White House version of partial transcripts of portions of presidential conversation. We did not subpoena a presidential interpretation of what is necessary or relevant for our inquiry. And we did not subpoena a lawyer's argument presented before we have heard any of the evidence.

The last phrase was a reference to the "summary" of the transcripts compiled by St. Clair and released to the press before the transcripts themselves had been made public.

Rodino was now confronted with a problem on his own Committee. Some members, angered by the President's obvious refusal to comply with a lawful subpoena, wanted to start contempt proceedings. Rodino and Doar and most of the Democratic members continued to see the danger of making the confrontation with Nixon on a narrow procedural question. They also understood that as a matter of law, the President could not be forced to comply, nor would any judge jail him for contempt until he did comply. They also foresaw that an attempt to enforce the subpoena by ordinary legal methods could only lead to a protracted battle in the courts, the outcome of which was dubious and which would almost indefinitely delay the impeachment proceedings.

In addition, Rodino felt there was an important constitutional principle to vindicate. The Constitution, as he read it, conferred upon the House of Representatives the "sole power" of impeachment, and that meant, to him and to the authorities upon whom he relied, that the House had, therefore, absolute power to compel the production of evidence from the very President whose actions it was called upon to judge. Therefore, he felt, not even the courts had the power to intervene should the House subpoena such evidence. It was an insoluble dilemma, but Rodino felt that restraint would at least not contribute to the overturn of the principle of sole responsibility, even if it could not confirm it.

Accordingly, he supported (and persuaded an overwhelming majority to support) a simple letter to Nixon stating the Committee's belief that the release of an edited set of transcripts did not constitute compliance with the subpoena. The same day, the letter went from the Committee, backed by a virtually unanimous vote:

Dear Mr. President:
The Committee on the Judiciary has directed me to advise you that it finds as of 10:00 A.M., April 30, you have failed to comply with the Committee's subpoena of April 11, 1974.
Sincerely, Peter W. Rodino, Jr., Chairman.

Like the legendary snake which thrashes until sundown even though its head has been severed, the subpoena issue continued to *appear* as an important one for another six weeks, even well into the hearings stage. But the action of the Committee on May 1 had determined the issue. It would not seek to enforce its subpoenas, it would not seek to cite Nixon for contempt, but the actions of Nixon in defying the subpoenas had created, not the "rush to judgment" for which the White House had hoped, but a measured resentment in the Committee which would find its expression in the third article of impeachment. Thus on May 15, a second subpoena issued * requiring delivery by May 22. On May 21, St. Clair, evidently still pursuing the strategy of taunting the Committee into premature action, declined to furnish the requested evidence on the ITT and milk cases, enclosing instead copies of the presidential White Papers which had been issued more than four months before. On May 22, the return date of the second subpoena, Nixon wrote Rodino refusing to comply.

The letter, even by what was known on May 22, 1974, was an astonishing one. In it, Nixon described his submission of the edited transcripts of April 30 as having been done "so that the record of my knowledge and actions in the Watergate matter would be fully disclosed, once and for all." He also described the subpoenas as "the continued succession of demands for additional presidential conversations," which had "become a never-ending process." Finally, he had the sheer gall to state that "the Committee has the full story of Watergate, insofar as it relates to presidential knowledge and presidential actions."

He then announced that he would "respectfully decline to produce [those things] called for in the subpoena of May 15, *and those allegedly dealing with Watergate that may be called for in such further subpoenas as may hereafter be issued.*" (Emphasis added.)

On May 30, a third subpoena issued, again by a 37-1 vote, emphasizing that Rodino and Doar were sticking to the course they had plotted, and on the same day the Committee responded to the President's defiant—and, as the nation would later discover, wholly and deliberately deceitful—letter of May 22. Representative McClory of Illinois issued a statement that he viewed "the President's present refusals to produce evidence with dismay," and he foreshadowed his later insistence that repeated refusals to comply with the Committee's subpoenas be made in itself a grounds for impeachment. It was largely to accommodate this feeling of McClory's that the third article of impeachment was finally voted.

* All subpoenas were voted 37-1, Representative Hutchinson voting no each time, not on the ground that he felt the Committee lacked the power or that the information sought was not relevant, but on his belief that since the subpoenas were unenforceable against the President, by contempt power or otherwise, their issuance was an idle act.

McClory announced that he "would support sending the President a letter expressing the displeasure and disappointment in the President's continued lack of cooperation, and advising him that his conduct would permit members of the Committee, in reviewing the totality of the evidence, to draw reasonable and natural inferences adverse to the President." In other words, McClory, a careful lawyer, had joined that growing body of public opinion which was becoming increasingly convinced that Nixon's refusal to furnish evidence was not based on any deep desire to protect "the presidency" but simply on the belief that revealing the evidence would destroy him.

The letter McClory had suggested was sent, stating that members of the Committee would be free to draw "adverse inferences" from the President's refusal to obey the subpoenas, and it drew a reply from the President which served as a sort of final irony to those who had followed the Nixon career.

On June 9 Nixon wrote Rodino, and on June 10 St. Clair sent a copy of the letter to Rodino, and on the President's behalf declined to furnish the material called for in the final subpoena—the one which was issued on May 30. That Nixon letter of June 9 demonstrated that Rodino's tactics of restraint had drawn some blood. Nixon went through a long redefinition of the doctrine of "executive privilege" and of the "separation of powers," reciting all of the arguments which lower courts had previously and which the Supreme Court would later reject. Then he turned to the question of any "adverse inference" which might be drawn from his refusal to comply with the Committee's demands for evidence.

"Such a declaration," wrote Nixon, "flies in the face of established law on the assertion of valid claims of privilege." Nixon quoted the Supreme Court as having stated that even allowing comment by a judge or prosecutor on the exercise of a valid constitutional claim would be itself "a penalty imposed by courts for exercising a constitutional privilege," and that "it cuts down on the privilege by making its assertion costly." Nixon went on to cite other court opinions to the effect that it was improper for a judge or jury to draw any inference from a claim of constitutional privilege.

But these cases were, of course, all related to claims by criminal defendants, under the Fifth Amendment to the Constitution, that they would not *testify* against themselves because their answers might tend to incriminate them, and the body of law cited by the President was a formidable one.

Nixon went on: "Those are legal arguments. The common sense argument is that a claim of privilege, which is valid under the doctrine of separation of powers and is designed to protect the principle of separation of powers, must be accepted without adverse inference—or else the privilege itself is undermined, and the separation of powers nullified."

But Nixon had gone too far. In the first place, his "common sense argument" had no basis in the law, since there were no cases supporting his proposition that an assertion of a constitutional claim by the subject of an impeachment inquiry prevented the Committee conducting the inquiry from drawing an adverse inference from the refusal to yield evidence. Nor would there be any such precedent; such cases as there were on the point went the other way. The protection of the Fifth Amendment is limited to testimony in criminal cases.

But there was a second objection to Nixon's "common sense argument," and it was a political one. Richard Nixon had based his entire political career—his election to the Senate from California in 1950 and his subsequent election and tenure as Vice-President, which led to his presidential campaign in 1960—on the proposition that there were such people as "Fifth Amendment Communists," defined as people who had claimed a constitutional privilege against testifying with respect to their membership in the Communist party, as to whose membership politician Nixon —as opposed to President Nixon—felt not only entitled to draw an inference of Communist membership, but to proclaim that inference publicly. Some stray poisoned chickens from the 1950s had come home to roost.

While all this was going on, the formal committee hearings had begun. On May 9, opening statements were made by Rodino and Hutchinson (who set the linguistic framework by announcing that impeachment was the most "awesome power" possessed by the House) and the Committee promptly went into executive session, from which it was to emerge only late in July. Congressmen Waldie and Conyers lead a brief rebellion against the rule of executive session (to which the public and the press would not be admitted), but a strong majority approved Rodino's plan.

The technique of staying in executive session for more than two months was to bear heavily on the final result. Without the press and without the public, the proceedings before the Committee became even less political and even more legal than they had been before. Rodino drove his troops hard, and each day would be consumed by the presentation of evidence by John Doar and his staff, the playing of selected tapes, and finally by some live testimony.

But the result of the long period of executive sessions was to fill each Committee member with a sense not only of the importance of the task, but to force them to consider carefully the evidence that was being laid out. This turned out to be crucial, because up to this time, among official Washington, only the staff and members of Senator Ervin's committee had ever paid close attention to the evidence.

We have seen, in the chapter on the press, how the most accurate predictions and the clearest understanding of Watergate and its inevitable result had come from commentators who eschewed the political arguments and had concentrated on the evidence, from those who ignored (or had never considered as important) the opinions of insiders but had instead observed that a mountain of evidence was available against Nixon if only someone would take the trouble to sort it out.

Sorting it out was John Doar's job, and he performed it better than it had even been imagined anyone could. He prepared—and had his staff prepare—books of evidence relating to each charge against the President, and bearing down most heavily on the ones where the most evidence existed—obstruction of justice and abuse of power.

The result was that when the curtain finally went up and the country was able to observe, by live television coverage, the Committee hearings in progress, what people saw was a group of 38 Representatives, each of whom had an enormous command of the facts of the case. For the first time, the country was to be made aware in a systematic manner of the case against Richard Nixon, and in less than a week the Committee made that case an overwhelming one.

For that, we owe a debt of gratitude to Rodino and to Doar (and to the largely anonymous staff assistants who labored night and day to produce those sheaves of evidence), particularly for the decision to keep the hearings closed and away from the public and the press until the great weight of the evidence had been thoroughly assimilated.

The press was not without complaints during this period. From time to time, articles would appear listing the difficulty which newspapermen were having in obtaining information, but somehow the public did not seem to care.

When the hearings became open to the public, the three television networks decided to rotate coverage, with ABC covering opening day and CBS and NBC following in turn. On the first day, after less than an hour of opening statements, a bomb scare forced the evacuation of the hearing room. The ABC commentators, who obviously had not studied the evidence, found they had very little to talk about. Howard K. Smith (who had supported Nixon as loyally as only a confirmed Vietnam hawk could have) and reporter Sam Donaldson spent their time asking the Congressmen what they thought of the bomb scare, and never what they thought of the evidence they had listened to for nearly ten weeks behind closed doors. It was a fairly typical performance by correspondents who had concentrated on the political and dramatic side, and had not comprehended the change in attitudes that had gone on behind those closed doors as the evidence was being presented.

After the Committee had voted for the first article of impeachment, Sam Donaldson unwittingly brought to mind the Andrew Johnson impeachment. In a "live" interview with William Cohen, the Maine Republican who had been one of the leaders among the six Republicans to vote for impeachment, Donaldson suggested that Cohen might be considered a "Judas." Cohen did not respond with Andrew Johnson's response to the same charge, but he might have. Johnson had also been called a "Judas," and his response was a savage one: "I have been traduced. I have been slandered. I have been maligned. I have been called Judas Iscariot. . . . Judas Iscariot! Judas! There was a Judas and he was one of the twelve apostles. . . . If I have played the Judas, who has been my Christ?"

The end came swiftly. On the day the public debate on the articles of impeachment began, the Supreme Court ruled unanimously that Nixon had no right to withhold the tapes from Special Prosecutor Jaworski. After a day of suspense, St. Clair announced the President would comply with the court's decision. On July 25, John Doar turned advocate for the first time, and presented a lengthy and powerful brief for impeachment, as anyone acquainted with the evidence must have realized he would. Hour after hour, the evidence was marshalled by Doar on the major charges and on some of the lesser ones. He had arranged the evidence, the tapes, the testimony, and the documents, and his arguments for impeachment were compelling and, finally, overwhelming.

From the beginning, the only question had been, how many Republicans would join the 21 Democrats in voting for the various articles? By the time Thornton, Flowers, and Mann had worked out with Railsback and McClory appropriate language on which they could all agree, the articles were ready to be submitted to a vote, and at least six Republicans were ready to support impeachment.

On July 27, with each member (except Rangel) trying to sound and appear more "awesome" than the others, Article I was adopted by a vote of 27–11. It recommended impeachment because Nixon's actions formed "a course of conduct" to obstruct justice in the investigation of the Watergate break-in and to cover up other illegal activities by his subordinates. All of the Democrats voted for the article, and they were joined by Republicans Railsback, Fish, Hogan, Butler, Cohen, and (a mild surprise) Froehlich.

Two days later, the Committee voted for the second article of impeachment, the one which embraced Madison's concept of "superintendency," and charged a general abuse of power by the President and his failure to "take care that the laws be faithfully executed." This article passed by a vote of 28–10, Representative McClory joining the six Republicans who had voted for the first article.

On the next day, Article III, "the McClory Article," recommending impeachment on the grounds of the President's refusal to comply with the Committee's subpoenas, was adopted by a vote of 21–17. On this vote Flowers and Mann, on the Democratic side, voted against the article while only McClory and Hogan among the Republicans voted for it. Hogan thus became the only Republican to vote for all three articles of impeachment.

There followed debate and defeat of two additional articles, one calling for impeachment on the grounds of Nixon's evasion of the obligation to pay income taxes in 1969 and 1970, and one relating to the illegal and concealed bombing of Cambodia. But the debate was desultory, and probably was sustained only because some of the members wanted to get all of the evidence on record—particularly on the income tax charge—in advance of the debate on the floor of the full House, then scheduled for three weeks later.

But the Committee's work was done, and Rodino and Doar and their colleagues in the Committee and the staff could take pride that they had resisted temptation and had gone the full course. They had done the job the Constitution had assigned them, and they had achieved—in the great conflict dividing Americans between the President and the Constitution, between the arrogance of power and the rule of law—a measure of peace with honor.

Appendix

LIST OF COURT ACTIONS BY OFFICE OF WATERGATE SPECIAL PROSECUTOR JUNE 27, 1973–DECEMBER 3, 1974

INDIVIDUALS

Subject	Status
Frederick C. LaRue, *deputy campaign director*	Pleaded guilty on June 27, 1973, to an information charging violation of 18 USC Section 371, conspiracy to obstruct justice. Sentencing deferred.
Jeb S. Magruder *deputy campaign director*	Pleaded guilty on August 16, 1973, to an information charging violation of 18 USC Section 371, conspiracy to obstruct justice and defraud the United States of America. Sentenced on May 21 to a prison term of four years. Sentence being served at U.S. Bureau of Prisons Camp, Allenwood, Pa.
Donald Segretti	Pleaded guilty on October 1, 1973, to an indictment charging one count of violation of 18 USC Section 612, Distribution of illegal campaign literature. Defendant was sentenced on November 5, 1973, to serve six months in prison. Released March 25, 1974.
Egil Krogh, Jr., *White House assistant, Under Secretary of Transportation*	Indicted on October 11, 1973, on two counts of violation of 18 USC Section 1623, making false declaration before Grand Jury or court. Indictment dismissed, January 24, 1974. Pleaded guilty on November 30, 1973, to an information charging violation of 18 USC Section 241, conspiracy against rights of citizens. On January

24, 1974, Judge Gerhard Gesell sentenced Krogh to a prison term of two to six years. All but six months of the prison term were suspended. Released June 21, 1974.

John W. Dean 3rd, *counsel to the President*

Pleaded guilty on October 19, 1973, to an information charging one count of violation of 18 USC Section 371, conspiracy to obstruct justice and defraud the United States of America. Sentenced August 2, 1974, to a prison term of one to four years.

Dwight L. Chapin, *President Nixon's appointments secretary*

Indicted on November 29, 1973, on four counts of violation of 18 USC Section 1623, Making False Declaration before Grand Jury or Court. Found guilty on two counts, April 5, 1974. Sentenced May 15 to serve 30 months in prison. Conviction appealed.

Herbert L. Porter, *chief of scheduling for Nixon campaign*

Pleaded guilty on January 28, 1974, to an information charging a one-count violation of 18 USC Section 1001, making false statements to agents of the FBI. Information filed January 21, 1974. Sentenced on April 11, 1974, to a maximum of 15 months in prison, all but 30 days suspended. Released May 23.

Jake Jacobsen, *White House aide under President Johnson*

Indicted on February 21, 1974, on one count of violation of 18 USC Section 1623, making false declaration to Grand Jury or court. Indictment July 29, 1974, on one count of making an illegal payment to a public official. Pleaded guilty August 7, 1974. Sentencing deferred.

Herbert W. Kalmbach, *personal attorney to Richard Nixon*

Pleaded guilty on February 25, 1974, to charges of violation of the Federal Corrupt Practices Act (2 USC Sections

Subject	*Status*
	242a and 252b) and a charge of promising federal employment as reward for political activity and for support of a candidate (18 USC Section 600). Sentenced to serve eighteen months in prison and fined $10,000.
Charles W. Colson, *special counsel to the President*	Indicted on March 1, 1974, on one count of conspiracy (18 USC Section 371) and one count of obstruction of justice (18 USC Section 1503). Indictment dismissed.

Indicted on March 7, 1974, on one count of conspiracy against rights of citizens (18 USC Section 241). Indictment dismissed.

Pleaded guilty on June 3, 1974, to one count of obstruction of justice, 18 USC Section 1503. Sentenced to serve three years in prison and fined $5,000. |
| Harry R. Haldeman, *White House Chief-of-Staff* | Indicted on March 1, 1974, on one count of conspiracy (18 USC Section 371), one count of obstruction of justice (18 USC Section 1503) and three counts of perjury (18 USC Section 1621). Trial in progress. |
| John Ehrlichman, *counsel to the President, chief domestic adviser* | Indicted on March 1, 1974, on one count of conspiracy (18 USC Section 371), one count of obstruction of justice (18 USC Section 1503), one count of making false statements to agents of the FBI (18 USC Section 1001), and two counts of making a false statement to a Grand Jury or court (18 USC Section 1623). Trial in progress.

Indicted on March 7, 1974, on one count of conspiracy against rights of citizens (18 USC Section 241), one |

Subject	Status
	count of making a false statement to agents of the FBI (18 USC Section 1001), and three counts of making a false declaration to a Grand Jury or court (18 USC Section 1623).
	On July 12, 1974, Ehrlichman was found guilty on all charges, except on count of making a false declaration before a Grand Jury. On July 22, Judge Gerhard Gesell set aside Ehrlichman's conviction on the Section 1001 charge.
	On July 31, 1974, he was sentenced to a prison term of five years on all counts.
John Mitchell, *Attorney-General*	Indicted on March 1, 1974, on one count of conspiracy (18 USC Section 371), one count of obstruction of justice (18 USC Section 1503), two counts of making a false declaration to a Grand Jury or court (18 USC Section 1623), one count of perjury (18 USC Section 1621), and one count of making a false statement to an agent of the FBI (18 USC Section 1001). Trial in progress.
Gordon Strachan, *White House aide, general counsel to United States Information Agency*	Indicted on March 1, 1974, on one count of conspiracy (18 USC Section 371), one count of obstruction of justice (18 USC Section 1503), and one count of making a false statement to a Grand Jury or court (18 USC Section 1623). (Case severed.)
Kenneth W. Parkinson	Indicted on March 1, 1974, on one count of conspiracy (18 USC Section 371) and one count of obstruction of justice (18 USC Section 1503). Trial in progress.
Robert C. Mardian, *Assistant Attorney-General*	Indicted on March 1, 1974, on one count of conspiracy (18 USC Section 371). Trial in progress.

Subject	Status
Bernard L. Barker	Indicted on March 7, 1974, on one count of conspiracy against rights of citizens (18 USC Section 241). Found guilty July 12, 1974. Suspended sentence. Three years probation.
Eugenio Martinez	Indicted on March 7, 1974, on one count of conspiracy against rights of citizens (18 USC Section 241). Found guilty July 12, 1974. Suspended sentence. Three years probation.
Felipe De Diego	Indicted on March 7, 1974, on one count of conspiracy against rights of citizens (18 USC Section 241). Indictment dismissed May 21, 1974. Action under appeal.
G. Gordon Liddy, *general counsel, Nixon campaign committee, White House aide*	Indicted on March 7, 1974, on one count of conspiracy against rights of citizens (18 USC Section 241). Found guilty July 12, 1974. Three year sentence to run concurrent with other sentence.
	Indicted on March 7, 1974, on two counts of refusal to testify or produce papers before either House of Congress. Found guilty on both counts May 10, 1974. Sentenced to six months on each count, sentences to run concurrently. Sentences suspended.
Howard Edwin Reinecke, *Lieutenant-Governor of California*	Indicted April 3, 1974, on three counts of perjury (18 USC Section 1621). Arraigned April 10, 1974. Found guilty on one count, July 27, 1974. Received suspended 18-month sentence October 2, 1974.
Richard G. Kleindienst, *Attorney-General*	Pleaded guilty on March 16, 1974, to an information charging violation of 18 USC Section 192. Sentenced to prison term of 30 days and fined $100. Prison term and sentence suspended.

Subject	*Status*
John B. Connally, *Secretary of the Treasury, counselor to the President*	Indicted on July 29, 1974, on two counts of accepting an illegal payment, one count of conspiracy to commit perjury and obstruct justice and two counts of making a false declaration before a Grand Jury. Pleaded not guilty August 9, 1974.
Edward L. Morgan, *Assistant Secretary of the Treasury*	Pleaded guilty on November 8, 1974, to one count of conspiracy to impair, impede, defeat, and obstruct proper and lawful governmental functions of the Internal Revenue Service (18 USC Section 371). Sentencing deferred.
Jack A. Gleason	Pleaded guilty on November 15, 1974, to one count of aiding and abetting a violation of the Federal Corrupt Practices Act; a misdemeanor. Sentencing deferred.
Harry Heltzer *(Chairman of the Board, Minnesota Mining and Manufacturing Co.)*	Pleaded guilty on October 17, 1973, to an information charging a non-willful violation of 18 USC Section 610, illegal campaign contribution. Fined $500.
Russell DeYoung *(Chairman of the Board, Goodyear Tire and Rubber Co.)*	Pleaded guilty on October 17, 1973, to an information charging a non-willful violation of 18 USC Section 610, illegal campaign contribution. Fined $1,000.
Dwayne O. Andreas *(Chairman of the Board, First Interoceanic Corporation)*	An information was filed on October 19, 1973, in Minneapolis, charging four counts of non-willful violation of 18 USC Section 610, illegal campaign contribution. A plea of not guilty was entered on behalf of Mr. Andreas. Acquitted July 12, 1974.
Harding L. Lawrence *(Chairman of the Board, Braniff Airways)*	Pleaded guilty on November 12, 1973, to an information charging a non-willful violation of 18 USC Section 610,

Subject	*Status*
	illegal campaign contribution. Fined $1,000.
Claude C. Wild Jr *(former Vice President, Gulf Oil Corp.)*	Pleaded guilty on November 13, 1973, to an information charging a non-willful violation of 18 USC Section 610, illegal campaign contribution. Fined $1,000.
Orin E. Atkins *(Chairman of the Board, Ashland Oil Inc.)*	Pleaded no contest on November 13, 1973, to an information charging a non-willful violation of 18 USC Section 610, illegal campaign contribution. Fined $1,000.
William W. Keeler *(Chairman of the Board, Phillips Petroleum Co.)*	Pleaded guilty on December 4, 1973, to an information charging a non-willful violation of 18 USC Section 610, illegal campaign contribution. Fined $1,000.
H. Everett Olson *(Chairman of the Board, Carnation Company)*	Pleaded guilty on December 19, 1973, to an information charging a non-willful violation of 18 USC Section 610, illegal campaign contribution. Fined $1,000.
Ray Dubrowin *(Vice President, Diamond International Corp.)*	Pleaded guilty on March 7, 1974, to an information charging a non-willful violation of 18 USC Section 610, illegal campaign contribution. Fined $1,000.
George M. Steinbrenner *(Chairman of the Board, American Shipbuilding Co.)*	Indicted April 5, 1974, on one count of conspiracy (18 USC Section 371); five counts willful violation of 18 USC Section 610, illegal campaign contribution; two counts, aiding and abetting an individual to make a false statement to agents of the FBI (18 USC Section 1001); four counts obstruction of justice (18 USC Section 1503), and two counts obstruction of a criminal investigation (18 USC Section 1510).

Subject	Status
	On August 23, Steinbrenner pleaded guilty to one count of conspiracy to violate 18 USC Section 610 and one count of being an accessory after the fact to an illegal campaign contribution. He was fined $15,000.
John H. Melcher Jr. *(Executive Vice President, counsel, American Shipbuilding Co.)*	Pleaded guilty on April 11, 1974, to a charge of being an accessory after the fact to a violation of 18 USC Section 610, illegal campaign contribution. 18 USC Sections 3 and 610. Fined $2,500.
Thomas V. Jones *(Chairman of the Board, Northrop Corporation)*	Pleaded guilty on May 1, 1974, to an information charging violation of 18 USC Sections 2 and 611, aiding and abetting firm to commit violation of statue prohibiting campaign contributions by government contractors. Fined $5,000.
James Allen *(Vice President, Northrop Corporation)*	Pleaded guilty on May 1, 1974, to an information charging violation of 18 USC Section 610, illegal campaign contribution. Fined $1,000.
Robert L. Allison	Pleaded guilty on May 17, 1974, to a non-willful violation of 18 USC Section 610, illegal campaign contribution. One month unsupervised probation and suspended $1,000 fine.
Francis X. Carroll	Pleaded guilty May 28 to a charge of aiding and abetting an individual to commit violation of 18 USC Section 610, illegal campaign contribution. Received suspended sentence.
David L. Parr	Pleaded guilty on July 23, 1974, to a one-count information charging conspiracy to violate Title 18, USC, Section 610, illegal campaign contribution. Sentenced to one year and fined $10,000.

Subject	Status
John Valentine	An information was filed on July 30, 1974, charging a one-count violation of Title 18, USC, Sections 2 and 610, aiding and abetting an illegal campaign contribution. A guilty plea was entered on August 12. Fined $500.
Norman Sherman	An information was filed on July 30, 1974, charging a one-count violation of Title 18, USC, Sections 2 and 610, aiding and abetting an illegal campaign contribution. A guilty plea was entered on August 12. Fined $500.
Harold S. Nelson	Pleaded guilty on July 31, 1974, to a one-count information charging conspiracy to violate Title 18, USC, Section 610, illegal campaign contribution. Sentenced to 1 year and fined $10,000.
William Lyles Sr. *(Chairman of the Board and President, LBC & W Inc.)*	Pleaded guilty on September 17, 1974, to two counts of non-willful violation of 18 USC, Section 610, illegal campaign contribution. He was fined $2,000.
Raymond Abendroth *(President, Time Oil Corporation)*	Pleaded guilty on October 23, 1974, to two counts of violation of 18 USC Section 610, illegal campaign contribution. Fined $2,000.
Charles N. Huseman *(former president, H.M.S. Electric Corporation)*	Pleaded guilty on December 3, 1974 to one count of violation of 18 USC Section 610, illegal campaign contribution.

CORPORATIONS

American Airlines	Pleaded guilty on October 17, 1973, to an information charging a violation of 18 USC Section 610, Illegal Campaign Contribution. Fined $5,000.

Subject	*Status*
Minnesota Mining and Manufacturing Co.	Pleaded guilty on October 17, 1973, to an information charging a violation of 18 USC Section 610, illegal campaign contribution. Fined $3,000.
Goodyear Tire and Rubber Company	Pleaded guilty on October 17, 1973, to an information charging a violation of 18 USC Section 610, illegal campaign contribution. Fined $5,000.
First Interoceanic Corp.	An information was filed on October 19, 1973, in Minneapolis, charging a four-count violation of 18 USC Section 610, illegal campaign contribution. Corporation entered a plea of not guilty to charge. Acquitted July 12, 1974.
Braniff Airways	Pleaded guilty on November 12, 1973, to an information charging violation of 18 USC Section 610, illegal campaign contribution. Fined $5,000.
Gulf Oil Corp.	Pleaded guilty on November 13, 1973, to an information charging a violation of 18 USC Section 610, illegal campaign contribution. Fined $5,000.
Ashland Petroleum Gabon Inc.	Pleaded guilty on November 13, 1973, to an information charging a violation of 18 USC Section 610, illegal campaign contribution. Fined $5,000.
Phillips Petroleum Co.	Pleaded guilty on December 4, 1973, to an information charging a violation of 18 USC Section 610, illegal campaign contribution. Fined $5,000.
Carnation Company	Pleaded guilty on December 19, 1973, to an information charging violation of 18 USC Section 610, illegal campaign contribution. Fined $5,000.
Diamond International Corporation	Pleaded guilty on March 7, 1974, to an information charging violation of 18 USC Section 610, illegal campaign contribution. Fined $5,000.

Subject	Status
American Shipbuilding Company	Indicted April 5, 1974, on one count conspiracy (18 USC Section 371) and one count violation of 18 USC Section 610, illegal campaign contribution. Pleaded guilty on August 23, 1974, to counts one and seven of the indictment and was fined $20,000.
Northrop Corporation	Pleaded guilty on May 1, 1974, to a charge of violation of 18 USC Section 611, illegal campaign contribution of government contractor. Fined $5,000.
Lehigh Valley Cooperative Farmers	Pleaded guilty on May 6, 1974, to an information charging violation of 18 USC Section, illegal campaign contribution. Fined $5,000.
Associated Milk Producers Inc.	Pleaded guilty on August 2, 1974, to one count of conspiracy and five counts of making an illegal and willful campaign contribution. Fined $35,000.
LBC & W Inc.	Pleaded guilty on September 17, 1974, to one count of violation of 18 USC Section 611, illegal campaign contribution by government contractor. Fined $5,000.
Greyhound Corporation	An information was filed on October 2, 1974, charging a one-count violation of 18 USC Section 610, illegal campaign contribution. No plea taken at filing.
Time Oil Corporation	Pleaded guilty to two counts of violation of 18 USC Section 610, illegal campaign contribution. Fined $10,000.

ATTORNEY GENERAL'S DIRECTIVE AND GUIDELINES FOR THE SPECIAL PROSECUTOR

TITLE 28—JUDICIAL ADMINISTRATION

CHAPTER I—DEPARTMENT OF JUSTICE

PART O—ORGANIZATION OF THE DEPARTMENT OF JUSTICE

Order No. 551-73

ESTABLISHING THE OFFICE OF WATERGATE
SPECIAL PROSECUTION FORCE

By virtue of the authority vested in me by 28 U.S.C. 509, 510 and 5 U.S.C. 301, there is hereby established in the Department of Justice, the Office of Watergate Special Prosecution Force, to be headed by a Director. Accordingly, Part O of Chapter I of Title 28, Code of Federal Regulations, is amended as follows:

1. Section 0.1(a) which lists the organization units of the Department, is amended by adding "Office of Watergate Special Prosecution Force" immediately after "Office of Criminal Justice."

2. A new Subpart G-1 is added immediately after Subpart G, to read as follows:

"*Subpart G-1—Office of Watergate Special Prosecution Force*

§ 0.37 *General Functions.*

The Office of Watergate Special Prosecution Force shall be under the direction of a Director who shall be the Special Prosecutor appointed by the Attorney General. The duties and responsibilities of the Special Prosecutor are set forth in the attached appendix which is incorporated and made a part hereof.

§ 0.38 *Specific Functions.*

The Special Prosecutor is assigned and delegated the following specific functions with respect to matters specified in this Subpart:

(a) Pursuant to 28 U.S.C. 515(a), to conduct any kind of legal proceeding, civil or criminal, including grand jury proceedings, which United States attorneys are authorized by law to conduct, and to designate attorneys to conduct such legal proceedings.

(b) To approve or disapprove the production or disclosure of information or files relating to matters within his cognizance in response to a subpoena, order, or other demand of a court or other authority. (See Part 16(B) of this chapter.)

(c) To apply for and to exercise the authority vested in the Attorney General under 18 U.S.C. 6005 relating to immunity of witnesses in Congressional proceedings.

The listing of these specific functions is for the purpose of illustrating the authority entrusted to the Special Prosecutor and is not intended to limit in any manner his authority to carry out his functions and responsibilities."

DATE: *2 Nov. 1973*　　　　　　　　　　　　Robert H. Bork

Acting Attorney General

Appendix

DUTIES AND RESPONSIBILITIES OF THE
SPECIAL PROSECUTOR

The Special Prosecutor—There is appointed by the Attorney General, within the Department of Justice, a Special Prosecutor to whom the Attorney General shall delegate the authorities and provide the staff and other resources described below.

The Special Prosecutor shall have full authority for investigating and prosecuting offenses against the United States arising out of the unauthorized entry into Democratic National Committee Headquarters at the Watergate, all offenses arising out of the 1972 Presidential Election for which the Special Prosecutor deems it necessary and appropriate to assume responsibility, allegations involving the President, members of the White House staff, or Presidential appointees, and any other matters which he consents to have assigned to him by the Attorney General.

In particular, the Special Prosecutor shall have full authority with respect to the above matters for:
—conducting proceedings before grand juries and any other investigations he deems necessary;
—reviewing all documentary evidence available from any source, as to which he shall have full access;
—determining whether or not to contest the assertion of "Executive Privilege" or any other testimonial privilege;
—determining whether or not application should be made to any Federal court for a grant of immunity to any witness, consistently with applicable statutory requirements, or for warrants, subpoenas, or other court orders;
—deciding whether or not to prosecute any individual, firm, corporation or group of individuals;
—initiating and conducting prosecutions, framing indictments, filing informations, and handling all aspects of any cases within his jurisdiction (whether initiated before or after his assumption of duties), including any appeals;
—coordinating and directing the activities of all Department of Justice personnel, including United States Attorneys;
—dealing with and appearing before Congressional committees having jurisdiction over any aspect of the above matters and determining what documents, information, and assistance shall be provided to such committees.

In exercising this authority, the Special Prosecutor will have the greatest degree of independence that is consistent with the Attorney General's statutory accountability for all matters falling within the jurisdiction of the Department of Justice. The Attorney General will not countermand or interfere with the Special Prosecutor's decisions or actions. The Special Prosecutor will determine whether and to what extent he will inform or consult with the Attorney General about the conduct of his duties and responsibilities. In accordance with assurances given by the

President to the Attorney General that the President will not exercise his Constitutional powers to effect the discharge of the Special Prosecutor or to limit the independence that he is hereby given, the Special Prosecutor will not be removed from his duties except for extraordinary improprieties on his part and without the President's first consulting the Majority and the Minority Leaders and Chairmen and ranking Minority Members of the Judiciary Committees of the Senate and House of Representatives and ascertaining that their consensus is in accord with his proposed action.

Staff and Resource Support

1. *Selection of Staff*—The Special Prosecutor shall have full authority to organize, select, and hire his own staff of attorneys, investigators, and supporting personnel, on a full or part-time basis, in such numbers and with such qualifications as he may reasonably require. He may request the Assistant Attorneys General and other officers of the Department of Justice to assign such personnel and to provide such other assistance as he may reasonably require. All personnel in the Department of Justice, including United States Attorneys, shall cooperate to the fullest extent possible with the Special Prosecutor.

2. *Budget*—The Special Prosecutor will be provided with such funds and facilities to carry out his responsibilities as he may reasonably require. He shall have the right to submit budget requests for funds, positions, and other assistance, and such requests shall receive the highest prority.

3. *Designation and Responsibility*—The personnel acting as the staff and assistants of the Special Prosecutor shall be known as the Watergate Special Prosecution Force and shall be responsible only to the Special Prosecutor.

4. *Continued Responsibilities of Assistant Attorney General, Criminal Division*—Except for the specific investigative and prosecutorial duties assigned to the Special Prosecutor, the Assistant Attorney General in charge of the Criminal Division will continue to exercise all of the duties currently assigned to him.

5. *Applicable Departmental Policies*—Except as otherwise herein specified or as mutually agreed between the Special Prose-

cutor and the Attorney General, the Watergate Special Prosecution Force will be subject to the administrative regulations and policies of the Department of Justice.

6. *Public Reports*—The Special Prosecutor may from time to time make public such statements or reports as he deems appropriate and shall upon completion of his assignment submit a final report to the appropriate persons or entities of the Congress.

7. *Duration of Assignment*—The Special Prosecutor will carry out these responsibilities, with the full support of the Department of Justice, until such time as, in his judgment, he has completed them or until a date mutually agreed upon between the Attorney General and himself.

ARTICLES OF IMPEACHMENT

ARTICLE I

In his conduct of the office of President of the United States, Richard M. Nixon, in violation of his constitutional oath faithfully to execute the office of President of the United States and, to the best of his ability, preserve, protect and defend the Constitution of the United States, and in violation of his constitutional duty to take care that the laws be faithfully executed, has prevented, obstructed, and impeded the administration of justice, in that:

On June 17, 1972, and prior thereto, agents of the Committee for the Re-election of the President:

Committed unlawful entry of the headquarters of the Democratic National Committee in Washington, District of Columbia, for the purpose of securing political intelligence. Subsequent thereto, Richard M. Nixon, using the powers of his high office, engaged personally and through his subordinates and agents, in a course of conduct or plan designed to delay, impede, and obstruct the investigation of such unlawful entry; to cover up, conceal and protect those responsible; and to conceal the existence and scope of other unlawful covert activities.

The means used to implement this course of conduct or plan have included one or more of the following:

[1]

Making or causing to be made false or misleading statements to lawfully authorized investigative officers and employees of the United States;

[2]

Withholding relevant and material evidence or information from lawfully authorized investigative officers and employees of the United States;

[3]

Approving, condoning, acquiescing in, and counseling witnesses with respect to the giving of false or misleading statements to lawfully authorized investigative officers and employees of the United States and false or misleading testimony in duly instituted judicial and congressional proceedings.

[4]

Interfering or endeavoring to interfere with the conduct of investigations by the Department of Justice of the United States, the Federal Bureau of Investigation, the office of Watergate Special Prosecution Force, and Congressional Committees;

[5]

Approving, condoning and acquiescing in the surreptitious payment of substantial sums of money for the purpose of obtaining the silence or influencing the testimony of witnesses, potential witnesses or individuals who participated in such unlawful entry and other illegal activities;

[6]

Endeavoring to misuse the Central Intelligence Agency, an agency of the United States;

[7]

Disseminating information received from officers of the Department of Justice of the United States to subjects of investigations conducted by lawfully authorized investigative officers and employees of the United States, for the purpose of aiding and assisting such subjects in their attempts to avoid criminal liability;

[8]

Making false or misleading public statements for the purpose of deceiving the people of the United States into believing that a thorough and complete investigation had been conducted with respect to allegations of misconduct on the part of personnel of the executive branch of the United States and personnel of the Committee for the Re-election of the President, and that there was no involvement of such personnel in such misconduct; or

[9]

Endeavoring to cause prospective defendants, and individuals duly tried and convicted, to expect favored treatment and consideration in return for their silence or false testimony, or rewarding individuals for their silence or false testimony.

In all of this, Richard M. Nixon has acted in a manner contrary to his trust as President and subversive of constitutional government, to the great prejudice of the cause of law and justice and to the manifest injury of the people of the United States.

Wherefore Richard M. Nixon, by such conduct, warrants impeachment and trial, and removal from office.

ROLL-CALL

FOR THE ARTICLE—27

Democrats—21

Peter W. Rodino Jr., New Jersey, chairman.
Harold D. Donohue, Massachusetts.
Jack Brooks, Texas.
Robert W. Kastenmeier, Wisconsin.
Don Edwards, California.
William L. Hungate, Missouri.
John Conyers Jr., Michigan.
Joshua Eilberg, Pennsylvania.
Jerome R. Waldie, California.
Walter Flowers, Alabama.
James R. Mann, South Carolina.
Paul S. Sarbanes, Maryland.
John F. Seiberling, Ohio.
George E. Danielson, California.
Robert F. Drinan, Massachusetts.
Charles B. Rangel, New York.
Barbara Jordan, Texas.
Ray Thornton, Arkansas.
Elizabeth Holtzman, New York.

Wayne Owens, Utah.
Edward Mezvinsky, Iowa.

Republicans—6

Tom Railsback, Illinois.
Hamilton Fish Jr., New York.
Lawrence J. Hogan, Maryland.
M. Caldwell Butler, Virginia.
William S. Cohen, Maine.
Harold V. Froehlich, Wisconsin.

AGAINST THE ARTICLE—11

Republicans—11

Edward Hutchinson, Michigan.
Robert McClory, Illinois.
Henry P. Smith 3d, New York.
Charles W. Sandman Jr., New Jersey.
Charles E. Wiggins, California.
David W. Dennis, Indiana.
Wiley Mayne, Iowa.
Trent Lott, Mississippi.
Carlos J. Moorhead, California.
Joseph J. Maraziti, New Jersey.
Delbert L. Latta, Ohio.

ARTICLE II

Using the powers of the office of President of the United States, Richard M. Nixon, in violation of his constitutional oath faithfully to execute the office of President of the United States, and to the best of his ability preserve, protect and defend the Constitution of the United States and, in disregard of his constitutional duty to take care that the laws be faithfully executed, has repeatedly engaged in conduct violating the constitutional right of citizens, impairing the due and proper administration of justice in the conduct of lawful inquiries, or contravening the laws of governing agencies of the executive branch and the purposes of these agencies.

This conduct has included one or more of the following:

[1]

He has, acting personally and through his subordinates and agents, endeavored to obtain from the Internal Revenue Service, in violation of the constitutional rights of citizens, confidential information contained in income tax returns for purposes not authorized by law, and to cause, in violation of the constitutional rights of citizens, income tax audits or other income tax investigations to be initiated or conducted in a discriminatory manner.

[2]

He misused the Federal Bureau of Investigation, the Secret Service, and other executive personel, in violation or disregard of the constitutional rights of citizens by directing or authorizing such agencies or personnel to conduct or continue electronic surveillance or other investigations for purposes unrelated to national security, the enforcement of laws, or any other lawful function of his office;

He did direct, authorize or permit the use of information obtained thereby for purposes unrelated to national security, the enforcement of laws, or any other lawful function of his office; And he did direct the concealment of certain records made by the Federal Bureau of Investigation of electronic surveillance.

[3]

He has, acting personally and through his subordinates and agents, in violation or disregard of the constitutional rights of citizens, authorized and permitted to be maintained a secret investigative unit within the office of the President, financed in part with money derived from campaign contributions, which unlawfully utilized the resources of the Central Intelligence Agency, engaged in covert and unlawful activities, and attempted to prejudice the constitutional right of an accused to a fair trial.

[4]

He has failed to take care that the laws were faithfully executed by failing to act when he knew or had reason to know that his close subordinates endeavored to impede and frustrate lawful inquiries by duly constituted executive, judicial, and legislative entities concerning the unlawful entry into the headquarters of the Democratic National Committee, and the cover-up thereof, and concerning other unlawful activities, including those relating to the confirmation of Richard Kleindienst as Attorney General of the United States, the electronic surveillance of private citizens, the break-in into the offices of Dr. Lewis Fielding, and the campaign financing practices of the Committee to Re-elect the President.

[5]

In disregard of the rule of law he knowingly misused the executive power by interfering with agencies of the executive branch, including the Federal Bureau of Investigation, the Criminal Division, and the office of Watergate special prosecution force, of the Department of Justice, and the Central Intelligence Agency, in violation of his duty to take care that the laws be faithfully executed.

In all of this, Richard M. Nixon has acted in a manner contrary to his trust as President and subversive of constitutional government, to the great prejudice of the cause of law and justice and to the manifest injury of the people of the United States.

Wherefore, Richard M. Nixon, by such conduct warrants impeachment and trial, and removal from office.

ROLL-CALL

FOR THE ARTICLE—28

Democrats—21

Peter W. Rodino Jr., New Jersey, chairman.
Harold D. Donahue, Massachusetts.
Jack Brooks, Texas.
Robert W. Kastenmeier, Wisconsin.
Don Edwards, California.
William L. Hungate, Missouri.
John Conyers Jr., Michigan.

Joshua Eilberg, Pennsylvania.
Jerome R. Waldie, California.
Walter Flowers, Alabama.
James R. Mann, South Carolina.
Paul S. Sarbanes, Maryland.
John F. Seiberling, Ohio.
George E. Danielson, California.
Robert F. Drinan, Massachusetts.
Charles B. Rangel, New York.
Barbara Jordan, Texas.
Ray Thornton, Arkansas.
Elizabeth Holtzman, New York.
Wayne Owens, Utah.
Edward Mezvinsky, Iowa.

Republicans

Robert McClory, Illinois.
Tom Railsback, Illinois.
Hamilton Fish Jr., New York.
Lawrence J. Hogan, Maryland.
M. Caldwell Butler, Virginia.
William S. Cohen, Maine.
Harold V. Froehlich, Wisconsin.

AGAINST THE ARTICLE—10

Republicans—10

Edward Hutchinson, Michigan.
Henry P. Smith 3d, New York.
Charles W. Sandman Jr.,
    New Jersey.
Charles E. Wiggins, California.
David W. Dennis, Indiana.
Wiley Mayne, Iowa.
Trent Lott, Mississippi.
Carlos J. Moorhead, California.
Joseph J. Maraziti, New Jersey.
Delbert L. Latta, Ohio.

ARTICLE III

In his conduct of the office of President of the United States, Richard M. Nixon, contrary to his oath faithfully to execute the office of President of the United States and, to the best of his ability, to preserve, protect and defend the Constitution of the United States, and in violation of his constitutional duty to take care that the laws be faithfully executed, has failed without lawful cause or excuse to produce papers and things as directed by duly authorized subpoenas isued by the Committee on the Judiciary of the House of Representatives on April 11, 1974, May 15, 1974, May 30, 1974, and June 24, 1974, and willfully disobeyed such subpoenas.

The subpoenaed papers and things were deemed necessary by the committee in order to resolve by direct evidence fundamental, factual questions relating to Presidential direction, knowledge or approval of actions demonstrated by other evidence to be substantial grounds for impeachment of the President.

In refusing to produce these papers and things, Richard M. Nixon, substituting his judgment as to what materials were necessary for the inquiry, interposed the powers of the Presidency against the lawful subpoenas of the House of Representatives, thereby assuming for himself functions and judgments necessary to the exercise of the sole power of impeachment vested by the Constitution in the House of Representatives.

In all this, Richard M. Nixon has acted in a manner contrary to his trust as President and subversive of constitutional government, to the great prejudice of the cause of law and justice, and to the manifest injury of the people of the United States.

Wherefore, Richard M. Nixon, by such conduct, warrants impeachment and trial and removal from office.

ROLL-CALL

FOR THE ARTICLE—21

Democrats—19

Peter W. Rodino Jr., New Jersey, chairman.
Harold D. Donohue, Massachusetts.
Jack Brooks, Texas.
Robert W. Kastenmeier, Wisconsin.
Don Edwards, California.
William L. Hungate, Missouri.
John Conyers Jr., Michigan.
Joshua Eilberg, Pennsylvania.
Jerome R. Waldie, California.
Paul S. Sarbanes, Maryland.
John F. Seiberling, Ohio.
George E. Danielson, California.
Robert F. Drinan, Massachusetts.
Charles B. Rangel, New York.
Barbara Jordan, Texas.
Ray Thornton, Arkansas.
Elizabeth Holtzman, New York.
Wayne Owens, Utah.
Edward Mezvinsky, Iowa.

Republicans—2

Robert McClory, Illinois.
Lawrence J. Hogan, Maryland.

AGAINST THE ARTICLE—17

Democrats—2

Walter Flowers, Alabama.
James R. Mann, South Carolina.

Republicans—15

Edward Hutchinson, Michigan.
Henry P. Smith 3d, New York.
Charles W. Sandman Jr., New Jersey.
Tom Railsback, Illinois.
Charles E. Wiggins, California.
David W. Dennis, Indiana.
Hamilton Fish Jr., New York.
Wiley Mayne, Iowa.
M. Caldwell Butler, Virginia.
William S. Cohen, Maine.
Trent Lott, Mississippi.
Harold V. Froelich, Wisconsin.
Carlos J. Moorhead, California.
Joseph J. Maraziti, New Jersey.
Delbert L. Latta, Ohio.

Index